MALTESE IN LONDON

Reports of the Institute of Community Studies

A catalogue of the books available in the series **Reports of the Institute of Community Studies** and other series of social science books published by Routledge & Kegan Paul will be found at the end of this volume.

MALTESE IN LONDON

A CASE-STUDY IN THE EROSION OF ETHNIC CONSCIOUSNESS

Geoff Dench

LONDON AND BOSTON

ROUTLEDGE & KEGAN PAUL

First published in 1975
by Routledge & Kegan Paul Ltd
Broadway House, 68-74 Carter Lane,
London EC4V 5EL and
9 Park Street,
Boston, Mass. 02108, USA
Set in Monotype Garamond
and printed in Great Britain by
Willmer Brothers Limited, Birkenhead

ISBN 0 7100 8067 0

CONTENTS

PREFACE

The Institute of Community Studies has been closely associated with this study right from the start, and although in a formal sense it was pursued independently, its character has been strongly influenced by the distinctive traditions of the Institute, and it is fitting that it should eventually find publication in this series. The first plans for the project were drafted while I was working at the Institute, and it was the encouragement of Michael Young, and his mediation in obtaining a small grant from the Elmgrant Trust to see me through the critical formative period of the research, which enabled me to undertake it. Peter Willmott has helped greatly in the production of this final version by carrying out extensive editing for me. Other colleagues at the Institute, in particular Peter Marris, have also maintained an interest in the study since I left Bethnal Green, and their support and criticism have been of great value to me. At a more mundane level, I have continued to have access to the Institute's mechanical resources, and this has eased the analysis of the voluminous materials which I amassed.

The main work in this project was carried out for a higher degree at the LSE, under the academic supervision of Ernest Gellner and David Glass – who was the first to suggest to me the need for some study of the Maltese. But for their patience and understanding the study would never have been completed. For as a part-time student I sometimes went for long periods without appearing to produce anything. During these pauses they remained undemanding; but whenever I needed guidance, criticism or official backing they gave it speedily and effectively.

A large number of individuals and bodies have assisted my researches, and it is inevitable that I can only hope to acknowledge my principal debts here. The Mediterranean Research Group at the LSE helped launch the study by covering the expenses of a short field trip to Malta, in which my ideas concerning the influence of British occupation on Maltese institutions were able to take a definite shape. The costs of the postal investigation among non-Maltese people in London were met by a grant from the Central Research Fund of the University of London; and the special tabulations from 1961 census data, used in Chapter II, were provided by the Institute of Race Relations. Simon Abbott of the IRR has also contributed suggestions at various junctures in the course of the enquiry, and his interest is very much appreciated.

Several people have influenced the direction taken in the study, by introducing me to new areas of source material, or important informants, or suggesting fresh approaches. The late Hector Bond, Employment Attaché at the Maltese High Commission in London, went to considerable trouble fixing meetings for me with officials in Malta. Arthur Scerri, founder of the Malta Labour Party (UK) and now High Commissioner here, created a number of useful contacts for me within the Maltese community, and has spent much of his valuable time in commenting for me on drafts. The Rev. Kenneth Leech's fund of knowledge about Stepney proved invaluable while I was finding my feet there. Edward Zammit, whose own study among Maltese in Britain overlapped mine, was generous in sharing his ideas and informants; and Jeremy Boissevain, drawing on wide experience of Maltese throughout the world, made a number of useful comments on the project. Jock Young and Nicholas Swingler, from very different perspectives, have helped me after the event to make some sense of the mass of data which I collected on Maltese criminality.

Some years have elapsed since these ideas and materials were pulled together for presentation as a thesis, and in amending this for general publication I have been faced with the problem of whether or not to bring the analysis properly up to date. Recent events in both Malta and Britain indicate that substantial changes are taking place. The return to power of Dom Mintoff in 1971 has triggered off a whole programme of domestic reforms which may go a long way towards secularising Maltese society. At the same time in Britain continuing economic stagnation, and absorption into Europe, have meant progressively tighter controls on economic migration from the new Commonwealth. The special quota of work vouchers for Maltese has been reduced twice to a level at which maintenance of the existing community is no longer possible.

These events do not however conflict in any essential matter with the original conclusions. They confirm that the paternalistic bond between Britain and Malta, in the context of which Maltese migration to Britain must be understood, is rapidly drawing to an end. The question of what new relationship may be taking its place is interesting; but it is a separate one which raises a different set of problems. The 1960s contain the natural termination of an epoch, and any attempt to bring the figures or argument of the case-study fully up to date would be not merely redundant, but analytically confusing.

On some limited and specific topics new data has been included in the course of revision, but generally speaking this analysis does not, and does not *intend* to embrace the current situation. A New Malta may have been born, and none too soon. But that is outside of the central concern of this book.

London 1973

INTRODUCTION

Maltese were among the first colonial citizens to embark on large-scale migration to Britain at the end of the Second World War, and they are generally assumed to have set up a sizeable community here. What is more, they played a very significant part in the emergence of a 'race relations' situation in this country, in the period leading up to the first Commonwealth Immigrants Act. But in spite of their undoubted interest and importance the Maltese in this country have not been the object of any detailed study; indeed, outside of the more lurid newspapers, they have scarcely received any public attention at all.

This almost total neglect is not fortuitous. There appears to have been a deliberate and widely observed policy of avoiding the topic, which in retrospect is itself highly symptomatic of the general position of the Maltese in Britain. In breaking the silence, it would be as well for me to examine how it seems to have come about, and to explain why I consider that it no longer serves a useful purpose – if it ever really has done.

Over a period of nearly a quarter of a century, sympathetic observers have kept quiet about the Maltese, in the belief that investigation and publicity would be detrimental to good community relations, and would compound the difficulties of Maltese immigrants themselves. At the heart of the problem has been the fact that a minority of Maltese has become involved in criminal activities of a type which public opinion defines as particularly loathsome and objectionable, and the popular press, especially those Sunday papers dedicated to sexual titillation, lost no opportunity in characterising Maltese in general as parasitic, indolent and vicious. This hostile reporting began soon after the arrival of the first wave of postwar migrants, and had its heyday in the 1950s. Since then it has been steadily on the wane, although even as recently as the spring of 1973 the *News of the World* attempted to launch a new crusade against Maltese criminals.

The bad public image which Maltese acquired in the wake of this one-sided and highly adverse treatment has inhibited many would-be investigators and commentators from producing more favourable accounts, for fear of unintentionally sparking off further antagonism. A consensus developed which acknowledged that the mass of Maltese immigrants was quietly and earnestly seeking assimilation into British society, and which held that anything more than the most discreet and veiled public reference to the misdemeanours of the troublesome few might damage the many.

A fairly characteristic, and typically brief, expression of this mood can be found in a piece by Lena Jeger in the *Guardian* in 1963.[1] Mrs Jeger portrays the Maltese as 'quiet' immigrants who are models of self-effacement in their concern to assimilate. They do not:

> except perhaps for a little while at first, cling to each other in obvious colonies. . . . They seem to have little language difficulty, do not demand newspapers in their own tongue, nor set up numerous organisations for their kith and kin.

Mrs Jeger quotes with approval a declaration by the Maltese High Commissioner to the effect that: 'we keep no records (of immigrants) and we don't want to. We only want our people who come here to live to settle down and become part of the British people here.'

To her mind, the existence of criminality among these exemplary immigrants is a most perplexing anomaly. Without specifying the nature of these crimes, she asks rather coyly: 'But why do even a few, usually young men who were well-behaved, God-fearing and priest-respecting at home get "into trouble": and what can be done to prevent it?'

No definite answers emerge; but Mrs Jeger does suggest tacitly that the problem is in part one of excessive public interest. For, paradoxically: 'It is perhaps because most Maltese live their unlabelled lives in simple goodness that the bad ones claim so much public attention.'

Therefore the most helpful thing that British readers and

---

[1] L. Jeger, 'London Maltese'. Full references to all works cited are given at the end of the book.

journalists can do is try looking the other way a bit; otherwise the problem of criminality among the Maltese 'can spread like a bad exhalation and damage the reputation of proud George Cross people'.

The message is clear. Public investigation and discussion of Maltese affairs, however well-meaning, can only make things worse than they need be. And this view seems to have prevailed among observers of the race relations scene right up to the present day. In the course of conducting the study reported in this book, however, I have parted company with this overwhelming consensus, and I now feel that on balance it is no longer helpful to maintain the silence. My change of opinion is partly a reflection of altering circumstances. The main period of press persecution is over, and the risk of provoking further public hostility has diminished. Since the arrival of darker-skinned, more alien immigrants, public interest and anxiety have transferred to them; and the recent attack on some Maltese in the *News of the World* seems to have fallen on stony ground.[1]

A more fundamental reason for departing from the consensus is that the liberal premises on which it appears to be based, and their implied model of individual and group relations, no longer appear to me to be tenable. Liberal theory asserts that the participation of people in a social system as unencumbered, self-fulfilling individuals is highly desirable, both in terms of social justice and social order. On the assumption that social and political behaviour in Britain closely approximates towards this ideal, many liberals supposed that immigrant settlers would seek to shed their separate identities as soon as they could in order to immerse themselves totally in the receiving society, and that natives would welcome them in goodwill. This was seen as an excellent opportunity to show the rest of the world the superiority of the open society, as patented in Britain, in resolving communal strife.

It is by now quite clear that this bland expectation was misconceived, as the 1960s have produced a series of obstacles to the effective extension to newcomers of full and equal citizenship – both in the attitudes of the majority group and in the immigrant communities themselves. The traditional liberal notion of

---

[1] An exposure of Maltese criminals started with a blaze on the front page of the *News of the World* on 29 April 1973, and petered out after three weeks.

individual assimilation has become qualified, and taken refuge within a somewhat incoherent concept of 'integration', whereby a degree of cultural pluralism and separatism is held to be quite compatible with universal enjoyment of equal and identical social and political rights for all individuals.[1]

But even in this modified and rather woolly guise, the idea that individualistic assimilation of immigrants in Britain is a natural and wholly beneficial process finds little support in the study presented here. The rationale for silence about the Maltese hinges on the belief that if individual migrants are keenly assimilating to British society, then not much can be wrong. The evidence collected here shows that there is indeed a widespread desire among Maltese immigrants for complete absorption into British society, but also that it is questionable how far this can be considered a normal and healthy phenomenon. In particular, it seems doubtful whether this 'assimilating' tendency is in any way jeopardised, as has been supposed, by the presence of criminality in the ethnic community. All the signs are that it is closely bound up with it, and even dependent on it. If the one is defined as natural, then the other should be too; and in so far as an aspiration to assimilation among immigrants is to be applauded, it may be necessary to give some recognition to less desirable concomitants. Perhaps this, as much as the unsavoury nature of some Maltese criminal activities themselves, is the unpalatable truth which the conspiracy of silence has sought to avoid. If so it is surely high time to break it, as realistic community relations cannot be based on wishful thinking.

Even if it can be accepted that public discussion of the Maltese case is potentially instructive, it may still be objected that such a debate must surely cause additional pain to innocent Maltese individuals. This is a very difficult issue to judge, but I think that it would be wrong to suppose that publication of the problems of Maltese must inevitably exacerbate them. This might be the case if the difficulties arising out of the poor public image were slight and avoidable; and perhaps most observers have assumed just this. But in fact they are a pervasive feature of the shared experience of Maltese people in this country, and notwithstanding waning public interest have dominated their relationships both within

[1] See E. J. Rose, *Colour and Citizenship*, ch. 33.

and outside the ethnic group. As long as the adverse commentary in the nationalistic press is remembered, no amount of self-denial by more sympathetic investigators is likely to help much. It may conceivably make matters worse. For silence on the part of commentators who could give a more balanced account of the situation, for example by drawing attention to the role of the British in shaping Maltese society and fostering Maltese deviance, must by default help reinforce the prevailing feeling that the Maltese are altogether unmentionable. I believe that, provided a reasonably full picture is given of the development and position of the Maltese community, publicity may do something to improve their collective standing.

There is no point in denying that there is some danger in a detailed study of the Maltese in Britain, as it cannot be guaranteed that all readers will in fact bother to acquaint themselves with the whole story. Those with hostile feelings towards Maltese may be able, by selective reading, to find information with which to rearm their antagonism. This cannot be avoided without completely emasculating the analysis. No half-way position is possible. Any attempt to gloss over a significant but unpleasant aspect of the situation, or cover up certain material, would merely perpetuate the suspicions, half-truths and erroneous assumptions that have prevailed for so long. However, the risk of malicious interpretation does not now seem very great, and is in my view outweighed by the possible benefits of fuller appreciation of the Maltese predicament.

The desirability of presenting a rounded and comprehensive account of the position of the Maltese community is one thing; the practical job of producing it another matter. Because so little information on the Maltese had been collected and published, I found that I had to start virtually from scratch on every topic I pursued. This meant that a great deal of available time had to be put into the compilation of usable material, and is one reason why the study spread itself eventually across several years. Each main stage in the attempted unravelling of interlocking factors entailed amassing and sorting out a fresh set of data, and the study tended to lurch forward as a series of semi-independent enquiries probing successive questions. It must be admitted at the outset that when fitting these diverse materials together into an overall picture, I sometimes found that I did not have direct evidence of the relationships between separate elements, and needed to speculate rather freely about the most probable connections. I have however made this clear in the text so far as this is feasible.

The first question to be taken up was the ostensibly straight-forward matter of establishing the general volume and composition of Maltese migration to Britain, and the distribution of the settlement here. This proved no easy job. Before drawing up the main lines of this study, I made a short, exploratory visit to Malta to look at the background of migrants and see what sort of enquiry might be possible. This field trip was useful in stimulating hypotheses, in particular about how far the social and political condition of Malta could be interpreted as a legacy of colonial rule; but in terms of hard figures all it did was to demonstrate how inadequate, and discrepant, were the various sets of British and Maltese official statistics on migration. So the first task I had to set myself on return was sorting out the major contradictions, in order to produce some realistic, if approximate, estimates of the size and composition of the immigrant community. The outcome of these investigations is summarised in Appendix B. Having done this I was then able to unscramble British census figures to separate out non-Maltese people born in Malta, categorised in our statistics with Maltese nationals, to reveal a more accurate profile of the actual Maltese community in Britain. This further stage in adjusting official materials is discussed briefly in Appendix C. Unfortunately the basic figures used for this have been out of date for some time now, as they were taken from the 1961 census. This source remains the best overall guide to the position of Maltese in London, for, unlike the 1966 census, it represents a full enumeration of the population, and covers a wide range of questions and at the time of writing the main results of the 1971 census had not yet been made available.

Although providing a useful general indication of the condition of the Maltese population, British census material gives little away about the spirit and organisation of the community, and so a programme of interviewing was carried out among Maltese migrants in London, mainly in 1967, to obtain more sensitive – as well as more up-to-date – information on the character and development of the group. This constituted the main enquiry in the investigation, and its findings are referred to at practically every stage in the argument. A description of the nature and conduct of this enquiry, and a summary of material collected in it, can be found in Appendix D.

Carrying out the London enquiry brought home to me just how central the Maltese bad name was to their experience here. So after completing this interviewing I made an analysis, in early 1968, of the convictions of Maltese men in two London magistrates' courts, to find out what behavioural basis the reputation might have, and see how trends in convictions related to fluctuations of public interest and anxiety. Detailed results of this analysis are reproduced in Appendix E. Following this I tried to establish what contribution the domestic situation in Malta might have had in shaping Maltese criminality, and I made a limited investigation of similar activities there. I was unable to collect primary data for this, and so my evidence had to be drawn from Maltese Government reports and legislation. This is a rather obscure area in Maltese social history, and my conclusions here are particularly speculative.

Finally I turned to the problem of what impact the reaction of the British majority to the Maltese, and to their reputation, might have had on the development and structure of the immigrant community. In 1969 I accordingly made a short survey, conducted postally, of the attitudes to Maltese of some non-Maltese residents of two London boroughs. The findings of this enquiry, parts of which are summarised in Appendix F, allowed me to close the circle of analysis by suggesting how British sentiments and conceptualisations may have interacted with those of the Maltese in creating the overall situation. In many ways this set of material, relating to British feelings about a minority group, generates the most far-reaching implications of this study. The Maltese community in Britain has a number of peculiarities which make its problems rather different from those of most minorities. Because of these odd features it may seem that their case holds little of general interest. But in fact just because it is unusual, this case-study is able to show up certain aspects of the minority situation in a particularly conspicuous form, and helps to highlight the existence of forces in British society whose operation is in ordinary circumstances easily overlooked. Hence it is in fact a most instructive case, and by virtue of its very singularity raises important questions about the general nature of our own society which might otherwise be more difficult to formulate. Ultimately this is perhaps the most compelling reason for subjecting the Maltese to public scrutiny.

I

MALTESE MIGRATION TO BRITAIN

The Anglo-Maltese connection is conventionally thought to have started with a letter sent by a Maltese delegation to Nelson in 1798, asking for his help in relieving the island from the scourge of Napoleon. Britain's speedy response, leading to their replacement of the French in 1800, may not have been entirely motivated by sympathy for the Maltese. Indeed, the fact that the possession of Malta was an important issue in the ensuing Anglo-Napoleonic wars, which ended with its formal acquisition by Britain under the Treaty of Paris in 1814, shows that consideration of Maltese feelings may have played a relatively minor part in shaping imperial strategy. Nevertheless the traditional idea that Britain was invited to occupy Malta reflects an important psychological truth, as the relationship has been seen on both sides as a friendly one, more between patron and client than master and subject.

This relationship was also very much in keeping with the general fortunes and experiences of the two nations whose destinies it bound together. For while Britain had a long and aggressive record of dominance in international affairs, and freedom at home from alien invaders, Malta's history had been one of almost unbroken occupation by imperial powers. Over the period of British administration of Malta, these complementary characteristics of imperial pride and submissive dependence together reached their zenith and then fell back – so that now, as Britain's former glory slips away, Malta has achieved nationhood and is looking for an independent role in world affairs.

But whereas the decline of Britain since the dissolution of its empire is probably irreversible, it is unlikely that Malta will ever achieve true independence, owing not merely to its small size, but also to the very nature of the place. Throughout Malta's known history her claim to be anything more than a barely-habitable rock

9

has been based on one supremely valuable resource – a secure natural harbour strategically placed at the slender waist of the Mediterranean.[1] This harbour is a natural fortress and entrepôt, and has been of interest to any state wishing to dominate the area. Before the British, there were successively the Phoenicians, Romans, Arabs, Spanish and French – via the ostensibly sovereign Knights. At present, in spite of the reduced importance of sea power, it is under the watchful eye of Russia as well as of the Nato alliance, which has formally taken the base over from Britain. Were it not for constant foreign interest, Malta would have had little to commend it as a site for human settlement.

This dependence on outsiders has led to a high degree of specialisation in the Maltese economy. Primary production is relatively unimportant, and the Maltese population has long since passed the point at which it could be supported from locally produced goods. The balance of income has derived from the expenditure of controlling powers, in return for – and in the course of exercising – their political and commercial rights in Malta.

The involvement of overseas powers in Malta has not always resulted in detailed control by foreigners over domestic Maltese affairs. Domination for mainly commercial ends, like that by France during most of the eighteenth century, has tended to assist indigenous economic initiative, since the market is a sufficiently decentralised system to allow occupying powers to tolerate a measure of local independence. In contrast, military occupation severely restricts local enterprise. A military administration must generally be highly centralised, and in so far as the interest of great powers in Malta has been strategic, the Maltese economy is necessarily controlled largely from outside, and becomes concerned particularly with servicing the military population.

This was taken furthest during the British period, in which the Maltese economy became increasingly dependent on the British garrison. Price, a leading authority on nineteenth-century Malta, has shown that Imperial expenditure accounted for an ever larger share of the national income over this period, and he argues that

---

[1] The name 'Malta' itself is believed to derive from the Punic word for harbour, and to date from the period when Phoenicians used the island as a trading base.

this made the whole economy extremely precarious.[1] Economic viability came to depend on purely strategic value – a commodity which for Maltese, if not for the British, was uncontrollable. During this period the economy lurched through a succession of strategic booms and depressions, beyond any local prediction or intervention, which gradually bemused the commercial classes into a supine fatalism.[2] The opening of the Suez canal led to a revival of the commercial dockyard in the last quarter of the nineteenth century, but this was too late and too little to prevent the economy from becoming almost totally subservient to the British garrison by the turn of the century.

In these circumstances the energy and interest of the Maltese seem to have become displaced, as often happens among powerless minorities, into religious activity and contemplation. It was with the arrival of the British that Malta came for the first time under the rule of a Protestant monarch. The Maltese were already a most strenuously Roman Catholic people; and by local repute Malta was the first Christian country, converted by St Paul following his shipwreck. Under the Knights it served as the bastion of Catholic Europe against the Moorish threat. Replacement of the Knights by Protestant governors created a situation in which the National church became projected into a new and more significant position as defender of the faithful population against an alien system of government.

Early British administrators were careful to respect obvious Maltese suspicions, and in their efforts to allay them ended up by strengthening the local church. One of the first sovereign acts was to free the church from Sicilian control and make the bishop directly responsible to Rome. This strengthened the church as a symbol of national identity. So from being in the eighteenth century near the hub of an internationally oriented Catholic system, the Maltese in the early nineteenth century had become a more obviously dependent people, with a national and rather isolated church, in religious opposition to their secular rulers.

Boissevain has shown that in the absence of alternative structures, a number of political functions have devolved on the church in Malta,[3] and it is likely that this tendency became entrenched under

[1] Charles A. Price, *Malta and the Maltese*, pp. 109 and 208–9.
[2] Ibid., p. 130.
[3] Jeremy Boissevain, *Saints and Fireworks; Religion and Politics in Rural Malta*, 1965.

the British. The increasingly centralised 'fortress' system of government inhibited the growth of secular political agencies, and the undermining of Maltese business stifled the emergence of a vigorous bourgeoisie. Instead the middle classes became bureaucrats in the Imperial administration. So for the Maltese peasants it was the church – as major landlord, national organisation and defender of the faith and of local, rural interests – which came to represent the nation and command their patriotism.

As the economy became progressively mobilised in support of the garrison, the only sphere of Maltese life which was allowed any proper independence was religion, in respect of which the British, although often scornful, were at least indulgent. Much of the passionate interest in religion displayed in Malta has therefore been escapist, and the alleged fatalism of the islanders simply a pursuit of spiritual goals rather than material – over which the Maltese individually and collectively enjoyed so little control. During the British period it is therefore likely that the religiosity of the Maltese increased. Certainly, while the remainder of Christendom had been undergoing secularisation, religious interest in Malta was maintained at a level described by many commentators as fanatical.[1] As recently as 1961, a parish survey in suburban Malta found that half the respondents attended Mass daily.[2]

The powerful position occupied by the church in Malta is closely bound up with the difficulties experienced by the Maltese in evolving an effective political system. The centralised administration of Malta as a fortress allowed no real internal political participation, but at the same time required a centralised organisation to express and inform local opinion. The church was particularly useful here because, while it was well equipped to serve as an authoritarian channel of communication, it was in the last resort not concerned with the material world and so presented no real challenge to the Governor.

It was precisely this facility to serve as an irresponsible voice of the people, though, which made the church so troublesome when the British did feel the need to promote more self-government. After the First World War, then again more decisively after the Second, the administration introduced new constitutions

[1] See, for example, Price, op. cit., p. 19.
[2] For more detailed figures see Table A.1 in Appendix A.

aimed at turning Malta into a modern secular state with a large degree of internal autonomy. However, because of the central position of the church in Maltese society there are very few issues on which the clergy have not felt impelled to speak and act. Since the Second World War they have not taken political office, but they have continued to exert influence informally. Notably, the church has at election times declared it a mortal sin to vote for certain allegedly anti-Catholic politicians, and has refused absolution to any who succumbed. This has created bitter conflicts between clergy and those who feel that complete separation of church and state is essential. Boissevain has referred to this as the fundamental problem of Maltese political life, and confessed to seeing no ready solution to it.[1]

The central position of the church has for generations channelled political debate into essentially symbolic and unrealistic issues. Governments and constitutions have collapsed over such questions as whether or not a prime minister had once attended a freemasons dinner, or on the hanging in a state gallery of a picture belonging in the cathedral. However, in retrospect, the nature of this conflict between church and state and the ostensibly ludicrous disputes to which it has led, can perhaps be seen as due not to the 'position of the church' as such, but rather to the fundamental incompatibility of local autonomy with a fortress administration. There was no need to be serious about politics as long as the British had a strategic interest in Malta, for whenever a constitutional deadlock arose, they would quickly and gratefully reassert direct rule. Hence there was never a compelling incentive for the Maltese to address themselves to problems realistically, as the important decisions were not likely to be taken by them anyway.

A mixture of petulant irresponsibility and fatalism was a perfectly rational response to British paternalism. Throughout the nineteenth and early twentieth centuries the church played the main part in this. Under the post-war constitutions secular bodies have joined in, but the role is basically the same.

The relationship between political irresponsibility and minority status is shown up clearly by what happened after the eventual granting of independence in 1964. Once the paternalistic, Protestant administration had been replaced by a local, Catholic government, realistic indigenous political forces quickly organised

<hr>

[1] Jeremy Boissevain, 'Malta; Church and State'.

themselves into a system in which the church was allocated a more strictly religious sphere of operation. The exercise of real political power soon brought the conflict between church and state to a head. Following a successful intervention in the 1966 election by the church against the Malta Labour Party, the Council of Europe ruled that civil rights were not adequately protected in Malta. Within months the church and the Labour Party – the current secularist protagonists – issued a concordat declaring that their differences were now resolved.[1] This is probably not the end of the matter, and further skirmishes will undoubtedly occur. But independence has greatly changed the prospects, and a spirit of national determination to settle the issues is now very much in evidence.

The population problem

One of the principal areas in which Maltese fatalism has most exasperated British administrations is that of population control. The problems associated with population growth have continually received official attention, and from as early as 1836, when the matter was examined by Royal Commissioners, the Maltese have been urged to change. The major cause of concern was initially strategic, as it was felt that a fortress with a large civilian population would be more vulnerable in a siege. But the general economic viability of the island was also an important issue.

The underlying causes of rapid population growth were seen to be located in the early age of marriage in Malta and also in the remarkably and persistently large size of completed Maltese families. Any attempts to question the prudence of these customs were interpreted by church authorities as attacks on the religious devotion of the people, and because of the national prestige of the church, British efforts to persuade couples to defer marriage and limit child-bearing failed signally. The debate itself may even

[1] Their joint statement emphasised that 'in modern society it is necessary to draw distinctions between the political community and the Church. The very nature of the Church demands that it should not interfere in politics. The Church authority has the duty and right to safeguard its spiritual and temporal interests and when necessary to teach which principles are correct and which are untenable. The Church does not impose mortal sin as censure. We are pleased to declare that in the spirit of the Second Vatican Council relations between the Church and the Malta Labour Party have improved considerably. We hope that with the help of God this goodwill will in future contribute towards peace among us' (*The Times*, 7 April 1968).

have inflated the patriotic and religious appeal of large families, for the Maltese have been slower in reducing their fertility than neighbouring Catholic countries. In 1948, for example, the Maltese census showed that a quarter of completed families still had over ten children. Later studies indicate that by the early 1960s this had fallen to around one fifth, but the average completed family size was still about six children.[1]

Over the last decade the idea of birth control has gained a small foothold in Malta, mainly through the work of the Cana Movement, a lay Catholic association which has introduced acceptable family limitation programmes evolved in more progressive Catholic environments. This recent development, which again seems to have coincided with the general trend towards realism since Independence, does seem to have resulted in a real element of positive control of population. During the last intercensal period (1957–67) a definite check in the growth of population was recorded for the first time, a contributory factor having been a fall in the overall birth rate.

It is still too early to say whether the Maltese are at last abandoning their predilection for large families. Until recently, the dominant theory of population held in Malta was that God would provide for his children. And this theory has always been upheld by events. The build-up of the British garrison continually provided extra employment for the growing population, and in spite of periodic difficulties and anxieties, none of the predicted catastrophes has materialised. Throughout the British period the Maltese man in the street would have been quite justified in the belief that on the whole there was no need to listen to jeremiads, all the more since they were so demonstrably offensive to his moral sensibilities. For in spite of chronic symptoms, a condition of real over-population has never really been reached.[2]

Casual nineteenth-century emigration

Given the propensity of the Maltese economy to accommodate the population presented to it, emigration was traditionally regarded simply as a short-term safety-valve or palliative to be used in exceptionally difficult periods. During the whole of the nineteenth century, and perhaps earlier too in a minor way, the

---

[1] Table A.2 in Appendix A gives more detailed figures on this.
[2] H. Bowen-Jones *et al.*, *Malta: Background for Development*, p. 161.

migrant flow consisted of persons drifting in an unorganised manner along the trade and shipping links with nearby Mediterranean ports. In many respects this emigration was just an extension and by-product of commercial networks. When the economy in Malta was sluggish, people would move out along these networks to operate elsewhere. As soon as the domestic situation improved, the great majority would return.

This tidal flow of migrants within a fairly small geographical area was feasible because booms and depressions in Malta generally occurred inversely with economic cycles in the rest of the basin. Again the cause of this was the garrison. Times of insecurity and war, when normal commercial activities were disrupted, were precisely the moments when British military expenditure in Malta was greatest. The more dependent the economy became on service expenditure, the more striking was this relationship.

Maltese emigrants did not regard their movement as permanent, and Maltese public opinion did not think it should be. Schemes were occasionally drafted for the promotion of permanent emigration. But the inspiration for these was mostly British, and they foundered through their inability to take into account Maltese preferences. Even Price has failed to appreciate the mood of most Maltese on this. He describes the tidal flow system of migration as economically irrational, and characterises the preference of Maltese for staying in or returning to Malta as a 'belief' or 'prejudice' that other countries were unsuitable for permanent Maltese habitation. He cites (Introduction and ch. 6) as proof of the erroneous nature of these beliefs the facts that some Maltese *did* settle permanently outside Malta, and that in the twentieth century many have done so right away from the Mediterranean region.

The real situation was probably less mysterious than he suggests. It is surely quite understandable that a proportion of casual migrants (15 per cent according to Price) should decide to settle in their place of work, irrespective of their original intentions.[1]

[1] Price gives the overall rate of settlement outside of Malta during the nineteenth century as 15 per cent (p. 189). This is quite compatible with an original intention to return to Malta. In the sample of Maltese interviewed in London, 40 per cent of the respondents who had come to the UK with very vague or casual settlement intentions in the first place, had decided that they would now probably stay permanently. Similarly, of respondents who had originally intended to stay only for a short or specific period, 31 per cent had since decided to stay here for good.

Considering the volume of these casual movements, the size of resulting colonies is small, and is not inconsistent with a general unwillingness on the part of Maltese to stay overseas.

The first main wave of emigration, after the Napoleonic war boom, was almost entirely casual, and closely reflected the state of the Maltese economy. But as some overseas settlements did begin to form, a more deliberate type of emigration became possible, although probably never very popular. Thus Price notes that as the nineteenth century wore on, movements out of Malta became less dependent on simple economic factors, and the existence of colonies abroad encouraged and sustained a certain amount of movement irrespective of domestic unemployment. Motives less purely economic, such as a desire for adventure, or to join up with or visit friends and relatives, were coming to play a more important part in the overall pattern.[1] Furthermore, as the social and religious organisation of Malta tightened, with the burgeoning of the parallel and interdependent military and ecclesiastical bureaucracies, a number of Maltese may have been seeking release through emigration from an increasingly oppressive society. As shown in Chapter IV, this has certainly been a feature of movements in the twentieth century.

Nineteenth-century emigration created little permanent settlement outside of Malta, but it did make some contribution to the population problem by helping to reduce the rate of marriage, and by removing young adults during their most fertile years. Like so many other features of Maltese life under the British, this pattern of casual movements was in the last analysis dependent on an indulgent, paternalistic administration. For although little public money was spent on promoting emigration, quite large sums were dispensed each year to support destitute Maltese abroad or to repatriate them. The initial reluctance of Maltese to leave the island would have been less easy to overcome without these facilities. But as will also be shown in later chapters, this indulgence had unforeseen consequences from which the Maltese are still suffering.

Organised emigration and economic planning

Maltese confidence in the providential capacity of Imperial

[1] Price, op. cit., p. 139.

expenditure to absorb population growth received its first major jolt with the termination of the First World War, and the heavy redundancy which followed in the dockyard. There was widespread distress and for the first time a sizeable segment of informed public opinion was prompted to consider organising emigration. Plans were made to send migrants to more distant lands, whence they would be less disposed to drift back, and where lasting colonies would be created to attract surplus Maltese thereafter. An official emigration agency was formed to negotiate entry with appropriate governments, and to screen and subsidise prospective emigrants.

Use of the English language had increased in Malta towards the end of the previous century, and small numbers of casual migrants had by this time been travelling to the English-speaking new worlds of Australia and North America. Emigration officials were encouraged by these private ventures, and set about opening up these countries to large-scale penetration. For a few years they enjoyed some success, but the wider sweep of events was against them. Growing economic depression and isolationism in receiving countries stopped the flow before it could get properly established. The status of Maltese as British, although never unambiguously acknowledged, maintained some minor openings for a while. Some Maltese, for example, were able to get visas for the USA during the twenties by travelling first to the United Kingdom, then onwards via the British quota.[1] But the main movements were soon curtailed.

The overall migration balance-sheet for the inter-war period was disappointing; the migration return rate in the 1920s was nearly as high as for the local and haphazard excursions of the previous century. Then, with the deepening insecurity at the end of the decade, followed by political instability in the 1930s, emigration was almost completely suspended. At the same time, as the international situation deteriorated, the Maltese economy itself picked up and was able to re-absorb the workers who were coming back. So by the outbreak of the Second World War, Providence had again found work for her children in Malta.

Emigration started again after the war. For the second time in a generation there was heavy postwar redundancy: but now there were also compounding fears about the longer-term prospects

[1] Henry Casolani, *Awake Malta, or the Hard Lesson of Emigration*, pp. 67–8.

for the garrison. Britain's relative decline as a world power and, even graver, a new uncertainty about the strategic value of Malta in an age of changing military technology, aggravated the immediate feelings of desperation. Those Maltese who had managed to emigrate after the First War were beginning to serve as magnets for relatives and friends, and a backlog of applications to emigrate was building up. So as immigration restrictions were eased in receiving countries at the end of the war, Malta was able to mount her largest-ever official programme of emigration to extra-Mediterranean countries.[1]

The over-dependence of the economy on service expenditure had by this time become evident to all, and programmes for broadening its base and returning a civilian role to the shipyard, in the form of entrepôt functions and bunkering, were under consideration. Emigration fitted into the plans as an essential measure for bringing about the restructuring of the economy, by removing the surplus population while all available resources were diverted into the growth sectors. Successive post-war redevelopment schemes have all emphasised this critical role.

In the event, the actual development of the Maltese economy following the run-down of the garrison has not been primarily industrial. Instead there has been a rapid growth in tourism and in meeting the demand for retirement homes in the sun, both of which entail some continuing dependence on Britain and greater-than-ever emphasis on personal service occupations. The boom in tourism was closely tied up with the British balance of payments difficulties and foreign travel currency restrictions. Malta was exempt from these regulations, and also enjoyed especially cheap air travel rates. Because of the arbitrariness and short-term nature of these encouragements, the tourist 'industry' has been a precarious investment, and by the later 1960s had already moved into decline.

The other profitable development – the creation of a tax-haven for prosperous, retired English people – was equally dependent on conditions in Britain, and soon ran into legal problems, for instance double death duties. Furthermore its economic effect has not been wholly benign, as it helped bring about rapid inflation – so that the real living standards of many Maltese suffered – without generating much extra employment. However until or unless the

[1] H. Bowen-Jones *et al.*, op. cit., p. 159.

Suez canal is re-opened, the alternative lines of development as set out in development plans will be hampered.

Although its basis seems fragile, the domestic boom since Independence has had a restraining effect on emigration. Annual rates have dropped steadily through the second part of the 1960s, and re-migration has increased. In 1964 over nine thousand more Maltese left the island than returned to it, and six and a half thousand the following year. By 1968 the net balance of outward movement of Maltese passengers was down to eight hundred, and in 1969 there was an *inward* balance of two and a half thousand.[1] It is still too early to judge whether this marks the end of another post-war emigration phase or just a temporary lull. Dom Mintoff's Labour administration, elected in 1971, is making very determined efforts to bring the Maltese economy under control by casting it in a less servile mould, in particular through concentrating on industrial investment. If Mintoff can attract capital or find exploit-able resources such as offshore oil, this may be possible. But in the meantime he remains dependent on foreign patronage and the traditional activities of servicing foreign sojourners, so that the economy and emigration seem likely to continue for some time to be towed along as before in the wake of decisions taken outside the island.

Emigration and politics

Permanent and distant emigration from Malta has become a reality this century. But it still goes very much against the senti-ments of most Maltese people. Not surprisingly, the issue has been the source of some acrimony in domestic politics.

Parties of the establishment, such as the current Nationalist Party, and which are closely bound up with the church, have accepted organised emigration with the same fatalistic nonchalance which formerly characterised Maltese unwillingness to do any-thing at all about population. Their public attitude has been that it is regrettable for any sons of Malta to have to leave but that because of gross unemployment, it must be faced bravely.

The present main secularist party, the Malta Labour Party (MLP) would prefer to solve the population problem through a

[1] Statistics of Maltese passenger movements are not yet available for later years, so it is impossible to say whether this trend has been maintained.

positive birth control programme, and sees the fostering of emigration as an establishment plot to erode support for the MLP itself. As it is mainly MLP supporters who have to emigrate, and as migration may remove something over 5 per cent of the electorate in a single year, this is a difficult charge to refute.

The heaviest emigration has undoubtedly occurred under the Nationalist Party.[1] It is widely believed in Malta that when the Nationalists are in power the most effective way to expedite one's treatment at the Department of Emigration is to turn up wearing an MLP badge. Under the Independence constitution and the new (Nationalist) citizenship laws, emigrants cannot retain dual nationality, even within the Commonwealth. So Maltese overseas must renounce local citizenship if they want to remain Maltese and keep their residence and voting rights. This is all seen by the MLP as a plan to deprive emigrants for life of their voice in Maltese affairs, and it has been badly received in the major Maltese settlements throughout the world, where many would still like to regard their stay as temporary.

Another reason why political support and emigration are connected is that in Malta there is a tendency for employment prospects to depend on political allegiance. It is an open secret that both the government and private employers exercise partiality on political grounds.[2] The electoral system of transferable votes encourages a network of patronage ties in which votes are traded for help in finding and keeping employment. This rule is one that all parties need to observe, and one of the reasons for lower emigration rates under MLP administrations is that the government is obliged to create mass work schemes to reward its followers.

Unemployment is therefore very much a political condition. Most private employers support the Nationalist Party, and the Nationalist Party has been the government – and therefore the public employer – for most of the time. So MLP supporters tend to be out of work more often for political reasons, which is why migrants are overwhelmingly MLP supporters. Unemployment also falls especially heavily on the young – both because they are less prepared to compromise themselves politically and because,

---

[1] The relation between the volume of emigration and political party in office has been summarized in the Malta Labour Party periodical *Voice of Malta*. A table published in the February 1968 edition, over Dom Mintoff's name, is reproduced below as Table A.3 in Appendix A.

[2] See Boissevain, *Saints and Fireworks*, p. 122.

62341

as single persons, they are regarded by employers as less deserving and reliable than the family man. Some employers have exploited single school-leavers by paying them subsistence wages until they are 19 or 20, then sacking them before they can marry. Consequently the common age for unemployment and emigration is between 18 and 25.

Not every emigrant is a reluctant exile, and many are only too glad of the opportunity to get away. This is usually related to disaffection with the dominant position of the church in Malta, from which emigration may appear to offer the only release. It is not easy to live in Malta and ignore the church. In the villages especially, the power of the clergy is almost total. Rarely is one out of sight of a church building or emblem to remind one of this. As a result the atmosphere can be extremely oppressive, and even Maltese who have never lived elsewhere are acutely conscious of lack of individual privacy and freedom. The island is so small and claustrophobic that physical movement within it is no solution; there is nowhere that one can go without being recognised.[1]

In late adolescence and early adulthood many Maltese feel an urge to escape and seek adventure and freedom. Often this is related to sexual frustration.[2] This desire for personal liberation probably played a part in the casual emigration and seafaring of the early nineteenth century, but it is unlikely to have been an important consideration until the church took on its almost totalitarian character, which seems to have occurred later in the century.

As political activity has become more open and realistic, many Maltese have looked to collective action for a solution to the problem of ecclesiastical power. With the rise of the Labour movement, and in particular since the introduction of mass suffrage, the individualistic desire to escape has become tempered by the belief that it is worth while staying in Malta to try to make it a better place to live. In the years of bitterest conflict with the church some Labour Party supporters still departed willingly enough, to get away from the intense – and in their view un-necessary – dilemmas of conscience that their political views

---

[1] A symptom of this lack of privacy is that letters to newspapers in Malta are almost invariably written above pseudonyms, especially if there is anything remotely controversial in the content.

[2] This point is elaborated in Chapter IV.

created. But since the concordat between the church and MLP this does not apply; and nor does being a socialist mean a lifelong opposition any more. Withdrawal of church interference in elections has predictably resulted in Dom Mintoff's return to power, and this time he seems to be getting some backing from the clergy in his attempted economic and social reforms. Open political debate seems assured for the foreseeable future, so that it is no longer necessary to go into exile in order to express opinions freely. Furthermore, under the new citizenship provisions, emigration is not a step to be taken lightly any more, and most young people with a serious desire to improve Malta are opting to stay there and sweat it out.

Emigration and population growth

Recent emigration has definitely had some effect in stemming Malta's population growth, and the only periods in which the population has not increased rapidly have been the two postwar spells of massive migration (see Table 1).

TABLE 1 *Emigration and population growth in Malta 1842–1967*

Intercensal period	Natural increase	Net population change		Net migration	
		Increase	Decrease	Outward balance	Inward balance
1842–51	11,310	8,620		2,690	
1851–61	17,470	10,060		7,410	
1861–71	7,860	8,490			630
1871–81	11,030	8,180		2,850	
1881–91	16,490	15,260		1,230	
1891–1901	15,830	19,710			3,880
1901–11	26,030	27,080			1,050
1911–21	17,300		110	17,410	
1921–31	25,280	28,260			2,980
1931–48	65,140	64,370		770	
1948–57	62,766	13,629		49,137	
1957–67	41,445		3,814	45,259	

Sources: 1842–1948 from H. Bowen-Jones *et al.*, *Malta, Background for Development*, table 30.

1948–67 from *Malta Demographic Review and Annual Abstract of Statistics*.

B

This effect has been produced by emigration in two ways – directly by counteracting natural population increase, and indirectly by removing young people during their most fertile span. Even casual and temporary emigration of young, single men has been important in this respect, as it has helped raise the age and lower the rate of marriage.

However the contribution of specifically permanent emigration in offsetting the natural population increase has been over-emphasised by official Maltese sources, which have naturally tried to give as much credit as possible to the Emigration Office. This has been done by using a curiously narrow definition of returning migrants, so that only a small proportion of them actually get counted in the official migration statistics. In official publications the category 'returning migrant' designates a person who has received government assistance or sponsorship, who returns to Malta within two years of this, and who informs the immigration police that he has come back to stay. Migrants who did not receive official aid, or who came back more than two years later, or who stated on return that they had only come back for a visit, would not be counted as returnees. It is in the interest of a migrant moreover not to be counted as a returnee, since this would make it more difficult to get sponsorship at a future date. So there is a strong bias in the system of compiling records towards the under-enumeration of returning migrants; and the wonder is not, as declared in government publications, that the rate is so low, but that any returnees should be officially detected at all.

Between the wars a more realistic definition was in use and a convincing return-rate was recorded. During the 1920s this was 83 per cent, which is a similar figure to that estimated by Price for nineteenth-century migration. But in recent decades the official rate has dropped to the suspiciously low level of 9 per cent. A more reliable assessment can be arrived at by analysis of the passenger balance statistics for Maltese persons, which yields a return rate of around 30 per cent up to 1967. Since then it may well have increased again, but the figures needed to show this are not available.

But even with the help of these passenger statistics it is difficult to gauge the true amount of movement back to Malta, as travel between Italy and Malta has not always been carefully attended to. Several Maltese censuses have discovered a population significantly in excess of estimates derived from returns on natural increase and passenger movements, and a large part of this discrepancy is likely to be due to such unrecorded arrivals via Italy. In the 1931 Malta census for example, 6361 more persons were enumerated than had been expected on the basis of natural increase and passenger statistics. As will be seen, the unreliable quality of these figures may have particularly important implications in estimating migration to the United Kingdom.

Migration to the United Kingdom

Britain is sentimentally a very special location for Maltese migration. For many Maltese it is a second home; and since they started to venture outside the Mediterranean, Britain has received them more openly than any other country. As the stronghold of personal liberties and the free society, Britain has been a particularly attractive destination for Maltese seeking refuge from religious oppression – and even perhaps from the colonial minority experience of living in the shadow of the garrison. Until the passage of the Commonwealth Immigrants Acts, Maltese could come and go freely in Britain. So as travel became easier, and use of the English language increased in Malta, Britain took over the role formerly filled by the Mediterranean ports of receiver of casual, short-term migrants. In addition, as English culture supplanted Italian among middle-class Maltese, London emerged as the centre of gravity for professional life in Malta, and numbers of students and other people came to acquire qualifications and experience.

To start with at any rate, few Maltese seem to have come here with permanent residence in mind. Britain's position at the centre of the Empire and Commonwealth has made it something of a clearing house for people unsure of exactly where they wanted to go, or unable to get there direct from Malta. From about the turn of the century, seamen have come to join the merchant navy, and this too has often been with the intention of getting to the distant dominions.

This special character of migration to the United Kingdom makes it difficult to estimate the amount of actual settlement. Large numbers of Maltese have certainly arrived; but many have later returned or moved on somewhere else. The statistics of formal migration movements are not much guide here; as is recognised by the Malta Department of Emigration, the unofficial, invisible journeys of migrants to and from Britain may be at least as large as those recorded.[1] Because of the ease and cheapness of imperial travel, it is only the less-well-off Maltese, or family groups, who needed assistance with their passage and who bothered to register with the Department before employment vouchers became necessary.

Passenger statistics do not add much to the picture, since they refer only to countries of embarkation and disembarkation – not to previous place of residence and final destination. Maltese returning overland are counted as travelling from Italy. This forms the largest component in Maltese passenger statistics, and could easily contain and conceal substantial movements to and from Britain. More generally, Maltese who acquire United Kingdom passports while living in Britain probably cease to be detectable as Maltese if they re-migrate.[2]

The official migration return-rate of 14 per cent for Maltese in Britain is lower than for other immigrant groups,[3] but for the reasons already outlined this figure should be disregarded. The true rate of return to Malta may be 50 per cent or more, and the total re-migration to all destinations even higher. So although many Maltese do come as migrants, the actual settlement is both more shifting, and much smaller, than generally supposed. This fact is important for an understanding of the state of community organisation among Maltese in Britain, and it will be referred to again.

Immigration controls in Britain over the last decade have done much to change the pattern of Maltese migration. At first sight the effect may appear to be negligible, as the volume of official migration has not been greatly reduced by British restrictions. The Maltese have in fact received preferential treatment under the

---

[1] See 1962 *Report of the Department*, p. 12. Statistics of Maltese *passenger* movements to the United Kingdom have only been kept for limited periods.

[2] Since Maltese independence and the creation of Maltese nationality, over 3000 Maltese resident in the United Kingdom have adopted UK citizenships, and would now hold non-Maltese passports.

[3] Estimates are given by the Economist Intelligence Unit in the first volume of *Studies on Immigration from the Commonwealth*. Malta's return rate is given as 14 per cent (from Malta government statistics) and the other rates given (based on passenger figures) are of the following order: India (39 per cent), Pakistan (63 per cent), West Indies (21 per cent) and West Africa (65 per cent).

Acts. Following the Mountbatten Mission in 1965, a special allowance of 1000 'A' employment vouchers was made for Maltese applicants. This allocation, made in recognition of Malta's dependent economy has exceeded the number of applications, and is in part wasted. Before this ceiling was imposed, only half of the vouchers issued to Maltese applicants were taken up, and the largest number of voucher holders actually admitted in a single year was less than 800.[1] So the special allowance, which was out of a total quota of 3000, was in reality comparatively generous. The numbers of applicants has declined since 1965, but this is probably not due to the restriction, as emigration from Malta has decreased altogether. Before 1971, when the allowance was reduced to 500, Maltese applications had consistently been fewer in number than the vouchers reserved for them. Also their rate of success in applications for the employment vouchers has been substantially higher than for other countries, and has suffered relatively less as a result of the tightening of British controls. The Maltese share of vouchers issued has increased steadily from 1 per cent of the total in 1962, to 20 per cent in 1972.

It might appear therefore that if Maltese migration to Britain has dropped off in the last few years this has little to do with the immigration legislation. But the Acts have completely ended the unofficial, casual immigration of Maltese, which formerly made up a large part of the total; and this fact has undermined perhaps irrevocably the role of Britain as a second home to Maltese, and has had significant effects on the volume and nature of settlement here.

Problems in estimating the volume of settlement

One reason why it is easy to overlook the temporary character of much migration to Britain, is because the official net migration figures coincide so remarkably well with the numbers of Malta-born persons enumerated at UK censuses (Table 2). The intercensal balance of migration (column 4) corresponds fairly closely with the increase in Malta-born persons in Britain (column 5), and it is tempting to regard the two sets of figures as mutually confirming. Official Maltese estimates of the volume of settlement in the United Kingdom tend to be taken straight from the censuses,

[1] For information on voucher application rates, etc., see Table A.5 in Appendix A.

and if any adjustments are made it is generally by *raising* the figure, to allow for supposed under-enumeration and for second and third-generation births within the settlement.

TABLE 2 *Emigration to Britain recorded in Malta, and Malta-born Population of England and Wales* * *1911–1966*

	Emigration to UK				Malta-born persons in E & W	
Period of emigration	Gross emigration	Migrant returnees		Net emigration	Intercensal increase	Malta-born popln at census	Date of census
		n	%				
	1	2	3	4	5	6	7
						5,703	1911
					1,033	6,736	1921
1921/2–30	3,628	1,218	34	2,410	1,264	8,000	1931
1931–50	9,551	1,232	13	8,319	6,503	14,503	1951
1951–60	12,246	1,807	15	10,439	10,176	24,679	1961
1961–5	6,614	731	11	5,883	6,900†	31,580†	1966

Source: Malta Department of Emigration Reports and UK censuses.
Notes: * Figures for Scotland and N. Ireland negligible.
　　　† Estimates, from 10 per cent sample census.

However, the British census figures are almost certainly far in excess of the true numbers of Maltese, as they include United Kingdom nationals born in Malta to service families resident there. This has been an extremely fertile group, owing to the high proportion of young wives of child-bearing age; and an analysis made of regimental birth registers suggests that at certain periods the average army wife in Malta was producing a child every two or three years. Estimates based on these sources indicate that up to the Second World War most of the Malta-born population enumerated in Britain would have been non-Maltese. Since the war the proportion is probably around one half.

Incidentally these births of non-Maltese British have also had an interesting influence on Maltese passenger statistics. The high fertility of British sojourners in Malta has created a persistent surplus of British passenger departures over arrivals, at all times except the end of the last war when many dependants of services personnel were re-admitted. This movement has helped to shield the passenger balance of returning Maltese migrants, and thereby to maintain the myth of a low return rate. The steady undertow of United Kingdom nationals leaving Malta has concealed the chronic inward flow of Maltese migrants; for when all passenger statistics are pooled together the sum is closer to the official figures for net emigration. For example, in 1931–9 the net inflow of Maltese passengers was 2589, and the net outflow of 'other British' passengers 2983. This effect is strongest in the last inter-censal period, 1957–67, during which a large part of the garrison and dependent families left the island. Their exodus made a valuable contribution to the apparent stabilisation of Malta's population over this period, as the total population decrease was only 3814, while the balance of non-Maltese British passenger departures was 10,001.

Sex composition of Maltese in Britain

Further substantiation of the largely non-Maltese composition of the Malta-born population in Britain is given by comparing its sex ratio with that of the migrant flow. Maltese migrants to Britain have always been predominantly single men. This was particularly true of the earliest arrivals, many of whom were seamen. It is probably more true of casual, unofficial migrants than of government-sponsored. The latter have generally been responsible people with a recognised need for assistance – and thus likely on all grounds to contain more married men. But even among these official migrants, and since the war when families have come in greater numbers, about two-thirds have been males.[1]

The actual proportion of males in the current settlement, including children, is likely to be even greater than this – nearer to three-quarters.[2] This is due in part to the continuing effect of very high rates among earlier arrivals, but also to the fact that

[1] Figures given in Table A.6, Appendix A.

[2] Support for this estimate is afforded by the analogous situation in Australia, where practically all Malta-born persons can however be assumed to be Maltese nationals. In the early stages of settlement the proportion of males enumerated in the censuses was very high; and even since the war, when massive family migration to the country has taken place, there is still a marked sexual imbalance. See Table A.7 in Appendix A.

re-migration from Britain occurs more frequently among migrant *families*. This is because Maltese women have a definite preference for Australia, where the climate is pleasant and where the existence now of a larger Maltese community makes domestic and social life more attractive for them. Although the amount of family migration to Britain increased in the mid-1960s, this has not been sustained, and was perhaps merely the combined effect of a gathering-in of dependants after the first Commonwealth Immigrants Act, and of the temporary bottleneck in migration from Malta to Australia. Taking the period 1962–72 as a whole, the arrivals of Maltese women have been almost cancelled out by their departures, so that the original male preponderance has been sustained.[1]

If Maltese nationals in the United Kingdom are assumed to be not less than 70 per cent males (or 65 per cent during the last decade), it is possible by adjusting census figures to make rough estimates of the volume, and even the location, of true Maltese residents in the country. This procedure is obviously not accurate for small numbers; but it is a useful guide to major trends and areas of concentration, and the overall figures this yields for each census are compatible with estimates derived from the births of United Kingdom nationals in Malta.

A complicating factor which needs to be taken into account in the analysis of sex ratios is that British servicemen (and some civilians) stationed in Malta have married Maltese girls who have subsequently returned to Britain with them. Sometimes when the girl's father has died, her mother has joined her here also. So there has been an additional movement of Maltese women to Britain which partially offsets the chronic male surplus in the main migratory flow. The numbers involved are not great, but nevertheless they constitute a sizeable chunk of the total Maltese national population in this country.

The pattern of Maltese settlement

In the light of all this, some estimates can be made of the real size of the Maltese immigrant community in Britain, which is clearly smaller than has been generally supposed. Before the war the settlement was negligible, almost certainly numbering less

[1] Statistics given in Table A.4, Appendix A.

than a thousand in the country as a whole, if service-brides are excluded. By 1951 the figure probably rose to around five thousand, and then doubled over the next decade. The 1966 sample census gives an indication of a further increase to a total of something in the order of thirteen thousand in the mid-1960s.[1] At present the number is unlikely to be much greater than this, and may even be less.

The community is also less well distributed than often assumed. Census figures for Malta-born persons tend to show at any particular time a clustering of about a third of the total in apparent concentrations, with the remainder widely and thinly scattered over the rest of the country. When these figures are adjusted to remove United Kingdom nationals the concentrations stand out more sharply, and account for almost all of the adjusted total.

The adjusted prewar concentrations were largely in ports such as Cardiff, Gillingham, Plymouth and Southampton, and most of the people enumerated were presumably seamen or ex-seamen.[2] In fact the actual total of Maltese seafarers based on these ports was probably several hundred more than was resident in Britain at census times, as those away at sea would not be counted.[3] Nevertheless the number involved is still small; the steady emigration officially recorded from Malta cannot have resulted in a very high settlement rate: and the bulk of Malta-born persons in Britain before the war were undoubtedly United Kingdom nationals.[4] At this time only a handful of Maltese appear to have been living in London; some around the dock area (centring then on Bermondsey), and others in the West End where a few students and professional people stayed.

This changed immediately after the war, with the substantial influx of migrants, and the 1951 census documents the emergence of the first decent-sized Maltese community, concentrated in

[1] See Table B.1 in Appendix B.

[2] Estimates of pre-war Maltese settlements in England and Wales are given in Table B.2 in Appendix B.

[3] Maltese seamen serving on British ships were enumerated under the 1894 Merchant Shipping Act, in 1901, 1906 and 1911, and figures published in command papers 1342, 3841 and 6442 in those years. Table A.8 in Appendix A summarises this material, showing the numbers, ratings and ages of these men.

[4] This fact was recognised when the censuses were taken. For example in the *General Report* to the 1911 census the comment is made that 'The large numbers from Gibraltar and Malta are apparently due in very great measure to the return to England of the families of soldiers who had been stationed at those places' (1911 census, *General Report*, p. 216).

London where about half – or, in central London, about a third – of the total Maltese lived. In later censuses the proportion in London has decreased slightly as a number of minor centres have grown up. But London has remained the chief centre, and the ports have ceased both relatively and absolutely to have any salience.

Movement of Maltese into London seems to have begun during the war itself. The capital experienced a shortage of labour in certain sectors, which attracted Maltese seamen currently unemployed or reluctant to go to sea in wartime. Relocation of Maltese away from the coastal areas was given further impetus after the war with the arrival of an unprecedented number of Maltese war brides, who have often served as sponsors for younger brothers and nephews. These brides are scattered throughout the country, and their existence has helped to diffuse the postwar influx of migrants along a large number of migration chains. It is difficult to gauge the amount of these diffused movements, but according to Maltese informants their effect is generally not long lasting. Many of the younger brothers and nephews leave after a year or two and either drift back to Malta or join compatriots in areas of major Maltese concentration. London is the principal receiver, but other cities like Manchester and Nottingham have similarly developed small communities.

Within London the most important grouping of Maltese has taken place in Stepney, which attracted seamen during the war and was the first area to develop a noticeable migrant community afterwards. Even in the 1960s, most new arrivals were still inclined to go first to Stepney, and the secondary centres draw people from there rather than direct from Malta. The main secondary developments have, accordingly, radiated out from this district to other parts of what is now Tower Hamlets, and to southern Hackney and Islington. Outside of this district the only habitations of any importance are in Brixton and small parts of the West End. About 80 per cent of all Maltese in London County, excluding service-brides, seem to live in these districts.[1]

Size of settlement

By the end of the 1960s it was clear that Maltese immigration to

[1] The main areas of settlement in London are shown in Table B.3 in Appendix B.

Britain was subsiding to a level where the inflow was only just adequate to offset natural wastage from death and re-migration, so that there was little chance of a larger community developing. The smallness of the Maltese population sets a limit to the possible level of communal organisation, and a highly independent or self-sufficient ethnic grouping would obviously be difficult to achieve with these numbers. It is significant that those Maltese here who have been keen to set up associations for their compatriots have generally supposed there to be many more of them awaiting mobilisation than there actually are; and their lack of success and eventual sense of failure can in some measure be seen as a consequence of their original over-estimation.

However there are certainly sufficient Maltese in Britain to sustain a fairly complex network of ethnic activities if they wanted to. As the Montserrat islanders in London show, small size is not necessarily a barrier to close-knit and lively ethnic grouping.[1] Geographical concentrations of Maltese exist in the sense that there are localities where enough live within reasonable travelling distance of each other. This is true most of all in London. Communications there are good. As the Metropolitan capital, London is where power over Malta has resided, and where pressure groups and political leaders have needed to operate. And since Independence the High Commission has channelled contact with Malta and Maltese affairs through London. So London is the natural hub of Maltese communal life in Britain.

But in spite of these potentialities the Maltese community in London displays little organisation or cohesion. As will be shown in later chapters there are several explanations for this, which go far beyond any possible consequence of the smallness of the community. Even if there had been many more settlers, it is doubtful whether things would have been very different. Small size may provide a comparatively low ceiling for ethnic interdependence and solidarity, but the sense of the community fails by a long way to reach even this level.

[1] Stuart B. Philpott, 'Remittance obligations, social networks and choice among Montserratian migrants in Britain'.

II

THE STRUCTURE OF THE
MALTESE COMMUNITY IN LONDON

Lack of cohesion in the community

Although the Maltese settlement in London is small, it was
assumed at the outset of this study that an active and organised
community existed. But the first contacts made with Maltese soon
cast doubts on this idea. The few formal associations turned out
to be weak, if not actually moribund, and general ethnic pride
and solidarity appeared to be at a low level. This seeming absence
of any real community was so glaring that it soon developed into
the central problem of the enquiry. Some systematic interviewing
was carried out among a cross-section of Maltese, to assess the
validity of these impressions, and the results confirmed the lack
of group cohesion.[1] This was manifested in a variety of ways.

First, and in spite of the recency of most migration from Malta,
nearly as many respondents defined themselves as English (35 per
cent) as Maltese (37 per cent), with the remainder unsure or
electing some composite or marginal identity. In addition to this
low level of ethnic consciousness, the extent of both formal and
informal association among Maltese proved to be limited. Less
than half of the respondents had regular and frequent meetings
(defined as once a week or more often) with Maltese outside of
their immediate household; and many came into contact with
compatriots only through purely chance encounters – in the
street, on a bus or in a betting shop and so on. Most voluntary
meetings were informal, consisting of domestic visits by a few
close friends and relatives, or of small gatherings in private clubs.
Very few of the sample had ever been involved in formal Maltese
associations in London, and indeed many were unaware of their
existence.

[1] For details of this '1967 enquiry' see Appendix D.

The weakness of the ethnic community is recognised by most Maltese. Only a third of the London sample considered that the Maltese living here were a cohesive group which could be regarded in any real sense as a community, and half of these made the revealing qualification that of course they personally were not involved in it. A half of the sample stated categorically that no Maltese community existed, and some actually laughed at the idea. The notions which respondents entertained about the nature of the community were related to the amount of contact they had with fellow-countrymen. In general, the more frequent their own contact with other Maltese, the more likely they were to assert that there was not a cohesive ethnic grouping. The only exception to this was a tiny minority who both attested without qualification to the existence and unity of a community, and associated frequently with other Maltese.[1]

Some Maltese in London attributed the poverty of their communal life to the geographical dispersal of settlers, arguing that they were so widely spread in the city that it was difficult to maintain regular contacts. This explanation was not applied to their own behaviour, but was used to help make sense of the supposed behaviour of others; in particular it resolved the discrepancy between the large number of Maltese believed to be living in London, and their personal experience in which they met very few. Most Maltese in fact assume that there has been fairly heavy settlement in Britain, with thirty to fifty thousand, not counting children, commonly offered as estimates. These figures are presumably derived in the first instance from the British census and then become inflated by allowances for supposed under-enumeration, and by the processes inherent in word of mouth transmission. Most of these Maltese are thought to live in London, but few respondents in fact knew of many others and some admitted to being astonished that their countrymen should manage to remain so inconspicuous. The theory of geographical dispersal bridges this gap between knowledge and experience.

But as pointed out in the previous chapter, Maltese are neither so numerous nor so scattered as assumed. Settlement is clustered in several moderately sized pockets. It may be misleading to call these concentrations, since even in Stepney the Maltese are quite

---

[1] For an expression of this relationship, consult Table D.3 in Appendix D.

thin on the ground, and are a visible minority in only a few streets.[1]

Nevertheless most Maltese in London do live quite near to a number of fellow-countrymen with whom they could socialise if they wished. Because of the small numbers, it is certainly possible to live close to a main area of settlement without having more than casual and infrequent contacts with other Maltese. But this is a possibility rather than a necessity. Within London the basic conditions for an active Maltese community are found, and if there is none some further explanation seems to be called for.

There is in fact an element of positive avoidance underlying the weakness of group structure. Far from being prepared to go a little out of their way in order to meet compatriots, many respondents went to some trouble in order *not* to do so. Only a third of the sample of men interviewed in 1967 expressed no objections to meeting *more* Maltese than they did already. Over half (55 per cent) stated that association between Maltese in London was not a thing to encourage; and the remainder (10 per cent) claimed to have no time for such activities. In terms of group consciousness and shared activities, a community barely existed.

Individualistic tendencies

The lack of cohesion among London Maltese is due in part to the nature of the migratory flow and the emigration motives of migrants. Although most of the migration to Britain has occurred within a narrow time-span, it has been a movement of individuals, rather than of family groups or small communities as has happened with contemporaneous migration to other receiving countries such as Australia. The majority of Maltese coming here have been young, single men. This is endorsed by the findings of the 1967 enquiry, in which 72 per cent of Maltese discovered in London were male, 65 per cent of sample members[2] had arrived between the ages of fifteen and twenty-five, and 79 per cent were bachelors on arrival. At the time of interview, nearly half (47

---

[1] Even these groupings had been diminished by the time of the main enquiry. Eastman Street in south Bethnal Green was largely a Maltese street in the late 1950s, but was demolished before field-work. Similarly in Christian Street, Aldgate, a pocket had been severely reduced by housing redevelopments by the time that interviewing was carried out.

[2] All of these were adult males.

per cent) had no close relatives anywhere in Britain, apart from wives and children.

Compared with other immigrants to this country, and with current Maltese migration to other countries, the *cafone* element is therefore strongly represented. Use of this term should not be allowed to suggest that the migrants are purely economic in their objectives; for although such considerations may be important, there is also a component of adventurism and escapism which is not always easy to separate out. A sizeable minority of the sample (29 per cent) did not have any clear economic reason for leaving Malta, and had often given up good jobs without any guarantee of finding equivalent work here. Their primary objective in leaving was to escape from the stranglehold which they felt the Maltese church exercised over political and social affairs. For other migrants this escapism was a secondary factor, not fundamental to their emigration as such, but perhaps determining why they had come to Britain rather than somewhere else – because the casual, disorganised nature of the movement to this country offers greater liberation than would participation in more organised migration to a different country, and because of the free way of life believed to prevail in Britain.

The escape afforded by emigration is not necessarily regarded as permanent. Sometimes it is seen merely as a means of asserting independence, so that when one returns to Malta, it will be on a new footing, as a man rather than a boy. For many young Maltese, a trip to England is by way of an adolescent cooling-off period. Few 1967 respondents had come with the intention of settling for good; in most cases they had entertained extremely flexible and vague expectations. This ties up with a further factor in the choice of Britain as a migration destination, namely the ease of travel to and from Malta. For many migrants this is a major reason for deciding to come here, and most men in the London sample had been back to Malta for holidays since their first arrival. So, again, migration to this country is distinctive in that it tends to attract those Maltese least committed to permanent settlement outside of Malta.

The discontent which drives many of these emigrants contains an element of sexual frustration. Sexual constraints in Malta are rigorous, and bear most severely on bachelors, from whose ranks most migrants to Britain are drawn. Marriage in Malta is a stratifying principle of some importance. Bachelors are not merely disadvantaged sexually, but, apart from the clergy, are socially defined as unreliable and irresponsible, and less deserving all round. Emigration offers a way out.

The situation of a married man is quite different. Unless he is deserting his wife,[1] his emigration motives will usually be more serious and more carefully worked out, as his conduct is bounded and tempered by family responsibilities. Normally a married man will prefer to go to Australia or North America than to Britain, since the composition of the migratory flow there is more balanced and his wife and children will have more Maltese families to mix with. Also settlement in a distant colony is seen as more permanent, and therefore as more responsible.

On all counts then the individuals attracted to Britain seem to be those with a minimal interest in cultivating a local Maltese community. Any who do wish to keep in touch with Maltese affairs can maintain direct contacts quite easily with friends in Malta. But most new arrivals are at a stage in their personal development when interest in Maltese culture and way of life is at a low ebb.

Adaptation of migrants

If migrants arrive with little interest in recreating a Maltese society in this country, their reception provides little incentive to change their minds. The majority are quickly able to look after themselves in Britain in essential matters. Most new arrivals,

---

[1] This seems to occur quite commonly, and several sample members had done it. In 1957 (the latest year for which figures could be found) over 300 maintenance orders were operative in Maltese courts for husbands domiciled in England and Wales. Some of these were on behalf of returned service-brides; but most were made on emigrants who had come to Britain without their wives. Some of these migrants subsequently remarry, bigamously, in Britain. This has been a delicate issue in Anglo-Maltese relations, for, if the second marriage is conducted in a civil registry, these migrants were not considered by the Maltese authorities to have contracted a further marriage, so that if *they* went back to Malta no maintenance order could be served on them there from London. (The same is true of course for non-bigamous civil marriages – but the same bitterness has not been created in these cases.) Since Independence the Maltese courts have put this right by deciding that a maintenance order can be transmitted in Malta on any marriage which is regarded as legitimate in the country where it was contracted. Although this does not help deserted bigamous wives, it has removed the impression that the Maltese church condoned such behaviour.

especially since the war, have sufficient knowledge of English to be able to work with non-Maltese people immediately. Some are rather small and swarthy, but they are not defined by English people as coloured, and do not experience great difficulties in finding employment.[1]

This is reflected in the occupational status of Maltese as recorded in the 1961 census.[2] Twenty-five per cent of Maltese held non-manual jobs, against a London average of 40 per cent, and there was a correspondingly higher proportion of unskilled workers. But their general status compared very well with other groups. The Cypriots, with whom Maltese are usually grouped for census tabulations, and who are frequently assumed to be similar to them, had a lower overall proportion of non-manual jobs in spite of a high managerial total, which was made up almost entirely of small businesses. Other immigrant groups in London registered much lower proportions of non-manual workers; for example Jamaicans had less than 5 per cent. These figures show that restrictions of opportunity are not so severe for the Maltese in London as they are for members of other immigrant minorities. Only once during the 1967 survey was a professional man met who was unable to get work appropriate to his qualifications, and even this had not been over a long period.

The over-representation of unskilled workers among Maltese may be due as much to the age of respondents, and differential immigration, as to real difficulties in the British labour market. It will obviously take young immigrants, as any young workers, some time to reach their employment peak; and as there are more young men in the Maltese settlement than old, there will be some bias towards lower status work. Comparing the current or last jobs of 1967 respondents with their fathers' main jobs, 12 per cent were upwardly mobile and 33 per cent downward.[3] For those who arrived since 1960, the respective figures were 3 per cent upward and 39 per cent downward; so age and duration of settlement are

---

[1] In the 1969 enquiry among non-Maltese people in London (see Appendix F) only 4 per cent of respondents considered Maltese to be coloured.

[2] See Table C.2 in Appendix C, where an account is also given of how the census figures were adjusted to separate Maltese nationals from other people born in Malta.

[3] This measure of social mobility is based on the three class division used in Table C.2 (i.e. non-manual; skilled and unskilled manual) and refers to movement between these categories.

clearly important factors. With the older settlers there was still a balance of downward mobility, but not great; it could probably be accounted for by differences in the overall occupational structures of Malta and Britain. In Malta's less developed economy the unskilled sector is smaller, and there are more craftsmen and small family businesses. If detailed allowance could be made for this the Maltese in London might compare favourably with the non-immigrant population.

Maltese also appear to be relatively better off than other immigrants in terms of the industries they worked in.[1] Cypriots were overwhelmingly concentrated in the pre-industrial sectors of catering and wood, clothing and leather work, with nearly two-thirds of employment in these. The Jamaicans were mainly in labouring and manufacturing. But the only sector in which there was a marked surplus of Maltese workers was catering and personal services, with a quarter of their total compared with an average of 9 per cent. Many of these were restaurant and hotel employees in the West End; and Maltese participation in this type of work can be interpreted to some extent as another heritage of the British presence in Malta. One of the main services provided by the local population to the garrison was culinary. A large proportion of Maltese recruits to the services and merchant navy have been employed as stewards in the galley; and the dock area of Malta has many small cafés and eating houses catering for sailors and servicemen.[2] Some members of the London sample worked in or even grew up in such establishments before emigrating. This servicing role has been exported to London now, in the sense that British people seem to consider the Maltese appropriate for this type of work. The image has been exploited by Maltese authorities seeking employment vouchers for migrants, and many controlled migrants have had their first taste of work in Britain in the kitchens of a large hotel.

The transference of the servicing role to London can explain some of the clustering in catering jobs, but it does not account for the small Maltese cafés, sometimes serving mainly Maltese people, which occur also outside of the West End. These grow more directly out of indigenous Maltese social life. Small cafés in Maltese villages have been the only real social centres not run

[1] See Table C.3 in Appendix C.
[2] See for example Table A.8 in Appendix A, giving numbers of stewards.

or dominated by the church. Consequently they serve as natural alternative foci of community life for migrants who have rejected the church and family-centred culture of straight Maltese society. A large proportion of the socialising which does take place within the ethnic group in London is in these cafés. And for those Maltese who enjoy the company of their countrymen, running a café is a means of combining work with pleasure. So around the areas of settlement are dotted numbers of little cafés, serving as informal centres for small and shifting clubs. As these are not primarily economic ventures, most of them are unprofitable and constantly changing hands. During the 1960s there were between one and two dozen such clubs operating in London at any particular time.

Maltese are perhaps slightly less well off in housing. They have more favourable arrangements than other immigrants, in the form of more council housing, and fewer furnished flats, and they are less overcrowded. But the difference between all immigrants and the general population in housing is not much greater than that between the Maltese and the London average.[1]

Intermarriage and attrition of the second generation

Another important aspect of the capacity of Maltese for settling as individuals in London, and one which is related to the large proportion of bachelors in the migrant flow, is the high rate of intermarriage of Maltese men with English girls. Only about a third of married Maltese men in London have Maltese wives, compared with a rate of intra-ethnic marriages among Cypriots of three-quarters, and an even high proportion for Jamaicans.[2]

This is not due simply to the fact that there are few Maltese girls living in London. It is true that few are available here, but as a result of male migration there is a chronic surplus in Malta, which is not difficult to get to. Those Maltese in London who want a Maltese wife easily can, and do, go back to find one. But non-Maltese wives are not regarded as substitutes or second best; several men said that they had come here expressly to find an English spouse, and a number of prospective migrants interviewed in Malta indicated similar sentiments before their departure.

[1] See Table C.4 in Appendix C.
[2] Detailed figures are given in Table C.6 in Appendix C.

This is all consistent with the forces underlying emigration. Young Maltese suffocating with sexual frustration find it easy to condemn Maltese girls for their stuffy ways, and to idolise the supposedly promiscuous English. Many come here to have a good time, and it is recognised by parents in Malta that this is an important motive for emigrating to Britain. A family in Malta will, because of the moral dangers, often try to discourage boys from coming to London. The Department of Emigration sometimes has to take the precaution of not writing to prospective migrants at their home addresses, because if the parents found out a boy was planning to come here they would stop it. The youth may therefore have to keep his plan quiet until the last moment, when it will be too late to prevent it. Even then the vigilance may continue. One highly-respectable, middle-class migrant who arrived in London in his late twenties, explained that a few weeks after he got here his father turned up unexpectedly from Malta in the middle of the night, and searched his cupboards and looked under the bed to make sure that there were no girls.

For their part, girls in London find Maltese men acceptable as husbands. A shortage, or dislike of Maltese girls on the part of migrants would not by itself produce a high rate of intermarriage; it would simply create a pool of bachelors. But in the London sample, predominantly young, the proportion of bachelors was only 26 per cent. The majority of men interviewed were married; and most had done so quite soon after arrival here. So in general they cannot experience much difficulty in finding wives. A small number of the non-Maltese wives were themselves immigrants from other parts of Europe, for example Spanish or Italian girls who had been au pairs in London, but most of them were English.[1]

Marriage to a local girl is an important step in the process of deciding to stay permanently in Britain. The survey in 1967 revealed that migrants with non-Maltese wives were firmly-established settlers, by comparison with the more recent arrival of those with Maltese wives, and were strongly represented in the skilled and supervisory occupations characteristic of this group. They were also perhaps basically more individualistic, having more often emigrated with escapist rather than economic motives. Marriage outside of the ethnic group takes this escape a stage

[1] The small number of wives of Maltese descent born outside of Malta are counted as Maltese in the 1967 enquiry.

further, by marking a weakening of the individual's contacts with other Maltese. There is a definite withdrawal into a more family-centred life, which may be accompanied by physical movement away from the centre of an area of Maltese concentration. Girls who marry Maltese men may sometimes offend their own families in the process, and several wives of respondents complained that their relatives had more or less ignored them since. So an intermarried couple may become rather isolated and self-sufficient. This is illustrated in the census, which shows that by comparison with other immigrant groups, and even with the general population, Maltese households are composed predominantly of simple nuclear families, with few in-laws living in or multiple-family households.[1]

Intermarriage weakens the ethnic community both by leading to a reduction in the range and volume of contacts with other Maltese people, and also, less directly, by producing children of mixed descent. In passing it is worth noting that mixed couples have rather fewer children than where both are Maltese; so intermarriage reduces the fertility of the migrant generation. One third of Maltese wives in the 1967 enquiry had three or more children, compared with a fifth of non-Maltese wives. Moreover as the Maltese couples in the sample were younger than the mixed, the real difference between the two is greater than these figures would suggest.

The greater fertility of Maltese couples is not enough to make the majority of children in the settlement full-blooded Maltese, as these families are in a minority. But no very great change in the proportion would be needed for parity to be achieved, and during the last decade there have been times when it seemed this might happen. Following the introduction of immigration controls, and the reduction of casual migration to Britain, the proportion of Maltese couples arriving definitely increased for a while. This may have had some effect on family sizes by the time of the 1967 enquiry, as the fertility of Maltese households in the 1967 sample was a little greater than that disclosed by the 1961 census figure.[2] The later sample also found a higher rate of intra-Maltese marriage.[3] At the time of writing, though, Maltese

[1] Comparative figures shown in Table C.5, Appendix C.
[2] Comparative figures are shown in Table C.7 in Appendix C.
[3] Compare figures for 'Maltese' and 'Inner London Maltese' in Table C.6, Appendix C.

family migration to Britain seems to have petered out and the increase in numbers of full-descent children during the mid-1960s will probably not be sustained.

But in any case the main effect of the larger proportion of mixed-descent children in the settlement is to help limit the involvement of second and third generations in ethnic community activities. Even children of full Maltese parentage who have lived in London for some years tend to think of themselves as primarily English – especially if they have been to school here. But this identification with the local population is greatly eased when the mother is not Maltese. This is not mainly a matter of physical characteristics, as in racial terms even full-descent children generally come well within the range of normal English variation. It is chiefly because an English mother passes on to her children a ready-made and justifiable alternative identity. Quite a few of the children with an English mother who were encountered in the course of the London enquiry had already adopted her ethnicity in some contexts. For example, in situations where their patronymic was not known, like at the cleaners, or when writing off for postal offers, they would use their mother's surname. The fathers did not appear to object to this, and sometimes even drew attention to how English their children were. Many seemed to feel that fathering English children enhanced their own claim to English identity, so that the absence of ethnic consciousness among the children is to some extent a reflection of its weakness in the migrant generation.

Because of this widespread complicity in electing a non-Maltese identity, there seems to be only a remote possibility of a self-conscious community surviving among second and third generation Maltese. Many mixed-descent children can be expected to adopt their mother's names formally when they set up their own households, and to become ethnically invisible.[1] Children of Maltese couples do not seem to be enthusiastic about perpetuating

[1] It was noticeable during the 1967 enquiry fieldwork that the surname sampling procedure came up with very few second- (or even half-) generation Maltese. The two or three who were located by it were adamant that although their fathers may have been Maltese, and their own names taken from this, they were themselves quite positively English. It is possible that to avoid annoyance and embarrassment many Maltese children adopt other names when they leave home – even if they don't have an English mother to provide one ready-made. All this shows that estimates of the size of the Maltese settlement which make a generous allowance

the group either; so unless there is further immigration the existing community must almost completely disappear in the fairly near future.

Communal activities

Most of the shared Maltese activities in London are informal, consisting either of domestic visits between close friends or of gatherings in small clubs to chat and play cards or billiards. Domestic visiting necessarily entails rather exclusive and narrow association. Within a context of wider communal affairs, and especially if there were heavy intra-group marriage, such visiting could help to sustain ethnic ties and sentiments. But in itself it is incapable of generating a community. Most of the members of the 1967 sample who no longer regarded themselves as Maltese still had one or two Maltese friends in London with whom they occasionally exchanged visits. But they did not consider the nationality of their friends to be significant. They were old friends; they also happened to be Maltese. Group loyalties and identity did not come into it.

It might be thought that socialising in Maltese cafés would succeed, where private visiting could not, in providing a basis for community life. Certainly at first sight these informal clubs do seem to be a real hub of intra-ethnic activities. The values which they embody are shared by many Maltese migrants. As already outlined, cafés like them have in Malta represented the only real fissures in the monolithic theocracy, and have served as meeting places for dissident elements. By comparison with the rest of Maltese culture, they are places of licence and moral relaxation, and they are accordingly the feature of Maltese life which migrant adventurers, liberated from religious and familial controls, have been most eager to recreate. Maltese settlements in this country have always had informal clubs of this sort, and most respondents in the London enquiry had at some time been connected with one.

But in several essential respects this café society is culturally

---

for locally-born children are being absurdly optimistic. It would make more sense to *subtract* a figure for Maltese children born in Malta who grow up in Britain and quickly *lose* their ethnicity here.

negative. The articulating ethos is a rejection of a religiously-grounded community life; but this does not generate roles and relations capable of supporting an alternative social order. Café society is at bottom anarchistic, and although it is the arena for much socialising, it is not an environment where any real spirit of community is propagated. In fact these clubs are veritable schools for individualism. Maltese men collect in them to share with each other in enjoying, and in being seen to enjoy, the freedom and good times afforded by the English way of life. Motivations are openly selfish, and friendships in this apparent fraternity are commonly exploitative and unstable. Great jealousies are excited by compatriots' sexual and economic successes, and many relationships and family ties are broken under the strain. Newly-arrived Maltese are often puzzled to discover that former friendships of long standing do not seem to count for much here, and that different standards of behaviour apply.

In the atmosphere of unrestrained hedonism and materialism which suffuses café society, migrants learn a defensive hardness and cynicism. Men interviewed in the 1967 enquiry were quite different people when I met them at a club. At home by themselves or with their families, most were relaxed and would talk freely on almost any subject. In the cafés the same men would be tense and excitable. If asked a question they would give an over-hearty joke answer or sullenly refuse to say anything at all. Afterwards they would excuse themselves by saying that you had to be careful what you said in the club as there were some 'funny people' there.

Informal associations centred on cafés are the most visible congregations of Maltese in London; but they do not furnish a basis for long-term communal activity in the settlement, and most migrants do not remain involved with them for any length of time. Many return to Malta, and those who stay in Britain soon withdraw into more private lives. At any particular time there is a group of newcomers caught up in café society, who do not know any Maltese outside of it, and who consequently believe that this *is* the Maltese community. But most settlers who have been here some time recognise the incoherent and individualistic character of club society, and appreciate its irrelevance in the lives of serious migrants.

Religious activity

Devout Roman Catholicism is pivotal to the whole social order in Malta, and has for generations provided the natural foundation for communal activities. Religious observance would be central to an overseas Maltese community organised on traditional lines, and the decline which Maltese religious behaviour undergoes in London is central to the decline in communal life.

The network of pressures maintaining religious observance in Malta do not exist in London. Priests in Malta derive a good deal of their day-to-day influence from the exercise of patronage, in recommending people for jobs, fending off the police and so on. This is not really applicable in London.

One fundamental factor behind the loosening of religious controls over Maltese in London is the relative absence of Maltese women. A good deal of Maltese church business ultimately comes down to regulating relations between the sexes, and much of the strength of the church in Malta, as in other Latin countries, arises from the alliance of interests between priests and women. The church upholds the position and above all the security of women through the institution of marriage. Women uphold the church by devoutly observing its rites and by pressurising their families to do the same. Men are altogether less interested in organised religion. They attend mass and communion less often and less willingly. Several migrants recalled how their mothers used to have to go round pouring water over their menfolk to get them out of bed and off to morning mass. And it is usually the mother who encourages a favourite son to enter the priesthood.

London life offers an escape from this bullying. There are very few mothers here, and not very many Maltese wives either. The display of devotion by London Catholics is pitched at a lower level than in Malta, and migrants' religious performance soon drops off. Over a third of the 1967 sample had not attended mass or made a confession for at least five years; and many had not been at all since arrival here. Some respondents claimed to have lapsed in spirit or even practice before leaving Malta, and said that emigration had been undertaken to prevent them offending the sensibilities of their family or bringing public dishonour upon it.

The desire to protect the feelings and reputations of relatives

47

in Malta is powerful and remains with migrants long after settlement. Most lapsed Maltese try to conceal their backsliding from
their families, and if the question is raised will pretend that they
are still regular church-goers. When they are in Malta for a holiday
they will accompany their parents to church sometimes in order
to go through a decent minimum of the correct motions. Many
appreciated that if they were to return to Malta permanently they
would start to follow local practice again; they realised that
church-going in Malta is for many people a matter of purely
social and secular convenience. This does not really make them
much more tolerant towards the church, though, and generally
speaking the lapsed settlers do not relish the possibility of returning. Since long-term lapsing is connected to marriage with a
non-Maltese girl, few of them are likely to do so.

Much lapsing is simply behavioural; few respondents had made
a total break with religious ideas, and a large number retained a
disposition towards a sort of basic, private religion. Some, however, mainly middle-class settlers, had used the intellectual freedom
they had found here to develop a completely new, humanistic
approach to life.

Over a third of the sample (36 per cent) continued to observe
what by the standards of British Catholicism seem to count as
minimum requirements, and had attended mass and communion
within the previous twelve months. As this figure includes the
most recent settlers it slightly overstates the true proportion. The
frequency of worship of even this group would be in Malta
regarded as poor. Some purely external difficulties can be cited,
like the distance to a church or problems of fitting it in with long
working hours. But the main factor is undoubtedly a change in
attitude towards the importance of ritual. Most of the faithful
had come to feel that church attendance in itself did not matter
very much, and that in fact the quality of religious life was
potentially higher in London, just because there was less emphasis
on formal sacraments and mechanical, habitual participation. The
act of public worship here was a much more conscious and
voluntary performance, as it was not constrained by moral blackmail and community pressures. So although church-going was
less frequent, it was more meaningful to them; and provided
that they could get in at least the obligatory annual mass, and
perhaps send their children to Catholic schools such Maltese

considered that they could count themselves as good Catholics. Devout compatriots unable to accept this level of local practice tend to go back to Malta pretty quickly.

Between those who had clearly lapsed and those who defined themselves as still faithful were a number of respondents in the process of lapsing. There was often a certain unease detectable among such men. Although they enjoyed the experience of personal freedom, they were hesitant and faltering in their use of it. External controls and pressures had been removed but no new internal mechanism yet evolved to take their place.

This marginal state is particularly evident in the behaviour of relative newcomers in the settlement, whom old-timers commonly liken to birds that have been let out of their cages.[1] An obvious manifestation of this is in their swearing. Blasphemous oaths tumble out every time they open their mouths – to the amusement of fellow-newcomers and discomfort or boredom of older migrants. This swearing would have been socially taboo in Malta – even a criminal offence. But there was no one in London who would bother to stop them, and the sense of freedom it gave them could be so stimulating that for a time they would be almost intoxicated. The Madonna would be invoked at the least excuse. This apparently carefree and unrestrained behaviour is at the same time for many newcomers a means of testing the new environment to find out exactly what they can get away with – not only in relation to other people, but also to God. As one young newcomer, an active member of café society, explained:

They are all bluff really. They say anything against Catholic. Here there are many things you see – so you can't be a good Catholic. You see things and you break your religion. So they all say 'Sorry God', because God is dead. But after a while they see that is wrong. After all there is somebody on top of us, and it might be God.

---

[1] The Metaphor of a bird in a cage has an especial poignancy in the Maltese context. Malta is a very barren little island, and birds which land there in passage between North Africa and Europe stay for as short a period as they can. To make up for the rarity of wild-fowl the Maltese trap whatever they can and keep them in tiny cages. Every little bus bumping along the road has a cage with a bird singing desperately inside it. The parallel with life in Malta for humans is often commented on by emigrants.

The Malta Catholic Centre

The weakening of religious traditions among migrants in London has not gone unnoticed, and a mission was set up in the early 1950s to serve the growing number of settlers. The church in Malta is aware of its role in maintaining social order, and recognises some obligation to extend its services to emigrant groups. Priests have often accompanied organised parties of migrants leaving Malta, or have been sent to settlements if there appears to be need. A Catholic Emigrants Commission operates in Malta to prepare migrants, and to co-ordinate pastoral work among them.[1]

Price (p. 192) has observed that during the nineteenth century there was relatively little religious lapsing in the Mediterranean colonies. This was in part due to the presence of Maltese priests; but they must have been greatly assisted by the fact that in these settlements their religion was an important index of high social status. In the African ports, to forget one's Christianity put Maltese in jeopardy of definition as Arabs, thereby losing their preferential position as members of the European community.

In a Protestant or largely agnostic setting there is no such danger, and there may even be a contrary incentive towards losing faith. Maltese colonists in the Mediterranean could regard themselves as superior to the local population; but as Catholics in a Protestant country, and as members of a dominated rather than dominating minority, their position is rather different. Maltese priests in London find that they do not enjoy great moral authority here, and this makes it hard to find a role which is either effective or acceptable to them. The Maltese Fathers who have come to the mission in London have not been held in high regard by most of the migrants, and have had little impact on community life. The mission has striven to become the centre of a traditional style of living, but as yet without any notable success. The priests have tried running a regular mass in Maltese, providing a centre for large social gatherings, and even chartering planes for summer flights to Malta. But only this last function has been

[1] This Commission in fact appears to be much better equipped and funded than the Emigration Department itself, and plays a very important role alongside it. Senior staff of the Commission include Emigration Department officials, sitting in a voluntary capacity. This reflects perfectly the values and division of labour in traditional Maltese society. Unpleasant realities are left to the administration; so the Department does all the hard grind. Anything that is 'social' is however properly the domain of the church, which commands the greater real resources.

received with anything approaching enthusiasm. In 1967 only one quarter of respondents had ever had anything to do with the activities of the mission, and less than half of these had a continuing connection with it. Several members of the sample had never heard of the mission or its priests. Those migrants who considered that it provided religious or social facilities not available to them at their local Catholic churches were a tiny minority.

The main beneficiaries of this mission, and the group which it now claims to exist on behalf of, are the Maltese in London for a short stay – such as students, diplomats, passengers in transit and, above all, Maltese who have come to London for specialised medical treatment. For this mainly middle-class, transitory group the centre has helped to reproduce some of the spiritual comforts they are used to in Malta.

Ordinary settlers in London are overwhelmingly apathetic towards the mission. The most important date in its religious calendar is the mass celebrated on Independence Day (formerly National Day) in a central London Church. Attendance is poor (a hundred or two would be considered good) and is made up chiefly of people marginal to the ordinary community.

The lack of impact cannot be blamed on the priests themselves, who are notable for their general open-mindedness.[1] The real problem for the mission is that its existence is incompatible with the cultural and political sentiments and interests of most settlers. Most migrants, including some who are religiously active in London, resent the part played by the church in Maltese political and social life, and identify the mission with the establishment in Malta. Even if they have never met the missionaries in person, many ordinary settlers criticise them for being too authoritarian or money-grubbing – that is, asking for donations. Several men interviewed insisted that they would prefer an English or Irish priest, now that they had discovered how different their manner was.

So the Maltese Fathers have been at a great disadvantage in London. They have not increased religious interest, and have only really managed to keep contact with those middle-class settlers or sojourners who could get by perfectly well without them. At the time of the main enquiry the mission seemed to have

---

[1] One priest in the 1950s who was critical of the English way of life was quickly found duties back in Malta. The job requires diplomacy as well as fervour.

given up the attempt to reach the lapsing migrants, and was concentrating on serving those Maltese who came to it willingly. The existence of the mission gives comfort to many parents in Malta, who are told that it is doing brave work. But its activities fall a long way short of providing a focus of ethnic community life.

The Malta Labour Party (UK)

A possible alternative axis of community activity is political association. The majority of emigrants are recruited from the ranks of the Malta Labour Party, and many leave Malta with an intention of continuing to serve the cause from overseas. Forty per cent of men interviewed had been members of the Labour Party before emigrating, and some others had voted for it on occasion. This proportion is more important than it might appear. Old-timers who left before the post-war emergence of the current party were politically apathetic. Between the wars the emigration officials even drew attention to the political passivity of the Maltese working man to endear him to prospective host countries.[1] Widespread political interest did not develop until the postwar constitution of limited self-government came into operation; and accordingly it is mainly migrants who left Malta during the 1950s and early 1960s who are Labour Party members.

The peak of political activity in Malta took place in the latter 1950s and early 1960s when the conditions for Independence were being thrashed out. During this period a UK branch of the Labour Party was formed among settlers in London, to mobilise local support and act as a pressure group here through channels like the Movement for Colonial Freedom, and to lobby at Westminster. Social functions were also arranged for members, in competition with those organised by the Maltese Fathers. Formal membership, in terms of subscriptions paid, reached several hundred for Britain as a whole, but even at its high tide the movement did not embrace many active participants. Less than 10 per cent of sample members in 1967 had been members of the organisation; and none of these had held office within it.

[1] Henry Casolani, first minister for emigration, reports that on a mission to London in 1922 he vigorously submitted, *inter alia,* that they (the migrants) were loyal and eminently religious, and that they led exceedingly clean lives; above all, they never meddled with politics and they were never concerned in labour troubles. Quoted in *Awake Malta, or the Hard Lesson of Emigration,* p. 54.

In spite of the fact that there were many MLP supporters living in London, the branch did not develop into a vigorous society capable of providing a long term framework for ethnic communality.

This is not to say that it had been created with an intention of developing in this way. Its formal objectives were specific and short term; and after the attainment of Independence there was no need for the parent organisation to maintain a separate group in London. MLP thinkers could still live in Britain and play a part in Maltese affairs, but they could best do so now by contributing direct to discussions and publications in Malta. Other types of political activity were no longer relevant here, and by the time of the main survey in London the association had been wound up.

Although it had served its declared purpose, there was perhaps no absolute need for it to suspend all its operations, and a gradual change of functions into a primarily recreational organisation for like-minded people would have been institutionally feasible. Associations of this sort exist after all among Maltese in Australia and Canada. The MLP did not transform itself in this way, however, because, as a pressure group in the metropolitan capital, its original functions were highly political, and through them its main activists became drawn out into other political formations which quickly absorbed this energy when Maltese Independence was settled. The association was affiliated to the British Labour Party, and through this a number of individuals had become involved in British politics. Members of the movement found themselves serving as Labour councillors for London boroughs, and the political concern of leading figures soon became diffused into local affairs.

Analogous processes of absorption into the local society whittled away the interest of the rank and file, so that there was no popular demand to turn the movement into a permanent social club. For newcomers to Britain the party affirmed their resentment against the Maltese church; and it may thereby have contributed to the weakness of the Catholic Mission in London, by reproducing this antagonism in a situation where the church itself was relatively powerless. But established settlers soon found that a satisfactory personal solution could be found through the individual act of lapsing. And in any case the iniquities of the situation in Malta seemed less provocative when you were living in London. Interest in collective solutions, in the liberation of Maltese from an oppressive priesthood, soon became of secondary moment, especially for those who had married English girls and fathered English children. Private lives were put first, and just as café society fails to hold migrants for long, the MLP has not evolved into a more permanent and general association for migrants.

Other formal associations

The only bodies with any real chance of serving as foundation for an active, organised Maltese community in London have been the Catholic Centre, reflecting traditional culture and leadership, and the Labour Party, which relates meaningfully to the background of most migrants here. Other organisations are much more limited in function or sectional in appeal.

The High Commission (Malta House) might be expected to take a positive interest in settlers, and to provide for their welfare. However, until recently, when it is perhaps too late to bother anyway, its staff have considered anything 'social' to be the responsibility of the church, and their own function as narrowly diplomatic. Just as in Malta the instruction and preparation of migrants was left to the Catholic Emigrants Commission, so in London the job of keeping in touch with migrants and tending their needs was judged a matter of interest only to the Malta Catholic Centre. The Commission was fully confident in the vigilant Fathers, and would refer to them any migrants seeking assistance. No register of Maltese in this country is kept at Malta House, and before the present administration took office the general impression was conveyed that the less known about their exploits here, the better for everyone.[1]

The oldest formal association of Maltese in London is the Malta League, set up between the wars among professional people to arrange social evenings and functions for visiting Maltese celebrities. Since the founding of the Malta Catholic Centre, the League has operated under its wing. League activities are almost purely sentimental and middle class, and are rather sporadic. Although it has been in existence for so long, it has not managed

[1] Consider for example the remarks attributed by Lena Jeger to the then High Commissioner, as quoted above at the beginning of the Introduction.

to attract into membership the locally born children of members. The league is small, with perhaps a few dozen personnel, and is utterly remote from ordinary migrants; it has no desire to serve as the pivot of a wider ethnic grouping, and never could.

A new organisation was founded at the time of Independence – the Friends of Malta G. C. Ltd. But this can scarcely be counted as a Maltese association. The Friends came together to help Malta adjust to the run-down of the garrison, and membership consists largely of English service persons, of rank, who have been stationed in Malta and retain a benevolent interest in the island. The association runs fund-raising dinners for the support of Maltese charities, channels some business aid to Malta, and helps generate employment possibilities in England for migrants. It operates strictly through official agencies, and at the highest level – the first president was Prince Philip, and vice-presidents include the Archbishop and the Prime Minister of Malta – and makes no direct contacts with Maltese immigrants in London.

Differential participation in the ethnic community

There seem to be two main dimensions of weakness discernible in the structure of the Maltese community in London. First there is weakness through the individualism of members. Most migrants who stay do seem able to manage quite well here as independent agents. They do not need a protective group to cushion their adjustment, and so there are no material incentives for ethnic association. Second there is a cultural and political gulf between those Maltese who accept, and those who oppose, the traditional church-based social order. Consequently there are conflicting ideas, among Maltese who might like to get together, over the appropriate institutional basis for doing so. The limited interest in ethnic association has been dissipated between factions which have, till recently at any rate, appeared irreconcilable.

The structural divisions within the settlement which result from these two axes of weakness, and the interplay between them, can be illustrated and summarised by looking at the main styles of involvement in the community which were manifested by members of the London sample. On the basis of replies to two questions in the standard schedule,[1] respondents can be grouped into four

[1] See Appendix D, questions 20 and 21.

categories indicating the style of their participation in ethnic affairs. The largest number of respondents came into contact with other Maltese only through domestic visiting or chance meetings. Many of them had in the past frequented Maltese cafés, or belonged to a formal association. But these ties had been dissolved by the time of interviewing and they positively rejected these modes of association. Since this group of respondents accounted for between a half and two-thirds of the total sample, they were divided arbitrarily into two sub-groups according to the rate of these informal meetings. Those who met other Maltese people weekly or more often were categorised as ethnic socialisers, while those who did so less than once a week were counted as essentially privatised and ethnically *non*-involved. For some of this latter group, contacts with other Maltese were extremely infrequent.[1]

Respondents who currently went to a Maltese café or cafés, albeit infrequently, were considered as belonging to café society. Several individuals in this category were definitely in the process of withdrawing from this type of company following, for example, marriage or the birth of a child; so it was difficult to draw a clear line demarcating participation. Because of the large size of the non-involved grouping, all marginal cases were included in the café society category: so if there was some real prospect of a future visit or visits to a Maltese club, a respondent was counted as having not yet withdrawn.

The fourth category adopted embraces all those respondents who currently belonged to a formal Maltese association. This was not a large group, amounting to only 10 per cent of the sample. This category did not overlap with café society, as in practice these formal associators were all people attached in some way to the Malta Catholic Centre, and concerned to recreate a traditional type of community.[2]

---

[1] This group of non-involved settlers is probably an even larger proportion of the actual settlement than it is of the 1967 sample, as it would logically include those Maltese who have withdrawn completely from the community and, by adopting English names, have disappeared from view.

[2] Maltese priests might sometimes visit Maltese cafés in the course of their duties – when looking for a missing person, or in a bid to communicate with ordinary migrants. But these would be purely business visits, and hardly constitute an overlapping of sectors of the community. At the time of the enquiry the MLP was no longer an active association, and so MLP 'members' were not counted as formal associators. If the movement had still been operative, some other classification would have been necessary, to separate the pro- and anti-church factions.

This fourfold classification of respondents according to their type of contact with other Maltese reflects the interaction of the two main lines of weakness in the structure of the community as a whole. As indicated in Figure 1, which shows the relationship between these different styles of ethnic group participation and gives the proportions of respondents in each category, the majority of Maltese did not engage in any ethnic group activity outside the home, and those who were communally involved subscribed to one or the other of two sets of antagonistic cultural values – secular as against traditional or religious. Among the privatised respondents there was no single attribute which could be treated as a direct reflection or manifestation of this fundamental ideological cleavage. However, the simple and rather arbitrary division made in terms of *frequency* of contacts turned out to correspond very broadly with this divergence, in that the more regular private socialisers tended to share the traditional religious and political views of the formal associators, while the withdrawn settlers generally agreed with café society on a secularist position. These points can be illustrated by looking at each of the four groups of respondents in more detail.[1]

FIGURE 1 *Forms of participation in the ethnic community*
(*percentage of respondents in each category shown in brackets*)

Extent of involvement in community life	*Cultural values of respondent*	
	Secular	*Traditional*
Group-based activity	*Café society* (32)	*Formal associators* (10)
Domestic or chance contacts only	*Non-involved settlers* (46)	*Private socialisers* (12)

Café society

Maltese involved in café society are those who are in reaction against traditional forms of Maltese social order and have not yet

[1] Table D.1 in Appendix D gives the statistical evidence for the generalisations made.

fully adjusted as individuals to life in this country. Café society provides a niche for such people, although it cannot really be considered to give them the support a more organised ethnic community would be able to supply.

Respondents in this group accordingly tended to have migrated to escape from the Maltese way of life, and to be religiously inactive and hostile to the Catholic Centre. There is a good deal of swearing and anti-clerical talk in the cafés, and a Maltese priest who ventures inside is assured a raucous reception. Those men who were politically interested in Malta largely supported the MLP. The occupations of these respondents were more often unskilled and many of them were either unemployed or economically unstable. This was due in part to the fact that café society contained a disproportionate number of newcomers, but there was also a hard core of old-timers who had been relatively unsuccessful as settlers.

A factor which seems closely related to continued involvement in café society is the absence of family ties. These respondents were more often single, or, if married, without children. Marriage, especially to a Maltese girl, seems to inhibit this form of socialising.

Members of café society spent more time in the company of fellow-countrymen, and were willing to meet even more. So it is all the more significant that awareness of the lack of cohesion amongst Maltese was at its highest in this group. The few among them who did believe in the unity of the community were mainly very recent arrivals.

Formal associators

Maltese active in formal associations were drawn from the traditionalist element in the settlement. None of the respondents so classified was a cultural or political exile, while most had supported establishment parties in Malta, and had arrived in Britain at an older age than other migrants, with their socialisation more complete. A sizeable contingent were middle-class sojourners – professional men like doctors or teachers, who were widening their experience before settling down in Malta or some other major Maltese settlement. Few of these expected to stay in Britain for long,[1] and many had arrived quite recently. Their class composition was heavily biased towards non-manual occupations.

The social networks of these middle-class Maltese in London were much less restricted geographically than those of other migrants. Friends and relatives from Malta often came to stay or were passing through, and they went to Malta themselves more frequently for holidays. So unlike the lower-class settlers, they had never really left Maltese society, and their socialising in London was just an extension of it. Consequently few had taken non-Maltese wives and none had lapsed from formal religious observance. Their knowledge about the main settlement in London was limited. Many supposed the community to be united, and blandly accepted the idea of meeting more Maltese; but it is probable that they were generally thinking in terms of other middle-class transients like themselves. A few, especially the middle-class sympathisers of the MLP, were concerned about the ordinary migrants. These men were critical of the neglect of settlers by the High Commission, and keenly aware of the inadequacies of the Catholic Centre. However, the short-term nature of their own residence here prevented them from becoming involved or really committed. Also the Maltese middle classes have not been used to assuming direct leadership, as the control and welfare of the lower orders has always been left to the clergy. So although the traditional type of community did not appear to work in London, there were not enough of these articulate and critical people here to initiate any alternative, and their potential for community leadership was strictly limited.

Non-involved settlers

Of those respondents whose only contacts with compatriots occurred through informal, domestic visiting or chance meetings, most had only infrequent encounters and must be counted as for most practical purposes uninvolved in communal ethnic activity. They included a large number of fully lapsed members of café society, as well as some former members of formal associations. The chief characteristic of these withdrawn settlers

[1] Students or other people intending to stay in the UK for less than one year were not included in the 1967 sample. So none of these respondents was a simple visitor here.

was that they had become reasonably successfully established in Britain and had little to gain by ethnic association. They tended to be old-timers, in relatively respectable occupations which they had held for a long time. Although some had remained bachelors for several years after arrival most were married, with a disproportionate share of non-Maltese wives. Many were religiously inactive but a fair number had come to adopt a régime of moderately regular church attendance. Very few of them desired greater contact with other Maltese, and their emotional distance from the community was reflected in their conceptualisation of the Maltese in London as a united group from which they personally were excluded. Their interest in Maltese group activities was minimal, and of all the migrants they probably had least to gain from a greater degree of ethnic organisation.

Private socialisers

Maltese who only associated privately with others, but who did so quite often, were in many respects marginal to the settlement as constituted at the time of the main survey. They were inclined to be pro-establishment in that they were not adventurers or escapists, were religiously active, and had supported non-socialist parties in Malta. However they were not themselves part of the establishment, as they were predominantly manual workers. In many ways they represented a rather new type of Maltese migrant to this country – a deferential and respectable working class which started to come here for a while when migration became restricted and regulated. These respondents were mainly recent arrivals and had arrived young, and in view of this could be deemed economically stable. Most significantly, they had a high proportion of Maltese wives, so that they were disposed towards meeting compatriots, while at the same time curbed from participation in wild café society. They expressed an interest in ethnic community life which would have been realised most appropriately through an extension downwards of the middle-class formal associations. Of the ordinary Maltese settlers in London they were potentially the most amenable to traditional forms of leadership. But in the period during which they have been arriving here, the Malta Catholic Centre had itself been withdrawing into a middle-class milieu, and many of these possible followers did not even know of its existence.

The significance of this category hangs on the scale of future migration to Britain. When the main enquiry was carried out they were a small and atypical minority. What is more, they are the type of Maltese who have contributed most heavily to the return migration movement of the last few years.[1] In principle, if controlled family migration to Britain were for some reason to expand substantially again, theirs is the style of communal participation which would grow most in relative and absolute importance, and which could perhaps serve as a bridge-head for the growth of a traditional community life in the settlement. Such an outcome is made all the more conceivable by the changes which have been taking place in Malta since Independence, and which have been gradually altering the balance of forces underlying emigration to Britain. The growing distinction between church and state, backed up perhaps by the Second Vatican Council, is leading to the modification of some more rigid church practices and doctrines, and to some relaxation of social controls. As a result the escapist element in migration to Britain is probably being reduced, and the antagonism among migrants to traditional culture qualified.[2]

But as already noted, the immediate indications are of a dropping off in emigration altogether, so that the more likely prospect for the community is that it will dwindle further as individuals either become absorbed into local society as ethnically non-involved settlers, drift back to Malta or go on elsewhere.

Marginal groups of Maltese in London

In his study of nineteenth-century migration, Price (pp. 135–8) comments that the settlement of Maltese in Muslim cities around the Mediterranean could not be regarded as a viable long-term proposition. Christian communities remained only upon sufferance, and in times of political tension might be attacked or expelled. Periodically numbers of Maltese would have to seek refuge in Malta while matters cooled down. This condition has continued into the twentieth century. With the post-war liberation

---

[1] See Table A.4 in Appendix A, for details of recent changes in composition of net migrant flow.

[2] This argument is pursued in Chapter IV below.

of North African territories there has been a resurgence of nationalism which in the later 1950s led to a series of crises unsettling some residual Maltese colonists in these areas. Many were expelled, in particular from post-Suez Egypt, and others chose to leave rather than risk loss of property or of European citizenship. Malta itself was at this time in the middle of its greatest-ever burst of emigration and was reluctant to receive these refugees. Thousands therefore came to Britain, although many have subsequently moved on to warmer habitats in South Africa and Australia.

Some of these exiles – Maltese or part-Maltese by descent, but born elsewhere – are now domiciled permanently in London, and are playing a part in the life, such as it is, of the Maltese community. Their identities are in many cases extremely ambiguous, as a result of the heavy intermarriage with other European groups in the Mediterranean colonies. Most of these hyphenated Maltese living in London seem to have a range of nationality options available to them, on the basis of birthplace and complex lines of descent. For example, a man born in Tunisia of a Maltese father, who had served in the French army, could have elected between Tunisian, French, Maltese or British citizenship, plus that of other ancestors if there had been intermarriage. Members of the same family may make different choices – Tunisian because of local interests or marriage, French for better family allowances, British for medical welfare and so on – and become scattered across several countries. Some may be unable to make up their minds about their identities, loyalties or best interests, and spend years shifting around trying to exercise several options.

On the whole those who have come to the United Kingdom have had a definite reason for wanting to elect British status. The Maltese in Egypt for example had property confiscated after Suez, and came to Britain to put themselves in the best position to press for compensation. A highly-organised 'Association of the Maltese Communities of Egypt' exists in London, which served originally to secure this compensation, through the Anglo-Egyptian Aid Society, and now operates as a charity to dispense that part of the property which had been corporately owned. Another common reason for taking British status and coming to Britain is that it is a convenient centre from which to re-migrate to other parts of the Commonwealth.

For many hyphenated Maltese then, the 'Maltese' part of their identity has been little more than a means of gaining British status. If the same people had wanted to go elsewhere – and many could have moved to France, Italy or Greece, for example – they would have referred to different ancestors and adopted an alternative ethnic label. Most of these migrants are culturally Maltese only in a secondary sense. Settlers from Libya commonly speak Italian amongst themselves, and those from Tunisia and Egypt mainly French. There are also some French-speaking Maltese from Marseilles, and the odd family from Corfu, Turkey, Gibraltar and so on. Few of them have ever set foot on Malta.

Ordinary Maltese migrants from Malta do not count the hyphenates, if they know of their existence, as proper Maltese. There is not much informal socialising between the groups, except where there are already family connections. They have no recent common experience to unite them, and the nature of their respective migration processes could hardly be more contrasting.

In the first place the foreign-born Maltese are exiles rather than economic migrants or individual adventurers, and they have arrived in groups cemented by shared danger and adversity. Families of marginal Maltese are extraordinarily cohesive, and their households are both complex and large – especially those from Libya and Tunisia. Unlike Maltese from Malta, who tend to be more friendly and forthcoming when alone, the marginals are uneasy and suspicious in isolation, yet relaxed and voluble in groups. The presence of more women and older people is important in maintaining this cohesion, but solidarity is evident not only at the family level. For example, a senior office-holder of the Egyptian-Maltese association once talked to me about the affairs of the society without the authorisation of the rest of the committee. Another member whom I met soon afterwards told me that this had been regarded by the committee as a great indiscretion, and that the offender had been reprimanded.

Second, the hyphenated Maltese are distinctly more alien to the British in cultural matters. English is spoken in Malta, though not always to perfection, and in spite of the religious divide Malta has been converging culturally with Britain in recent decades. Migrants from Malta do not generally have a great problem in communicating with English people and entering the labour market at an appropriate position. This is not so true of the marginal Maltese – except for some of the Egyptian contingent, whose range of skills and languages is wide. The cohesion of marginal Maltese families often extends to joint ownership and operation of small businesses, which limits their penetration as individuals into wider society. Several Tunisian Maltese families, for example, have set up networks of small hotels in London.

Third, the class composition of Maltese hyphenates is generally higher than that of ordinary Maltese settlers. Those Maltese who retained their European identity in Arab cities, and resisted absorption into the local populations, were often in some degree property-owning. Many were businessmen. Because of the group form of their migration, these families have brought their capital intact with them. As a result of all this, the life they adopt here has much more in common with that of the middle-class Maltese from Malta than of the majority of migrants. They are religiously active, having retained their faith during generations of exile. Support for the Catholic Centre in London would be much thinner without them and, while this is of little moment to working-class Maltese in the settlement, it is reassuring for the middle classes.

So paradoxically it is the marginal Maltese – many of whom do not consider themselves truly Maltese, and who are not regarded as such by the bulk of migrants – who have been underpinning the formal, traditional communal activities of Maltese in London over the last dozen or more years. They are the really professional and seasoned migrants, drawn from the organised cores of ancient settlements. Their own experience, although not typical, predisposes them towards a more active community life. Again, this is especially true of the Egyptian-Maltese, who run a regular newsletter and mount frequent social events.

Another factor in this is that, as relative outsiders in the conflict between the MLP and church, these marginal Maltese occupy a structurally neutral position in the community, which enables them to ride over some of the factionalism. A Migrants Convention held in Malta in 1969 owed much to their interest and international contacts. And the formation of a united British delegation to it, although formally made possible by the MLP-church concordat, seems to have been greatly helped by the fact that the co-ordinating role was played by an individual who was a hyphenate and therefore a stranger to the old dispute.

This structural significance of the hyphenates was not appreciated when the 1967 enquiry was being prepared. They were known to be around, but because of sampling and interviewing difficulties they were excluded from the design of the investigation.[1] A number who were unearthed in the course of this enquiry were interviewed informally, but no systematic study of them was attempted. At the time of the main survey there may have been as many as two thousand of them living in Greater London. No precise information is offered here about them, but references will be made in the text to their activities when these have a bearing on the life of the main Maltese settlement.[2]

[1] The main difficulty would have been in devising a reliable sampling frame. These groups cannot be identified through census returns, and estimates of where they live in London and of how many there are of them vary enormously. Language may have presented some interviewing problems, but this could have been resolved more easily.

[2] The figure of two thousand may give an impression of greater relative importance in the settlement than is warranted. It must be remembered that the households of these marginal groups are large and complex, with many more children (most of them foreign-born also), so that two thousand in fact represents a far smaller number of families than two thousand ordinary Maltese migrants, most of whom would have separate households.

III

MALTESE CRIME IN LONDON

The preceding chapter raises a central question. Why should the migrants so quickly lose interest in each other as fellow-Maltese, and be so eager to adopt new identities? The highly individualistic mode of migration, and the compromised position of traditional Maltese institutions in the eyes of many settlers, go some way towards explaining the lack of demand for a formal community life. But they cannot by themselves account for the strength of negative feelings, and often explicit avoidance, shown by many respondents in the main enquiry. If the factors already dealt with were the only ones operating, a much higher incidence of purely sentimental intra-group socialising would surely have been found.

The absence of such behaviour can, I believe, only be properly understood if the reputation for specifically vicious criminality under which Maltese in Britain have laboured is taken fully into account. The collective bad name seems to have been of critical importance in structuring both the intra- and extra-communal relations of Maltese in London, and the remaining chapters will all in some way or other be concerned with analysing the inhibiting effect that this reputation seems to have had, in conjunction with the other factors already introduced, upon the growth of a richer Maltese community life in London. In this chapter and the next, the development of the bad name will be traced, and some review made of its basis and probable determinants. In the final chapters, the nature of the problems arising for Maltese out of the bad name and the ways in which they have responded will be presented and analysed, and a short assessment made of the implications of this analysis for our understanding of community relations in Britain.

The Messina Brothers

The bad name of the Maltese undoubtedly owes a great deal to the Messina Brothers affair, which gave wide publicity to a vicious image of Maltese men, and which also played some part in generating that image. The Messinas were five brothers who ran an international vice empire based on Soho, from early in the 1930s to the 1950s.[1] For most of this period the police seem to have been fairly lethargic towards them, and it was the Press which took the main initiative in their eventual downfall. The dramatic nature of this public exposure and campaign, as much as the vice operations themselves, made the overthrow of the Messinas into the notorious affair it was.

As early as 1936 a vice charge was brought against three of the brothers, but the police were unable to get convictions, and over the next ten years they seem to have been left to continue quietly extending their empire. Public attention was first drawn to them in 1947, when one of the brothers (Eugene) received a sentence arising out of a Soho gang fight.

The first conviction occurred almost by accident, and could not be seen as the outcome of long and careful police endeavour. In April of 1947 a group of five Maltese men had been convicted at the Old Bailey of demanding money with menaces from women in the West End of London. At their trial the five had asserted, in defence against the charge, that they had in fact been out seeking for a rival gang known as the Messina Brothers, to get revenge for an injury one of them had lately received.[2]

The popular Press followed the trial of these Maltese with pronouncements about organised vice in London. The *People* declared (27 April 1947): 'For the first time it was publicly revealed how girls were being organised and exploited by gangs of men who terrorised them into accepting their lives of shame, and made huge profits from immorality', and went on to explain how the convicted men had organised recruitment to vice through 'theatrical agencies' in the provinces. It asserted that several other gangs existed, and that: 'Another of these vice-rings now operating in London has specialised in bringing girls over from the

[1] According to the *Sunday Times* on 13 August 1967 (p. 1) the three who were still alive then had a continuing stake and income in London, although of course no longer residents here.

[2] *The Times*, 25 April 1947.

Continent – hence the feuds that have taken place between the rival promoters.'

The *Daily Mirror* (24 April 1947) made more specific propositions.

We say that there exists in London a powerful gang of men known to the police as the Messina Brothers, who are living on the immoral earnings of women of the streets, powerful and rich, on the evidence of one of the women called, who said that they had two Rolls-Royces and who are able to make journeys for what purpose you may surmise to Brussels, Paris and Barcelona.

Two months later Eugene Messina was convicted of grievous bodily harm against one of the five men sentenced in April. In the meantime the public was regaled with estimates of the fortune amassed by the Messinas, and after the conviction of Eugene the Home Secretary was asked by a private member in the Commons to appoint a commission to look into white-slave-trade gangs. He refused on the grounds that an enquiry would not help the police, whose main difficulty lay in getting reliable evidence.[1] The conviction of Eugene does not seem to have relieved the police in this difficulty. No further prosecutions of Messinas followed, and still no vice charge had been sustained against them. Public interest in them began to subside, although speculation continued among journalists.

When the Messinas finally exploded into full public notoriety, it was as a result of the private investigations of Duncan Webb of the *People*. Beginning in September 1950, Webb published a dramatic exposé of the gang and their methods, and presented the police with the evidence they said they needed to ensure conviction.[2] Four of the Messinas left quickly for the Continent, leaving behind as caretaker the brother not known to Webb or the police at that time. He was however soon revealed and sentenced, followed by the brother who slipped back to take over. Webb continued to track and expose the rest, and over the next few years the empire was largely dismantled and the

[1] *Hansard,* 3 July 1947 (vol. 439, columns 1505–8).

[2] The main exposure started in the *People* on 3 September 1950, and continued for nearly a year.

brothers one by one imprisoned. For his single-minded efforts, Webb was several times attacked in Soho, and not long afterwards died in circumstances which seemed to indicate revenge.

The public interest created by this exposure was enormous. Coming after long years of post-war austerity, it was a case which had great imaginative appeal. The scale and panache of the vice ring were unprecedented and thrillingly shocking; the contrast between protracted police inactivity and Webb's heroic initiative was all too revealing and suggestive; the long chase was exhilarating and in the end almost moving. The affair had something for everyone, and for several years press references to these 'Maltese Kings of Vice' and their associates remained excellent copy.

It is, however, the great publicity accorded to the Messinas which has caused most Maltese to deplore the affair so wholeheartedly. For the case established a clear link in the public mind between white slave trading and Maltese ethnicity. In the opinion of many Maltese this was the blackest irony and injustice, for they contend that whatever the Messinas may have been, they were certainly not Maltese.

The nationality of the Messinas is a complex issue. When Webb began the exposure in 1950 he apparently assumed that they were Maltese in the ordinary and full sense of the word. But as more evidence came to light he realised that, although the brothers had claimed Maltese origin and descent, this had been done in order to qualify for British citizenship, and that their true nationality was more ambiguous. Although their mother seems to have been Maltese, their father Giuseppe was an Italian. The two elder brothers (Salvatore and Alfredo) were born in Malta where Giuseppe himself was a well-known vice-racketeer. Early in the 1900s the family moved to Alexandria to evade criminal proceedings in Malta, and the remaining brothers – Eugene, Carmelo and Attilio – were born there.

The family vice business flourished and spread along the North African coast to Morocco. Then in 1930 a concerted police drive was made against the Messinas right across the Mediterranean, and one by one they travelled to continental Europe and thence on British passports to London where they met up again and established a new, northern empire.

Duncan Webb had fitted this all together by July 1951 and wrote that 'although they claim to be Maltese, the Messinas come from Italian stock'.[1] The Messinas eventually had their British passports withdrawn, and yet in spite of this they have continued to be regarded and referred to as Maltese, to the dismay of the real Maltese in London. When their record became known no group wanted to be publicly associated with them and share their guilt.[2] The English Press execrated them more enthusiastically because they were not English – and commented on their foreign origin whenever possible. For their purposes it made little difference whether the Messinas were identified as Maltese and thus technically – but only technically – British, or as Italian. Maltese people on the other hand have been keen to make that distinction, and have emphatically contended that the principal nationality of the Messinas is Italian by paternal descent. Naturally the Italians took another line. Dispatches from Italy published by Webb during the 'chase' period indicate that the Messinas staying there were known publicly as 'Englishmen' – although Italian nationality and domicile were officially accorded later, after representations by the British government.

The Maltese in Britain feel the nationality issue keenly, because they see the Messinas as having played a crucial role in the formation of their collective reputation. If the Messinas were *not* Maltese, then the affair can be seen not simply as bad publicity, but as most undeserved defamation. The willingness of English people to continue to think of the Messinas as Maltese after reasonable doubts had been raised is bitterly resented by many in the community as prejudice and perversity. In so far as the Maltese bad name was in fact grounded in the Messina Brothers affair, their sense of grievance is understandable and legitimate.

The Messinas and the origin of the Maltese reputation

Up to a point it is reasonable to blame the Maltese bad name on to the activities of the Messinas. The great publicity given to them certainly propagated throughout London and the rest of the country an image of the Maltese as vice-racketeers. There was a flowering of anti-Maltese sentiment during the 1950s, for which the affair surely created the necessary climate. But on close

---

[1] *People*, 29 July 1951.
[2] Some of the mechanics of group blame situations are discussed below in Chapter V.

examination it seems unlikely that the Messinas themselves explain this stereotype – certainly not on their own.

There is some evidence that in areas where numbers of Maltese had settled in Britain, purely local and verbal reputations of a similar nature were in circulation before the Messina exposure, and even before their arrival in Britain. This seems to have been the case for example in Cardiff, the chief Maltese settlement prior to the Second World War. Kenneth Little, writing at the end of the war, from field-work completed earlier, has shown that the Maltese in Cardiff were locally renowned for disproportionate involvement in the running of the café-brothels for which Bute Street was notorious. Among a community with a generally bad reputation, the Maltese had a specifically bad name:[1]

> Of the 'café' proprietors, as already indicated, men of Maltese origin provide the majority, and they are given a very bad name in the district by the coloured people as well as by officials.

This reputation probably dated back to the end of the First World War.[2] There are moreover grounds for supposing that the vice activities of Maltese in Cardiff were closely linked with those later revealed in London. In its revelations about Soho vice rings in 1947, the *People* named Cardiff as one of the provincial recruiting centres for the gang of sentenced Maltese:[3]

> One clearing centre of the organisation was in Bute Street, Cardiff. Young women were drawn to the centre by promises of lucrative and respectable employment in London. Once at the collecting centre some of the girls were actually bought. It was not unusual for a girl to change hands over a game of cards.

Another area where local field-work suggests the existence of a local vice reputation before the Messina exposure is Stepney, where Maltese became established during the Second World War. Under wartime conditions, with many unemployed seamen in the area and numbers of servicemen stationed nearby, Cable Street in Stepney blossomed into another Bute Street. A report circulated

---

[1] Kenneth Little, *Negroes in Britain*, pp. 51–2.
[2] Private communication from K. Little.
[3] *People*, 27 April 1947.

among dismayed local residents showed that here too cafés provided the focal-points for drifting dockland society, and that Maltese figured prominently among café-owners.[1] No direct reference was made in this report to a specifically Maltese reputation, but Banton, who started his own work in the area not long afterwards, hints rather primly that these Maltese did have a local name for vice: 'In this stretch of Cable Street there are also five Maltese cafés each of which provides lodgings for six to twelve young males whose womanising activities have given two of the cafés a particularly bad reputation.'[2]

Journalists and area representatives made several protests to the borough council, who in turn asked early in 1948 for increased police activity.[3] No special reference was made publicly at this stage to the Maltese, who were treated formally as just one sector of a generally troublesome immigrant community. But from Banton's remarks it appears that verbally, at a local level, a Maltese reputation may have become formulated here, as it had earlier in very similar circumstances in Cardiff. It is quite feasible that other early Maltese settlements, most of which were in docklands, were of a similar character and enjoyed similar reputations; but no field-work has been found with a bearing on them to confirm this.

So when the 1947 protection money case caught public attention, it is probable that localised vice images of Maltese were already spreading in some areas, although no public, national stereotype had yet been articulated. Despite the publicity given to the 1947 vice case, the nationality of the five men sentenced was at first not emphasised. There was a good deal of speculation about the number and size and organisation of other gangs involved in the business, but the possibility that any of them might be Maltese too does not seem to have been aired. Papers did not even suggest that the gang reportedly known as the 'Messina Brothers' might be Maltese, or even that their nationality might have any relevance at all.

The only interest shown in the nationality of the five men sentenced at this time was that of James Callaghan in the House

[1] Phyllis Young, *Report on an Investigation into Conditions of the Coloured Population in Stepney,* April 1944.
[2] Michael Banton, *The Coloured Quarter,* pp. 92–3.
[3] Ibid., pp. 81–3.

of Commons, during the discussion on the possibility of a commission of enquiry into white slave trading, who asked:[1]

> Is the Home Secretary aware that Maltese residents deplore
> the emphasis placed on the country of origin of these
> wretched men? Is he aware that a large number of decent
> citizens of Malta consider that they are prejudiced by this
> undue emphasis?

What Mr Callaghan seems to have been doing here was simply
airing the opinions of his constituents. As Member for South
Cardiff, he represented the then largest Maltese settlement in the
country. Clearly the sensitivity of the Maltese in Cardiff to their
local image predisposed them to imagine that their bad name
extended to London and the rest of the country. But other
members of the Commons do not seem to have grasped the point
that Mr Callaghan was trying to make; and certainly press coverage
at the national level did not indicate the existence of a widespread
Maltese reputation.

However, by the time of Webb's exposure of the Messinas a
national stereotype of Maltese vice-racketeers seems to have gained
currency. Webb himself repeatedly refers to the Messinas as
'Maltese merchants of vice', and seems to have considered their
nationality significant. The tenacity of the Press in calling the
brothers Maltese, even after their origin had been placed in doubt,
suggests that a firm image had by then been formed.

The event which must have done most to cause the image to
crystallise was Webb's exposure itself. But the exposure does not
seem to have itself been the real origin of the reputation. The true
effect of the Messina affair may have been to publicise an image
which was already beginning to develop anyway. With the
extension to London of Maltese settlement and vice activities, a
reputation could have been on the point of emerging, independently of the Messinas. The sensitivity of Maltese to the bad name,
as evidenced in Mr Callaghan's question in the Commons, would
no doubt help the stereotype to travel with them.

Hence, although the Messinas boosted tremendously the
circulation of the reputation, one of the reasons why the Messinas
were *themselves* so newsworthy may have been that they confirmed
ideas and rumours already bubbling under. This would explain

[1] *Hansard,* 3 July 1947 (vol. 439, columns 1505–6).

why the stereotype became set so soon after the beginning of the exposure. The Messinas were themselves in part prisoners of the public image of the Maltese, rather than the other way round. The fact that they had some Maltese connections, albeit minor, made them eligible to go on being regarded as Maltese, since the image was fitting, even after the ambiguity of their nationality had been shown.

Paradoxically, for the English newspaper reading public, the Maltese-ness of the Messinas may even have served to mitigate their individual sinfulness. A prostitute, who gave evidence against them, said in extenuation of old Giuseppe and Mrs Messina: 'They had lived most of their lives in Malta and Alexandria and accepted vice as quite a normal business.'[1] The cultural imperatives explained and reduced personal culpability.

Naturally such thinking is anathema to most Maltese. But perhaps the very bitterness with which some Maltese have castigated and denounced the Messinas, and blame them for the bad name, can be understood better on the hypothesis that it is the Maltese who are using the Messinas as scapegoats for their collective reputation. The Messinas help some Maltese avoid the fact that the bad name might perhaps contain an element of truth, as a highly developed sense of injustice prevents any open assessment of the image. And, as shown in Chapter IV below, maybe it is a truth which little can be done about, and which is therefore very hard to come to terms with.

The real significance of the Messina nationality issue may therefore be that it gives a let-out to those Maltese who do not wish to think that the reputation could in some sense be valid. If the Messinas had not had an Italian father, some other characteristic would perhaps have been singled out to show that really they were not proper Maltese. This scapegoating allows the preservation of a remarkable degree of complacency in some sectors of society in Malta itself, which has prevented them honestly recognising the problems faced by Maltese people in this country.

The nature and extent of Maltese crime in London

Scapegoating of the Messinas by real Maltese commonly takes the form of arguing that any apparent criminality of Maltese in

[1] *People*, 2 September 1951.

London, especially any connection with vice, is simply the outcome of prejudiced police actions following the Messina exposure: it is a classic case of a self-fulfilling image. This argument asserts that police are immediately suspicious of Maltese men and, because of the humiliation suffered by the force as a result of Webb's exposure, they have retaliated by prosecuting as many Maltese as they can get their hands on.

This contention is not one that can be settled easily by reference to criminal statistics, as these are themselves ambiguous, and lend equally to various opposing interpretations. As often pointed out by criminologists, official figures of crime are as much indices of public concern and administrative action as they are of deviant behaviour. And the two things may not vary together. Concern about certain modes of behaviour may grow – as, for example,

TABLE 3 *Convictions, by selected countries of origin, for living on immoral earnings in London, 1951–69*

i *Annual average convictions per country of origin*

Period	Malta	West Indies*	Eire†	West Africa	Cyprus	United Kingdom	Total annual average
	1	2	3	4	5	6	7
1951–4	15	3		7	1	32	62
1955–9	34	16	9	13	2	40	118
1960–4	23	36	16	7	6	72	169
1965–9	17	58	18	4	9	75	191
Total convictions	428	565	213	148	86	1063	2634

ii *Percentage share of total convictions in period*

1951–4	24	6		12	1	53	
1955–9	29	13	7	11	1	34	
1960–4	13	21	9	4	4	43	
1965–9	9	30	9	2	5	39	
1951–69	16	21	8	6	3	41	

Source: Metropolitan Police.
Notes: * Including Guyana.
† Not separately counted in period 1951–4.

TABLE 4 *Estimated annual rates of conviction, of selected groups, for living on immoral earnings in London, 1951–69**

Period	Malta	West Indies	Country of origin Eire	West Africa	Cyprus	United Kingdom
	1	2	3	4	5	6
1951–4	1,000	38		280	12	1·2
1955–9	1,700	53	11	260	14	1·5
1960–4	960	65	16	70	30	3
1965–9	570	77	18	27	38	3·3

Note: * Estimates are of the annual number of convictions per 100,000 men (in ethnic group) living in the Metropolitan Police area. (See Table A.9 in Appendix A for details of population estimates.)

with violence during the last fifty years – while the incidence of such acts stays the same, or even declines.[1] Therefore little meaning can be attributed to simple trends in conviction rates. An additional difficulty with the London Maltese and vice offences is that the compilation of official tabulations did not begin until after the Messina affair, when public interest had been aroused. The figures collected by the police since 1951 of the countries of origin of men convicted in London of living on immoral earnings are as shown on the previous page (Table 3).

As shown in Table 3 the number of Maltese offenders increased quite markedly during the 1950s, but has dropped back since. Their annual rate of conviction for this offence has been high throughout the period for which the police have kept special statistics, but was greatest during the years of maximum public anxiety about vice, in which questions were frequently asked in Parliament about the national background of vice offenders,[2] and which culminated in the Street Offences Act.

Other immigrant groups cannot be regarded as having suffered the same fate as the Maltese. Firstly, the *per capita* conviction rate for the Maltese is much higher than for any other group, as the large number of offences was achieved by a small population. An attempt to take this into account is made in Table 4, which

[1] See for example the discussion in Hermann Mannheim, *Social Aspects of Crime in England Between the Wars.*
[2] The question was usually put by Norman Pannell, MP who played an important part in the passage of the Street Offences Bill. More detailed discussion of this period can be found later in this chapter.

indicates that if the numbers of men at risk in different national groups are allowed for, the rate of Maltese convictions was at its highest point around one thousand times greater than that of British men, and at its lowest still nearly ten times that of the highest West Indian rate.

Secondly, the trend in Maltese convictions is contrary to the overall trend. From 1951 to 1969 there was a steady increase in convictions (see Table 3, column 7). The only groups *not* sharing in this general movement were the Maltese and the West Africans, both of whose rates have declined over the last decade. Although the number of West Africans involved was never great, they are the only other group whose conviction rate was anywhere near that of the Maltese. It is interesting therefore that both groups should have had a peak at the same, atypical period. West Africans had their own vice reputation in the 1950s, and if there was a police drive against the Maltese in the years after the Messina affair, as these figures rather suggest, there may have been a similar, though lesser, campaign against Africans at the same time.

There are several *a priori* arguments which would lead one to expect increased police interest in the Maltese after the Messina Brothers affair. It is notorious that convictions for living on immoral earnings are liable to extreme distortion by public and police interest, and that immigrant or other minority groups suffer disproportionately from this interest.[1] There are several reasons. To start with, poncing is a very elastic offence. It is difficult for police to collect hard evidence; and since the actual behaviour of a ponce is passive in many cases, courts are often prepared to settle for circumstantial evidence. Any man staying with, or repeatedly in the company of, a reputed prostitute, and who is in possession of money for which he cannot closely account, would find it difficult to defend himself on this charge. The testimony of an alleged prostitute seems generally to be heeded by the court only when it supports the police case. When a girl asserts that she has given a man money, no one doubts her word. But if she declares that she has not, or is not even a prostitute, this is discounted as an understandable attempt to save him.

A man who keeps company with a prostitute cannot therefore be defended by her – although he may easily be framed. And if

[1] See for example Derrick Sington's article 'Immigration and Crime' in *New Society* (no. 57), 31 October 1963.

she doesn't do this, the police still can, as so much depends in poncing prosecutions on the evidence of the police. If they do not choose to accept a man's explanation of his income, there is not much he can do about it.

So the offence is elastic in the sense that there are a large number of men who *could* be prosecuted for living on immoral earnings if the police wanted to. Actual convictions at any time represent only a proportion of potential convictions. The limiting factors are police time and interest in the offence – both of which are determined by the level of public concern. This is however probably never so great that the police resources are sufficient to tackle every available suspect, and they always have to exercise some selectivity. The police are aware that all they can hope to do is to deal with a few people, and therefore tend to use exemplary prosecutions to keep matters under control. At any particular time, then, police attention will be concentrated on those categories of suspects who appear to pose a special threat.

Immigrants are particularly vulnerable. They are more likely to be associating frequently with prostitutes; they understand the operation of the law less well; and being economically weaker, they are likely to have difficulty proving financial independence. Also as members of identifiable minority groups they may be more prone to experience the wrong end of police discretion. Immigrants involved in vice are more visible than other men would be, and excite greater sexual jealousy. So public opinion will be more inclined to define them as a special problem, and selective police activity will consequently focus on them.

Because of this undoubted flexibility in poncing conviction rates, it is conceivable that some of the apparent vice business of Maltese after the Messina exposure was the simple outcome of public and police prejudice. Like other immigrants, they were liable to police suspicion of a general sort; and as Maltese, they were regarded as specifically vicious and subjected to much greater exemplary police attention than other groups. Perhaps their great volume of convictions was more an expression of public anxiety, than a manifestation of behavioural tendencies. In this way, Maltese loyalists argue, in the years which followed the Messina affair the image of the Maltese ponce was fulfilled and publicly confirmed several hundred times over. Hence the poignancy of the Messina nationality question. For if these arch-racketeers were really Italians then it was surely an erroneous conception which was being thus fulfilled.

But, as already suggested, it does not seem likely that everything can be blamed on to the Messinas and the British police. Many Maltese may have been victims of police discrimination in the 1950s; but this is not the whole of the story and no service is done by pretending that it is. Maltese in this country were being sentenced for vice offences before the Messinas were known about. A wider analysis of Maltese crime in London, going back to before the affair, will help to show the limits of the self-fulfilling image hypothesis.

Analysis of court records

In order to help unravel the impact of the Messina affair on the convicting of Maltese in London, an analysis was made of court appearances of Maltese people in two magistrates' courts in London, one in the West End and the other in Stepney, over the period from 1940 to the mid-1960s.[1] The main findings of this analysis will be outlined first, followed by a more detailed discussion of the probable interplay of Maltese crime and the Maltese image over this period.

It would not be possible to use the findings of this analysis to make accurate estimates of the overall volume of Maltese crime in London, as it covers only certain areas, and it would be difficult to assess the proportion of London Maltese at risk in these court catchment areas. Thames Court in Stepney embraces a large part of the main East End settlement, but not all of it. Marlborough Street Court similarly draws cases from an important segment of Soho. Between them these two courts include some of the most important locations of Maltese criminality, but by no means all. For the period 1951–64, when figures for both these courts can be compared with the police statistics for London as a whole, slightly over half of Maltese poncing convictions occurred in *other* court areas.[2] At a rough guess, and assuming similar distributions of offence types in different areas–which is no small assumption – these two courts have between them probably dealt with from a third to a half of Maltese crime in London, so that

[1] For details of the analysis see Appendix E.
[2] For these comparative figures see Table E.4 in Appendix E.

some broad conclusions can be drawn about its composition and main trends.

The material collected shows that the general proportions of types of offences remained constant throughout the period covered, almost regardless of the numbers of convictions. This is particularly true of serious offences – that is, those for which Maltese were imprisoned without option or sent for trial. Except for a slight increase in the later 1950s, vice offences consistently amounted to about a third of serious cases. The proportion of violent crimes also remained steady, at around a fifth of total serious cases, and with a similar brief rise at the end of the 1950s.[1]

The Messina Brothers exposure does not appear to have had much influence on this overall composition of Maltese convictions, although it may have affected their distribution. If the two courts are examined separately, it can be seen that in the West End the proportion of vice crimes was highest in the war years – with 17 per cent of all offenders – before an image of Maltese as traffickers in vice had apparently emerged in London, and then dropped to less than 5 per cent in the 1950s.[2] In Thames court on the other hand the rate increased in the 1950s, to a fifth of all crimes for the decade as a whole, a period in which Thames court dealt with over half of the London total of Maltese poncing convictions. This suggests that if there was a drive against Maltese vice, it was quite localised, and that the main aftermath of the Messina exposure took place in Stepney. This point is elaborated later in the chapter.

The Messina affair may also have had some impact on the overall volume of Maltese convictions, as there was a sharp rise in sentencing in the 1950s for all types of offence, especially in the Stepney area.[3] However this increase also closely followed the arrival in London of the first of the main wave of postwar migrants. During the war years only a few hundred Maltese men can have been living in London. At the end of the 1940s this figure had quickly become several times greater, and throughout the 1950s fairly heavy immigration continued. This increase in the Maltese population was as steep, if not actually steeper, than that in convictions. In relation to the numbers at risk there may therefore

[1] Numbers of different types of offence, by period, are shown in Table E.2 and proportions in Table E.3, in Appendix E.

[2] See Table E.5 in Appendix E.

[3] Annual numbers of convictions, by court, are shown in Table E.1 in Appendix E.

even have been a drop in the rate of convictions over the years in question. This does not rule out a police drive against Maltese after the Messinas exposure, but it does modify the significance of such a drive by indicating that additional factors were involved.

The findings of this analysis also show that some interesting shifts in the characteristics of offenders were taking place over the years dealt with, in both courts alike. In the first place, offenders were becoming younger. In the period 1941–5, 19 per cent of men convicted (21 per cent of serious offenders) were aged between 15 and 25. By 1961–6, these proportions had risen to 42 per cent and 49 per cent respectively.[1] Second, there was a change in the nature of their employment. During the war years seamen and café proprietors figured prominently, as 61 per cent of offenders – and 53 per cent of those with serious convictions. But these gradually declined to make way for a wider range of job types, and also for higher rates of *un*employment, which rose among serious offenders from 14 per cent in 1941–50 to 42 per cent in 1961–6.[2]

These changing proportions were linked with a general shift in the age structure of the settlement – or at any rate that part of it which came before the courts. It was mainly younger men who were unemployed, and older men who were seamen and café owners. The first Maltese men to settle in London were not, on the whole, young men straight from Malta, but older migrants drawn from other settlements in Britain. As the community in London grew through direct migration, it came to contain a greater proportion of younger newcomers unconnected with seafaring.

Finally, although no reliable estimates of the volume of Maltese crime in London can be drawn from this analysis, it is possible to make some assessment of the general incidence of crime among settlers, by using the court record findings to identify those members of the 1967 sample with criminal convictions in these two areas. Thirty-four of the respondents were discovered to have convictions, plus a further eleven men who were in the sample but refused to be interviewed or were not fully contacted. So

[1] See Table E.6 in Appendix E.
[2] See Table E.7 in Appendix E.

forty-five men of the gross sample were found to have criminal records at these courts.[1]

Taking this group as a 'criminal sub-sample' of the main 1967 sample, a rough estimate can be made of the incidence of crime in the settlement as a whole. Just over half of this sub-sample were serious offenders in the sense of having at some time been sent to jail without option; this represents about 15 per cent of the gross 1967 sample. If some further allowance is made for convictions of different sample members at other courts[2] and for non-contact with current young criminals, including those actually in prison during the enquiry, among whom the rate of serious convictions had been increasing, it seems reasonable to suppose that about a quarter of current settlers had served or were serving prison sentences, and possibly between one third and one half had been sentenced on some criminal charge in London. The chance of conviction at some time during settlement, or the 'completed' criminality rate, would be greater than this.

This does not mean of course that these proportions of Maltese who had arrived in Britain were liable to conviction – only those who had stayed here. But to put it this way may be to mistake the direction of causality, for what had happened frequently was that criminal experience and labelling increased a migrant's chances of staying here. Several men interviewed commented that with their records they could never go back to live in Malta; it would bring too much shame on their families.

There is some confirmation from the court record analysis itself that a criminal conviction may play a significant part in the decision to stay permanently in Britain. The criminal sub-sample

[1] Men interviewed in the 1967 enquiry were asked about their criminal activities and records, and several discussed them in some detail. However some who had denied a record were discovered in the court record analysis. The sub-sample of criminals considered here represents the overlap of the 1967 sample and the 'sample' of Maltese offenders identified through the court records, and consists of all 1967 sample members for whom convictions were *found,* in the 1968 analysis. Those 1967 respondents who admitted convictions, either at the courts analysed or elsewhere, but who were not encountered in the court record analysis, were excluded from this 'sub-sample'. A comparison of the characteristics of this sub-sample with those of the offender group in general is made in Table E.9 in Appendix E.

[2] That is, to include cases of 1967 respondents who admitted offences, but who were not encountered in the course of the 1968 analysis, and also of respondents who had not admitted convictions, nor were found to have any in the two courts analysed.

accounted for between 6 and 7 per cent of all the court appearances analysed. The 1967 sample itself was a 10 per cent sample of London Maltese. There is no reason for supposing that the sample was drawn disproportionately from the catchment areas of the two courts used, as its geographical distribution was good. So if all the offences from 1941 had been committed by men still living in London, and if they were reasonably sampled in the 1967 enquiry, then the share of all convictions attributable to sample members would have been unlikely to be much in excess of ten per cent. When allowance is made for the deaths of offenders – and there were more older men sentenced in the earlier periods – and for some degree of non-contact in 1967 with current young offenders, then little margin of offences is left which can be allocated to the large numbers of returned migrants and short-term settlers who no longer formed part of the settlement. In view of the complex nature of the 1967 sampling procedure, no statistical significance can be attached to this finding. But it is consistent with the 1967 interview material.

On this evidence, some experience of criminal proceedings is common among members of the ethnic group here – both in the sense of occurring frequently, and also as an important consideration leading to permanent domicile here. In spite of the high migration return rate, the current settlement probably contains most of the Maltese who have been convicted in London since the war. This is an extremely material factor in the life of the community.

The interplay between Maltese crime and their reputation

During most of the 1940s there does not seem to have been a definite stereotype in circulation at a national level of Maltese men as ponces or vice-racketeers. Localised, verbal reputations may have been forming in London; but only in the final year or two of the decade does the Press appear to have taken these up, and no explicit public suggestions of this image have been found prior to the actual Messina exposure. So the criminal convictions of Maltese in London during most of this period can be regarded as having taken place before the emergence of a collective bad name.

Few Maltese in London seem to have been convicted before

the outbreak of war. Random volumes of court registers were scrutinised back to the early 1920s, without yielding any definite cases. There may have been a few hundred Maltese living in London then, but they do not seem to have had much bother from the police, at least in the districts analysed. The first cases brought to light took place in 1941 and 1942, mainly in the West End, and Maltese seem to have been new to the courts at this time. For example, one man convicted of 'wandering abroad' in 1943, after several other offences in the previous few months, had the following comment entered into the court notebook against his appearance:[1]

> He doesn't reply to questions. The gaoler knows him and says he has been here often. But when interpreters are sent for – Russian, French and so on – it's no good, as he seems to speak a gibberish of his own.

By the next year, when court appearances of Maltese had become more common, the nationality of this man had been appreciated and he was treated as a little less mad.

These first Maltese demonstrated a lack of self-consciousness consistent with the absence at this time of even a localised reputation. One Soho café concealing a wartime brothel was named the 'Sons of Malta'. If this appellation had possessed then the connotation which it certainly would have in later years, this would indicate a scarcely credible candour on the part of the proprietors. It is much more reasonable to suppose that no such inferences would have been made then. This same establishment crops up again under Maltese ownership and operating in the same way in the 1950s, but the name of the premises had been changed.

The general turning point seems to have occurred in the later 1940s, perhaps in the aftermath of the 1947 protection money case, and as rumours and speculation built up about the Messinas. In Soho a local Maltese reputation is likely to have preceded the actual exposure of the Messinas, but not by a wide margin of time.

As shown earlier, it was actually in the war years that vice offences made up their highest proportion of Maltese convictions in the West End. Nearly all the serious offenders during the war were sentenced on poncing or brothel-keeping counts. It is

[1] Entry in Court 1 notebook at Marlborough Street Court in 1943.

pertinent to the argument to note also that many of these first Maltese vice offenders, in Stepney as well as in Soho, had *previous,* pre-war, convictions for vice activities, in older Maltese settlements such as Cardiff, Barry and Southampton.[1] So they are unlikely to have just been innocent victims of a vice squad frustrated by failure to trap the Messina Brothers.[2]

Several of the early defendants stated these other places as their main residence at the time of the hearings. So what seems to have been happening is that older settlers, already possessing criminal records in this country, were moving into London, partly perhaps because of unemployment in the provinces, and partly because of the boom in the London entertainment and vice industries which mobilisation had brought about. In addition, and for the same reasons, those Maltese leaving the merchant navy were now coming to London instead of the older maritime centres. It has already been noted that wartime offenders were mainly café owners and workers, or seamen, and many of the latter were described in the court notebooks as being absent without leave from the merchant navy pool.

This would explain why the numbers of Maltese offenders in London managed to grow in the war period, in spite of the curtailment of emigration from Malta, and how by comparison with later periods the criminality of these first arrivals was so high. Hardened, seasoned criminals were being drawn selectively to London by the special circumstances from Maltese café society around the country. The allegations made in the Press after the 1947 case, about organised vice networks reaching out into the rest of the country, may have been somewhat overdrawn, but were perhaps grounded in reality.

The war years were a busy time in Soho, and the number of vice convictions of Maltese may not give an adequate indication of the volume of business. Large numbers of prostitutes had Maltese surnames, presumably most by marriage, and if an image had been current of Maltese men as pimps and *souteneurs,* police would surely have been able to increase the rate of sentencing several times over. One Maltese charged in 1944 with living on

---

[1] Records of previous sentences, and personal histories of offenders, are often entered in the court notebooks. Some of the men from Cardiff had records going back to the 1920s.

[2] In fact the police do not seem to have been concerned at this time about the Messinas, or their nationality.

immoral earnings retorted indignantly in the court: 'Why pick on me; there's plenty of others who have done nothing in this war except ponce. I am no worse than the others.'[1] This hardly suggests an excess of police zeal at the time.

At the end of the war the market dried up quite quickly, and gangs formed to protect shares in the dwindling trade. Conflicts between rivals became more overt. As a result of this competition, and perhaps too of the public attention being given to it, several Maltese moved business to Stepney. In the later years of the decade a number of veteran Soho offenders started appearing in Thames Court. Stepney was emerging as the major Maltese settlement in London, and, in addition to some old-timers moving there from areas like St Pancras, new migrants were arriving from Malta. The volume of Maltese crime rose steeply there.

This transference of Maltese activity to Stepney coincided with, and was contributory to, the increase in dockland vice which was alarming local residents. Repeated pleas were made by residents to Stepney Borough Council to clean up the area, and a retired Port of London policeman wrote in the *People,* a year or two later, that a 'Great Wave of Vice threatened to overwhelm the port as at the end of the first world war'.[2] At this stage the Maltese in Stepney were not yet being singled out publicly for special reference and attack; but the Messina affair was soon to change that.

The 1950s: public reaction to the Messinas' exposure

The turn of the decade coincided with the breaking of the Messina Brothers affair, and there can be little doubt that the publicity had great repercussions for the Maltese. Local rumours and speculations were transformed almost overnight into a coherent stereotype with national currency. This mass image in turn filtered back through public and police concern to bring about an immediate increase in the convictions of Maltese and to boost their ostensible criminality. In both the courts analysed, but mostly in Stepney where Maltese were now visibly congregating, the number of court appearances rose dramatically and suddenly. Webb's articles about the Messina Brothers began in September

[1] Comment recorded in Marlborough Street Court 1 Notebook, 1944.
[2] William Simmons, 'How we rescued women who were lured on to vice ships'.

1950. The number of convictions of Maltese in Thames Court in 1950 was three times as great as in 1949, and then in 1951 five times as great.[1] This rise is consistent with a season of exemplary measures against the Maltese from the autumn of 1950 to the end of the summer in 1951 when Webb's main series ended.

There is further evidence of this in the kind of offences for which Maltese were convicted in these years, for a significant feature of the early 1950s was that for a few years there was a notably higher proportion of trivial charges. For example, convictions for gaming were high, suggesting that the police had taken to routine raiding on Maltese clubs. Offenders were younger than in the 1940s, reflecting the growth in the community from young migrants. But the newcomers would surely not have received so much police attention so quickly but for the collective bad name they had suddenly acquired. The actual criminality of these newcomers can hardly have been so great as that of the wartime settlers, many of whom had been selectively recruited to London for criminal purposes, after apprenticeships in the provinces. So, although immigration was a contributory factor to the growth of convictions, without the Maltese bad name it would not have had the same effect in the short term.

The form of the Messina exposure gave the police a special incentive to clamp down severely on Maltese activities. Duncan Webb's articles had taunted them with intimations about their reluctance to prosecute the Kings of Vice, and this may have goaded them into stronger reprisals than usual, in an effort to restore public confidence by demonstrating that they had taken command.

Distressed local residents were also stimulated into public attack on the Maltese. Whereas in the 1940s the Maltese had been referred to in Stepney as part of a general dockland problem, in the 1950s they were more and more singled out for vitriolic commentary, and public anxieties came to focus on them particularly. The Messina affair may not have caused this; but it certainly unleashed and endorsed it. It was argued earlier in this chapter that the tenacity with which people hung on to the idea that the Messinas were Maltese can be understood most easily on the assumption that their being Maltese made sense to many people, either by supporting an existing local reputation, or by being

[1] See Table E.1 (columns 4 and 5) in Appendix E.

D

seen to fit local realities. It was these potentialities which gave the affair its impact; and it would be precisely in an area like Stepney, where the image bore some relation to the developing local circumstances, that it would take root most readily. General anxieties which had been building up about immigration and vice were lent a specific content by the exposure, and were legitimised by the national concern which the exposure represented.

Encouraged as though by an oracle, indignation in the East End waxed strong, with an inevitable snowballing effect. As public opinion became more inflamed, police vigilance was stepped up; the vice convictions in the Cable Street and Whitechapel areas multiplied, and were accordingly given more attention in the Sunday newspapers. In this way the local campaign against the Maltese, originally drawing its meaning and momentum from the Messina affair, gradually came to replace the Messinas as news, even at the national level. As interest in the vice kings subsided, attention was transferred to the Maltese cafés and brothels of Stepney. This progressively reinforced and compounded the fears of ordinary East Enders.

Local reaction to this apparent surge in Maltese crime came to be centred round the Vicar of St Paul's in Dock Street, the Rev. Joseph Williamson.[1] In 1957 he and his associates published a pamphlet entitled *Vice Increase in Stepney*. This opened with the assertion that vice had spread from the dock area of Cable Street and was invading the residential parts of Stepney. This rise in prostitution was accelerating at an alarming rate:[2]

> In recent years, the decent residents of Stepney have been powerless to prevent immorality imported into the district by pimps, and blatantly practised in the streets. Charges for soliciting at the local Magistrates Court were:
>
> 2 in 1946
> 9 in 1949
> 585 in 1956
>
> Prostitution is a social disease. If a small area in Stepney is allowed to continue and grow as a breeding-ground for prostitutes, the whole country is affected.[3]

[1] See his autobiography, *Father Joe*.

[2] This increase was itself probably occasioned in part by the extra police effort, following earlier representations in 1947 and 1948.

[3] Rev. Edwyn Young, Miss Edith Ramsey, Miss M. C. Paterson and Rev. Joseph Williamson, *Vice Increase in Stepney*, p. 1.

The Maltese were identified as the principal bearers of this disease:[1]

Recruitment for Prostitution:
Much could be written on this subject, but the dominating factor in this context is ALL-NIGHT CAFES – mainly owned by Maltese, kept open not for the convenience of stranded travellers or workers in night-shifts, but for the promotion of prostitution, and often gambling. In 1956, out of a total of 35 men convicted at the local Court for 'living on immoral earnings', 27 were Maltese. . . .
A steady stream of girls – often young girls – arrive at the Cafés, attracted by tales of easy money without work or supervision. The phraseology among Café proprietors is 'A mystery has arrived'. Within-a matter of days, perhaps hours, the 'mystery' has joined the ranks of professional prostitutes, and a man is taking her tax-free earnings.
. . . The entry to prostitution is made easy through these Cafés.

Many other voices were raised against the Maltese. Court cases involving them commonly had front page treatment in the local newspapers, and in the court itself one magistrate regularly justified imposition of a heavy sentence on defendants by direct reference to their Maltese nationality.[2]

This publicity emanating from church, bench and press cannot have done much to calm already over-heated emotions. If it did nothing else, it clearly signposted the route to easy money for runaway girls. So no one should have been surprised, whatever his standpoint, when Maltese convictions in the area, especially for serious offences, reached a new peak in the second part of the decade. Over the same period in Soho there seems to have been a drop in activity, reflecting the displacement of concern and emphasis.[3]

[1] Ibid., p. 3.
[2] The formula 'Owing to the nationality of the defendant' would be entered in the court register to indicate the exemplary nature of the judgment.
[3] Events in the two court areas were of course not entirely independent. Some ponces living in and charged in Stepney were also involved in Soho, and there was police co-operation between the areas in bringing prosecutions. During this period though, because of the shift in emphasis, most of the convictions of men involved in both areas were effected in Stepney.

An interesting by-product of this shift in attention to East End vice was the gradual modification of the representation of the Maltese ponce. After the Messinas' exposure, the Maltese had been characterised as heartless vice lords relentlessly engaged in brutal warfare on the streets of Soho. Public anxiety about vice gangs was sharp at the turn of the decade, and this was reflected in legislative action. For example, the 1951 Criminal Law Amendment Act, aimed basically at giving known prostitutes equal protection in law to that of other women against procurement, was promoted as a civil rights measure. But it owed something of the ease and speed of its passage through Parliament to the fact that it was also seen to help the police in moving in on the organised vice racketeers considered to be so powerful.

This type of image could not survive for long in the flood of Stepney corner café cases. In addition to the poncing, a few brawls took place, and even the odd murder; but these were unrelated events. There were no networks of vice lords revealed, only a number of seedy, relatively homely amateur ponces. Maltese defendants appearing in the court were becoming constantly younger, and included newer arrivals, and so the stereotype of the racketeer inevitably yielded place to that of the Maltese 'boy' fresh off the plane.

The better-informed sectors of public opinion had already been moving in a compatible direction. Serious research was being conducted which questioned and went a long way towards allaying popular ideas about organised white slavers. For example, C. H. Rolph showed through a number of case studies that the relationship between prostitutes and their ponces was normally an extremely close and personal one. The prostitute's trade presented her with a constantly changing public, and her ponce was important because he could provide a stable and supporting relationship. Rolph found no evidence of widespread organisation of vice; in fact the market seemed very free. Thus the ponce was far from the ruthless deployer of passive female flesh as usually portrayed.[1] Similar conclusions were reached by the Wolfenden Committee, although they adopted a slightly sterner attitude towards ponces, whom they considered guilty of exploiting human weakness.[2]

[1] C. H. Rolph (ed.), *Women of the Streets.*
[2] *Report of the Committee on Homosexual Offences and Prostitution.*

This shift of emphasis can be seen clearly in the line taken at different times by the *People*. In the early 1950s this organ of mass opinion was the prime scourge of vice kings, and capitalised heavily on popular fear and hate of the inhuman white slavers. However, by the end of the decade it regarded the Maltese ponce as little worse than a misguided youth. This is exemplified in an article by Robert Hill in 1959 entitled: 'PASSPORT TO VICE – That is all it costs Malta's young men to come here and prey on women'.[1] The basis of the problem was identified as the ease and cheapness with which young and immature Maltese could come to Britain, and the temptation in which they were placed by the availability of quick money through poncing. A Maltese priest in London was reported as saying:[2]

> One café I went to had some 40 Maltese men sitting round the tables. . . . As I talked to these men, English girls came into the café and went up to their 'protectors'. I was disgusted. These were Maltese boys, my countrymen, living off the earnings of these women. I argued with them, pleaded with them to give up this way of life and take an honest job. They just laughed. 'It's easy money, Father', they said.

The old allegations about disciplined, ruthless gangs had by now been abandoned, and Maltese vice had come to be represented almost as another form of adolescent delinquency. The main blame had accordingly been lifted from the individuals themselves, and now was seen to reside in lax parents and negligent authorities. And in the view of the *People*, the most negligent authority of all was the British government for allowing unrestricted immigration.

Climax of reaction in the Street Offences Act

The change in the Maltese stereotype during the 1950s had a wider political significance. By drawing attention away from supposedly specific national characteristics to the more general features of immigrants, this change of emphasis enabled Maltese ponces to be used as vehicles for anti-immigrant feeling in general. The strength of concern aroused at a national level by the events in Stepney can only really be accounted for on the hypothesis that

[1] *People*, 8 February 1959.
[2] Ibid.

emergent ethnocentric sentiments were being channelled into anti-Maltese feelings. At this time respectable political figures were reluctant to attack immigration openly, and so symbolic debates were held instead. Control of vice was one appropriate arena, since it overlapped at several points with the immigration issue. The Maltese themselves were a particularly useful target group, because they seemed to be active in vice but were not defined as a coloured group. So it was feasible to attack immigration via them, without appearing racialist. These points can be substantiated by an examination of the passage of the 1959 Street Offences Act, which represented the culmination of public disquiet about postwar vice in London, and marked the beginning of the end of public reticence on the immigration issue.

The Stepney problem played an important part in the shaping and passage of the Bill. Support for legislation was at its most hysterical in the East End, and the local pressure group was so successful in mobilising and channelling national interest that some provisions of the Act were included almost entirely in response to the Stepney situation.

Spearheading this pressure was the Member for Stepney, Walter Edwards, a man whose own sensibilities were thoroughly in harmony with the anxious majority of his working-class constituents. Walter Edwards's mass following was greatly welcomed by the government, as it compromised Labour Party opposition to the Bill.[1] The representations from this area carried greater weight than the recommendations of the Wolfenden Committee on certain issues. Mr Butler himself admitted that clause two of the Bill, tightening up on all-night cafés:[2]

> arose from strong representations made to me about nuisances created, particularly in Stepney, and I decided to listen to the advice given to me by a deputation from Stepney. Evidently, all-night cafés frequented by prostitutes need dealing with most strenuously.

Similarly, in deference to pressures from Stepney, and against the explicit recommendation of the Wolfenden Committee, the

[1] Patricia Hornsby-Smith gratefully acknowledged the support given by Walter Edwards, when she moved the third reading of the bill. See *Hansard*, 22 April 1959, vol. 604, col. 529.

[2] Introducing the second reading; see *Hansard*, 29 January 1959, vol. 598, col. 1287.

government raised the maximum sentence for living on immoral earnings from two to seven years.

The pattern of vice in Stepney had come to dominate public discussion by the end of the decade. One or two questions were raised in this debate about the problem of organised gangs; but these were quickly dismissed. In fact the problem had so receded in public consciousness that major provisions could be made in the Bill – for instance, making soliciting an offence in itself, without nuisance necessarily being caused – which were almost unanimously thought likely to encourage the organised rackets, as in the event they have done. In one member's opinion the Bill was a Pimp's Charter,[1] but few people seemed to care. The prime objective of the legislation was to remove prostitutes and their company from public places – cafés and the streets – where they offended public decency.

It was no accident that the fiercest support for this Bill came from an area in which the growing public sensitivity to prostitution was linked with a popular identification of immigrants as the people responsible for the vice. An important and perhaps indispensable factor behind the postwar concern about vice was precisely this fact that some immigrants were involved in it. In real terms it is unlikely that prostitution in London was greatly increasing. More probably there had been a gradual decline in recent decades, associated with the movement away from Victorian life styles. But from the end of the war to the passage of this Bill there was accelerating public anxiety. Paradoxically this may have been due in part to rising expectations of order and decency in working-class areas, which the long-term reduction in actual prostitution was permitting. However, the main factor seems to have been the increasing visibility of vice, as immigrants, above all coloured immigrants, became involved. This greater visibility was due to the physical distinctiveness of most immigrants, and the fact that, as members of outside and competing groups, immigrants were more liable to excite the sexual jealousy of indigenous males and draw their attention to the existence of vice.

An immigrant ponce arouses greater sexual jealousy and anger than a local one. Firstly, in general terms, the immigrant is seen as a natural competitor for any scarce resources in the territory to which he has moved. Conflicts over women can be severe,

[1] Mr Paget. See *Hansard*, vol. 604, col. 476.

because of the strictly limited supply of this 'resource' and the difficulty of sharing it. Sexual conflict has been behind several of the racial incidents that have occurred in this country, like the riots in Cardiff after the First World War, and the events in Nottingham and Notting Hill in 1958.[1] An immigrant ponce, more specifically, is a figure to excite sharp feelings, as he is apparently getting money for what most other men would willingly do freely, and many are prepared to pay for. This is too invidious to be borne with good grace, and inevitably prompts suspicion either that some compulsion is being exercised, which is vile, or that the immigrant's performance is tangibly superior, which is unfair competition.

Throughout the debate on the Street Offences Bill, it was clear that sexual jealousy of immigrants was a strong underlying force in popular opinion. Walter Edwards repeatedly indicated that the ethnicity of an offender was important, since immigrants had no right to our women:[2]

> The committee is certainly agreed on this occasion that living on the earnings of prostitution is one of the worst and vilest offences committed in this country ... If honourable Members were to see the actions of some of the pimps and the way they behave they would agree that an absolutely filthy atmosphere completely surrounds these people.... They are the scum of the earth and should be treated as such. Many of them are people from the Colonies and Commonwealth who have hardly done a day's work here since they landed. They have been spending nearly all their time here living on the earnings of our white women.

Mr Rees-Davies, distilling a great wealth of experience in the field of vice, endorsed the view that this was an alien crime:[3]

> I agree with [Walter Edwards's] last observation about ponces. The great majority of ponces and pimps in this

[1] Sexual jealousy is evident in some interviews carried out by Barry Carman, BBC reporter, with Teddy Boys at Shepherd's Bush in the autumn of 1958 following the Notting Hill disturbances. Ruth Glass gives a transcript in Appendix C of her *Newcomers*. A typical item (p. 262) reads: 'Voice "Just that a lot of ponces live round here. I mean, it's not very nice to see a coloured bloke with a white girl out in the streets, is it? I don't mind white people doing it but not black."'

[2] Report of Standing Committee F, for 8 April 1959, cols 353-4.

[3] See *Hansard*, vol. 604, col. 542.

country are not Englishmen. They are principally Maltese,
Ghanaians and Jamaicans. Over two-thirds are men who
come from these territories, and there are a small number of
Sicilians and Italians. . . . They are a pest to this country, and
the crime of poncing is a singularly unEnglish crime.

During the 1950s politicians were under great pressure from
constituents to speak out against immigration, but there was a
feeling that to do so was somehow indecent – to do so too
directly at any rate. The Street Offences Bill and the issue of
poncing offered a welcome opportunity to raise the issue obliquely.
One of the most heated sessions of the debate occurred in the
committee stage when Norman Pannell moved a deportation
clause for Commonwealth immigrants convicted of this offence.
This was defeated only after firm government assurances that
consultations were in process and separate legislation was being
considered. This debate on the deportation clause marked an
important phase in the emergence of an explicit anti-immigration
lobby. And the Maltese enabled a distinction to be made between
immigration and race relations. When moving the insertion of
the clause, Mr Pannell gave figures showing that the Maltese
regularly had the lion's share of poncing convictions in London,
and pointed out disarmingly:[1]

It is not essentially a colour question, because the number of
these immigrants who were coloured was far smaller than
those who had white skins. . . . Many hon. Members are
anxious about the undercurrent of prejudice that exists here
regarding immigrants. We have had certain unfortunate
manifestations of that prejudice in recent months, but I do
not want to dwell on that, because my Amendment is not
chiefly concerned with coloured immigrants. The prejudice
that has grown up is not unconnected with the offences committed by certain immigrants, coloured and otherwise, which
are dealt with in this Bill and mentioned in this Amendment.
I am convinced that if they could be deported, as aliens are
able to be deported, that prejudice would tend to diminish,
if not disappear, to the great advantage of the law-abiding
immigrants here.

[1] Report of Commons Standing Committee F, 8 April 1959, cols 339 and 341.

Although this amendment was rejected, the government had been made aware of the strength of the anti-immigrant lobby, and thereafter the real debate was open, with foregone conclusions. Walter Edwards and others continued to campaign outside of parliament,[1] and immigration control legislation with deportation provisions was to follow soon after.

Once immigration was opened to free discussion, public interest in vice quickly burned out. Convictions in London for living on immoral earnings continued to rise throughout the 1960s but it is no longer an issue. In retrospect the Street Offences Act can be seen as the route by which anti-immigrant sentiments emerged fully into the arena of respectable public debate, and as the first legislative expression of these sentiments.

The rising tide of feeling against immigrants in the 1960s, which came to focus more explicitly on coloured people, has relatively benefited the Maltese. After playing a central role in the opening stages of the debate, the Maltese have in recent years ceased to be of any real public interest. Their specific reputation still exists, but its severity has abated as the vice problem has lost its hold on the public imagination. This improvement may even have been hastened by the adoption of Maltese as a prime target of hostility by the anti-immigration lobby in the late 1950s. The publicity given to them as immigrants may have assisted their re-absorption, once the general debate was opened up, into the broader category of immigrants from which the Messina exposure had helped to lift them ten years earlier. And since they are not coloured, the more open the race issue has become, the better they have fared.[2] At the beginning of the decade Maltese offenders, including rightly or wrongly the Messinas, were to some extent regarded as vicious in themselves, on account of their nationality. This is implicit in the prostitute's testimony cited earlier in this chapter. But as the Press became more concerned with the mass offences of young newcomers, greater attention was given to general factors in the migration process and situation, and in the volume of migration. This line of development was consistent with the needs of the anti-immigration lobby,

[1] See Joseph Williamson, *Father Joe,* chs V and VI.

[2] Their increasing share of employment vouchers under the Commonwealth Immigrants Acts, as shown in Table A.5 in Appendix A, is almost certainly related to their whiteness.

and may have been partly constrained by it. But whatever the cause of the shift, its consequence has been gradually to liberate the Maltese from the more crippling elements of their reputation, by locating the source of their vicious behaviour in more general aspects of immigration procedures and policies.

The 1960s: consequences of controls

The reaction against immigrants at the end of the 1950s, which was in some respects channelled through the Maltese ponce stereotype, resulted in the erection of a network of restrictions and new sanctions which materially altered the context within which Maltese criminality took place. The consequences of these new controls have accompanied and perhaps contributed to the dwindling of the Maltese bad name, and most Maltese who have lived in Britain for a long time believe that, although there are still many difficulties, the worst is now definitely over.

The most important pieces of legislation dividing these periods were the Street Offences Act and the first Commonwealth Immigrants Act. The first of these hit Maltese café owners hard, by raising the penalties for allowing unlawful gaming and the assembly of prostitutes and other disorderly persons in late-night cafés, tightening up on the café licensing system to make it more difficult for licences to be transferred quickly between colleagues in the event of prosecution, and the outlawing of simple loitering and soliciting by prostitutes in public places. The Act also increased to seven years the maximum sentence for poncing.

The Commonwealth Immigrants Act introduced the concept of limited and controlled migration, and provided for the deportation of recent immigrants convicted in the courts. Up to this time casual movements by Maltese had been a central feature in the pattern of migration to Britain. These new provisions transformed the attitudes of Maltese to the mother country, and led to some immediate changes in the composition of the migrant flow.

The changes referred to earlier in this chapter in the characteristics of Maltese offenders and their criminality during the 1960s are clearly in part the result of these various controls, though since several different measures were instituted around the same time it is not always easy to see which of them were responsible for what effects. The reduction in the numbers and proportions of café owners and employees, and of seamen, can be seen as related both to the imposition of migration controls, with the consequent reduction in casual settlement, and to the tighter regulation on running cafés. What is perhaps less easy to understand is why the proportion of *young* offenders should have continued to rise in the 1960s: for with the reduction of immigration, the settlement would have been ageing in this period. The younger offenders were not second-generation Maltese,[1] so clearly the reduced number of newcomers were taking over an even larger share of criminality. The most plausible explanation for this is that the deportation provisions of the immigration act were encouraging the police to be especially hard on the newcomers. Since deportation orders could be made only within five years of entry to Britain, if the police were to take advantage of these new powers they needed to build up a case against an immigrant rather quickly; this would tend to put younger members of the community at greater risk of prosecution.

It is difficult to trace the effects of these controls in detail on the volume of Maltese convictions in London. The totals of offenders and convictions dropped in the 1961–5 period, and the fall in vice crimes was greater than average. But the trends in the two court areas were very different, and separate analysis is needed to unravel the differential consequences of controls in each of them.

The situation in Stepney was probably the more typical of London as a whole. There was a decrease in all types of crimes, except those against property, which slightly rose. Vice and violence convictions both fell distinctly.[2] There are several possible alternative explanations for this. Common sense would suggest that the pre-eminent cause of this reduction in criminality was fear of harsher penalties and deportation. But in respect of vice offences at any rate, the reduction of Maltese convictions went against the general trend. Other Commonwealth immigrants, no less subject to these sanctions – including non-coloured groups like Irish and Cypriots – steadily increased their activities in this field, as did men in the local British population.

---

[1] The dates of arrivals of offenders are commonly noted in the court evidence notebooks, enabling non-immigrants to be identified – had there been any.

[2] Gaming convictions fell away almost completely, as a result of relaxations in the law.

An obvious factor in the decline in Maltese figures was the closing of many all-night cafés following the Street Offences Act. The exploits which local opinion had found so offensive were reduced substantially; and at the same time, compounding this effect, public interest in these cafés was flagging. Much of the concern had in any case been spurious, in that the real issue had been race and immigration, and when it was no longer necessary to conduct that debate symbolically, anxiety about the cafés would have subsided even if convictions had continued to rise. But of course the fact that people no longer cared so much ensured that the figures did fall, and fell fast. In parts of London where concern had not been so hysterical, a commensurate reduction in convictions did not take place. If the Stepney total of Maltese poncing convictions is subtracted from the London total, the balance turns out to be fairly stable, so that the reduction was indeed pretty localised.

A consideration which complicates this analysis is that from the late 1950s onwards the Maltese settlement in Stepney was beginning to lose its importance, with the emergence of secondary centres in such places as Lambeth and Islington. Some Maltese were moving to these districts to get away from the anti-Maltese hysteria infecting parts of the East End, and this movement was encouraged by the local authorities, who demolished several streets with large Maltese populations. So the apparent stability of vice convictions in other parts of London may have been the outcome of a general diminution, temporarily offset by the re-location of some activity from the Stepney area, where the reduction had been particularly rapid. Without looking at court records for a number of other districts there is no way of resolving this point. What is, however, clear from the figures available is that there was an immediate slump in Maltese vice convictions in Stepney in the early 1960s, while those in the rest of London remained steady, and that this was in contrast to the rising rates for other ethnic groups.

The figures on deportations of Maltese since the Commonwealth Immigrants Acts, although a very small sample of total Maltese criminality, suggest that the tailing off of Maltese convictions continued gradually throughout the decade. Although the statistics refer formally to the whole of Britain, in fact the Maltese were mainly in London; the figures show that the average of around ten deportation orders on Maltese offenders each year in the early 1960s had dropped to five by the end of the decade.[1] It is noteworthy too that even in the latter part of the decade, vice offences still constituted the largest category for which deportation recommendations against Maltese were made. These figures are especially interesting as they are the only official statistics on Maltese crime which refer to all types of offence; and so they do tend to confirm that Maltese criminality *generally* declined over the last decade.

There seem to be two general reasons. As the specific virulence of the Maltese bad name faded, police attention would have naturally abated towards a level general for immigrants as a whole. The effect of this was perhaps less marked in London generally than in Stepney, where the drive against Maltese had been concentrated; but the overall trend would have been similar.

Second, the volume of Maltese immigration was being sharply curtailed. As already demonstrated, the proportion of young offenders amongst the Maltese was high and increasing. With a reduced inflow of young newcomers, some diminution in crime would be likely. Immigration from other Commonwealth countries also declined in this period, in most instances much more precipitously, without similar apparent reductions in criminality, at least in vice offences. This does not necessarily invalidate the proposition. One of the most significant features of the Maltese community in Britain has been the absence of authority figures, and the individualistic and adolescent characteristics of many migrants. Disorganisation among Maltese is therefore likely to occur soon after arrival, instead of some years later as a consequence of cultural or familial conflicts. Maltese criminality may therefore be rather different in type from that of most immigrants, and much more closely related to the migration process itself. This point is developed further in Chapter IV.

It is also worth noting here that although there was a drop in the overall conviction-rate of Maltese in the 1960s, there seems to have been some rise in property offences.[2] Vice crimes are sometimes considered to be characteristic of immigrant groups in an early stage of settlement, when they have not yet adapted

[1] These figures are shown in Table A.10 in Appendix A.
[2] See Table E.3 in Appendix E.

to urban, industrial life.[1] As the group adjusts itself culturally its pattern of deviance will move towards that of the local population. The rise in property crimes among Maltese indicates that some such settling down process may have been in train.

Consequences in Soho of legislation

The changing pattern of convictions in Soho before and after the imposition of new controls was different, reflecting the unique character of this area and the very different results there of the Street Offences Act. The Act undermined the open market formerly enjoyed by prostitutes, and created conditions in which greater organisation was inevitable. Expertise and facilities for such organisation were concentrated in the West End, so the legislation served to put Soho firmly back into the centre of the picture. This was perhaps an implicit aim of the Act, which was primarily concerned with combating prostitution in residential districts of London.

The organisation of vice of course remained illegal, and did not manifest itself openly. But there was a spawning of clubs operating indirectly and parasitically on the margins of the vice trade, usually by providing private premises in which discreet soliciting would take place. The commonest form was the clip joint, which was basically a private 'club' employing girls who were generally assumed, but not admitted, to be prostitutes as hostesses to entice clients and promote their consumption of drinks. Functionally, in relation to the vice trade, these clubs were analogous to the public cafés where prostitutes formerly gathered.

These private clubs were commercially more rewarding than the old cafés. As prostitutes could no longer solicit in public places, would-be clients were prepared to pay high entrance fees for admission to places where contacts might be made. And of course there was no guarantee of satisfaction. The club had the complete backing of the law to tease customers for as long as they were prepared to pay. The Street Offences Act, dubbed originally as a pimps' charter, turned out even better for the extortioner. This type of organisation lifted the art of living on

[1] See for example Julius Isaac, *Economics of Migration*, 1947, p. 195, and also the discussion in Chapter IV below.

immoral earnings to a subtler and commercially more rewarding level. No offence was committed unless immoral acts by prostitutes on the premises could be proved, and this was not easily done. As street soliciting had been reduced, the police found it harder to identify girls as prostitutes, so that a denial by a hostess or club manager was difficult to disprove. The Act removed girls from the streets, at the expense of clients and to the great profit of intermediary organisations.

In the early 1960s several Maltese in the West End invested their capital in this legal business, and many others were employed as managers and assistants. The only members of the organisations who were exposed to prosecution were the touts or doormen who brought in the clients. To operate effectively they needed to attract attention; and this often entailed causing obstruction or nuisance in the street. It is this type of offence, together with property offences as in Stepney, which increased most for Maltese in Soho in the early 1960s. Another type of venture in which Maltese became heavily involved in Soho which was similarly reliant on touts for attracting custom was the traditional strip club; and by the middle of the decade quite a high proportion of these establishments were owned and run by Maltese.[1]

Touting is boring and exhausting work, and there is a high turnover of staff. Most Maltese touts were young men, new arrivals, who had not yet been able to get better jobs. Old-timers retired as soon as they could to quieter occupations, or operated as club managers and proprietors, safely off the streets. So it was the young men who became the visible instruments of Maltese activity in Soho, and who bore the brunt of police interference. And it was these touts who accounted for the lower age of Maltese offenders in the area. Before the Street Offences Act convictions of Maltese men in Soho were outnumbered by the soliciting convictions of women with Maltese surnames, usually wives of Maltese men rather than Maltese girls themselves. After the Act this was reversed, and it was young men who preponderated.

To a limited extent the Maltese ownership and character of many of these clubs may have served to relocate the stereotype of the Maltese back in the West End again. Club touts have been treated in Sunday newspapers as a species of licensed pimp, and

---

[1] An editorial note 'The salesmen of Soho', in *New Society* on 18 July 1968 estimated that half of the touts working in Soho were Maltese.

only a slight modification or embellishment of the existing Maltese image was needed to accommodate this role. Furthermore the re-appearance of Maltese gang warfare in the mid-1960s may have revived some ideas about the organised nature of Maltese crime. During the winter of 1966 to 1967 an 'explosives war' was waged by some competitors against the owner of a chain of clubs who was a leading figure among Soho Maltese. Over a period of several months, three or four of his premises were badly damaged by bombs and several people injured. The case was given wide coverage in the national press, and the violent aspect of the Maltese image was endorsed by it.

The Street Offences Act may have given some direct stimulus to the formation of gangs in Soho. The types of clubs which grew up after the Act required substantial investment, and were more viable in chains. This was particularly true of the strip clubs. Strippers can work at a lot of clubs in the same day so it was economic to group the clubs in chains worked by a single team of girls. This structuring of resources would have been likely to promote organised competition and conflict, as it was groups of clubs, not small individual units, which competed for customers and for the best girls. Such a network of interests could therefore easily result in gang warfare.

But as after the last war, the actual break-out of violence may have been indicative of a weakening of the economic basis of organisation. As long as business was good there was no need to mount direct attacks on rivals; but the boost given to Soho by the Street Offences Act was beginning to falter by the middle of the decade. Redevelopment blight was beginning to discourage investment in the area. More specifically, from the middle-1960s onwards local authorities were starting to relax regulations governing stripping, and such shows blossomed all over London, in public houses as well as private clubs; so that in order to maintain business the clubs in Soho had to cater for increasingly specialised demands. Similarly as public concern about vice waned, prostitutes were venturing back on to the streets and the market was opened up again.[1] So after a few years the restrictions which underpinned the organisation of vice and commercialisation of soliciting had started to atrophy, and the trends in Soho Maltese criminality

[1] Nicholas Swingler, 'The Streetwalker Returns', *New Society*, 16 January 1969.

evident in the first half of the decade were probably not long sustained.

These statistics of formal convictions may represent only part of the contribution of Maltese to West End life, as there might have been invisible involvement of more circumspect Maltese criminals throughout the last thirty years or more. The most recent press allegations about Maltese criminals have specified individuals – currently accused of organising high-class call-girl rackets, in the guise of innocent landlords – who seem to have been linked with the original Messina network, and who have managed to keep their tracks well covered.[1] Suggestions concerning highly organised Maltese crime do crop up from time to time, and by their nature are very difficult to dispose of. I have come across no conclusive evidence of the existence of secretive, businesslike rings of Maltese criminals; but this does not rule them out, as I deliberately have not stuck my neck out too far in this direction. As I argue in the next chapter, though, if they do exist they probably account only for a minor part of Maltese activity in Soho, and they are hardly likely to be the inner, articulating core of known Maltese crime.

In any case, and what is more germane to the argument here, recent disclosures about Maltese criminals, such as those in the *News of the World,* have not excited much public interest, so that the Maltese reputation seems to have lost its hold on public imagination – irrespective of its behavioural basis. Now that the debates on immigration and race have opened up, leading to the increasingly rigid control of immigration and the formalised exclusion of minorities from full British citizenship rights, public attention to objectionable behaviour among them is no longer sustained by so great a feeling of urgency.

Summing-up: the Maltese and vice in London

The 'bad name' which Maltese have been given in London refers specifically to vice activities. Shifts in their image have taken place, as publicity has focused on different areas. But the changes are less important than the continuities; the core of the reputation has remained constant.

Some Maltese would consider that this reputation was foisted

[1] *News of the World,* 29 April, 6 May and 13 May 1973.

on them unjustly, as a result of the erroneous identification of the Messina Brothers. They would argue that the Messinas were the sole basis of the bad name and that all other vice convictions of Maltese derive in some way from them. On the evidence examined in this chapter it does appear likely that the Messina exposure stimulated police activity against Maltese men. But it is equally clear that many vice offences occurred prior to the affair, and that this itself may have owed some of its news value to the confirmation it provided for local reputations which were already in existence or forming.

The exposure of the Messinas may have been critical in fostering the adoption of the Maltese in the 1950s as a main target for the anti-immigration lobby. This was at the time politically expedient, for as the Maltese were generally defined as whites they could be attacked openly by respectable people loath to appear racialists. To some extent therefore the Maltese may be considered as having paradoxically been made scapegoats by public opinion on behalf of *more* alien groups. But this is only a small part of the story, and it does not follow that hostility towards the Maltese was not itself genuine. If the Maltese had not themselves been considered outsiders they could not have been cast in this role. In the climate of opinion at the end of the 1950s, when many people – especially public figures – were afraid to make any negative statements about coloured immigrants, the position of the Maltese as white outsiders meant that they indirectly attracted more than their share of antagonism, and were attacked more strongly than they might otherwise have been. But even if there had not been the same reluctance to speak against coloured immigrants, the Maltese would still have been subject to public recrimination for their distinctive form of deviant behaviour. Nor was their association with this type of crime simply the result of malicious fabrications, directed at them on account of their minority status. Unless the Maltese had some real tendency for involvement in vice there would not have been a sufficient basis to support this public identification of them with poncing. The Maltese population in London was tiny. Attacks on them would surely have been quickly revealed as hollow fabrication unless there was some grounding in reality.

The existence of a penchant for vice is on the whole confirmed by events since the passing of the Street Offences Act. Maltese in the West End have invested heavily in commercialised sex. In spite of their small numbers they control a large share of this trade. Other sectors of the leisure business – restaurants, gambling houses and so on – have scarcely received any Maltese capital. Strip clubs and clip joints are quite legal, so it cannot really be argued that, in any direct sense at any rate, this bias is the consequence of police prejudice. It is a voluntary specialisation. This point is elaborated, and qualified in the next chapter.

The Maltese reputation cannot be dismissed as completely unjustified. There does seem to be a leaning among Maltese in London towards the sex trade. Before looking at the consequences of the reputation for the Maltese, it will be useful to examine some of the main determinants of this behaviour, as the causes and consequences of the reputation may prove to be intimately connected with each other.

IV
CAUSES OF MALTESE CRIME

The distinctive form taken by Maltese deviance in Britain can be traced back ultimately to a central dilemma in colonial Maltese society, revolving around the discrepancy between an extremely strict set of moral principles on sexual matters, and a practical reality of extensive prostitution in the island, meeting the needs of the large garrison. Perhaps nowhere in Maltese life has their dependent status and inability to control their own lives been felt more keenly than in this sexual subjection. Because it was so offensive to religious sentiments, it has been an unmentionable subject; for the intractability of the problem did not ease its acceptance, but merely helped to render all sexual issues even more highly charged.

It is perhaps in fact because of their impotence in this matter that the Maltese came to demand and affirm such uncompromising moral standards. Social reality was so humiliating that they have collectively turned their backs on it in favour of the contemplation of an ideal and unattainable state of purity. The fervour with which moral and religious values have been celebrated in the island suggests that they were absolute ends in themselves, and not just guides to real behaviour.[1]

This polarisation between moral principles and unpleasant actualities created at the individual level a great deal of sexual neurosis. Maltese were required on the one hand to exercise complete personal restraint, while on the other expected to maintain a high level of interest in other people's sexual behaviour in order to help uphold general standards through constant mutual censorship. It was a difficult balance to keep.

[1] Malta would serve as a well-stocked hunting ground for anyone seeking to substantiate Wilhelm Reich's propositions relating to sexual repression and religiosity. See his *Mass Psychology of Fascism*, in particular chapters 6 and 7.

Emigration has been an escape from all this for individuals unable to tolerate the strain. The migrant flow has probably always contained a disproportionate number of people whose interest in sex was greater than their capacity or willingness to practise self-control, and even normally-sexed Maltese might be liable to disorientation when they left Malta, as departure removed or severely weakened the network of mutual controls which had bounded their previous activity.

The actual degree of sexual restraint which has been enjoined in Malta must rank as high as that demanded in any society. Sexuality is defined by the Church as the sacred property of God, to be exercised only in religiously meaningful acts. The key concept is chastity – either in the absolute sense of total abstinence from physical sexuality, or in the relative sense of fidelity and procreation within human marriage. A comparatively large proportion of the Maltese population follows a religious vocation with vows of complete chastity; and their sexuality is given purely symbolic expression in the relation of Christ and his church. That of the rest of the population is tolerated solely for the purpose of propagating the Maker's image and augmenting his congregation; and any discussion of sex outside of the context of family building is strictly taboo in most circles.[1]

Dom Mintoff's new Labour government has recently relaxed the secular laws relating to sexual behaviour and its public discussion; but until then at any rate censorship of films and printed matter was keen. Imported materials – even technical and academic publications – underwent extensive cutting if they contained anything which might arouse sexual feelings. For many palates, though, these scissors were not used enthusiastically enough, and some films were shown on church premises so that priests could hold a hand over the projector to shut out offensive passages left in by the censor. The only formal sex education was that conducted by religious associations, for the benefit of married or engaged couples.

Any sexual relation outside marriage is a mortal sin requiring

[1] A group of researchers from the Catholic University of Louvain criticised this reticence on sexual matters, and were particularly disturbed to find that the Maltese population was ignorant of Church teaching on birth control: 'the majority believing that their duty is to have as many children as possible.' Their report was not allowed free circulation in Malta. See *The Socio-Religious Study of Malta and Gozo,* by the Centre de Recherches Socio-Religieuses, Brussels, 1960.

immediate and sincere confession. If the parties to it are single, then the priest will usually exert his influence to salvage family honour by making a marriage out of it. If either of the parties is married the offence is greater, because other people are harmed by it, and there is no way of legitimising the liaison retrospectively. Adultery by a married woman is a bit worse than that of a married man, as she is presumed to be subject to weaker desires; but there is not much in it.

Because of the definition of sexuality as a religious commodity, swearing in Malta has a religious content. Curses tend to be obscene references to God or, more commonly, the Virgin Mary.[1] Indecent language has accordingly been a matter of public concern in Malta, and even in recent years such 'crimes against religious sentiment' have occupied a place in the work of the courts. Between 1960 and 1965 – the latest years for which figures could be found – 58 men were committed to prison for uttering 'immoral words', in addition to numbers for blasphemy.[2]

The attitudes of Maltese priests to legitimate, marital sexual activity are suffocating enough; but deviant behaviour and vice are almost unmentionable. The only occasion when priests will discuss them is during confession – and this is not the best setting for an exchange of views. Recourse to a prostitute is a mortal sin, like other sexual acts outside of marriage, for which absolution is necessary. And it is not likely to be given unless the supplicant displays proper contrition and promises not to do it again. Open reference to vice is considered utterly offensive, and respectable Maltese try to close their eyes and ears to the topic.

When it does occur, public discussion of vice excites a curious sensitivity in which evident consternation combines with half-hearted and equivocal denial that such a thing might be possible – in Malta at any rate. This was illustrated a few years ago by the reception in the Maltese press of a provocative article in *Titbits* about prostitution in Valletta. The author, 'Eric Saxon', pretended to be concerned to advise the Maltese how to attract British tourists, but the main intention was obviously to paint a lurid picture of the blue quarter of Valletta, for the same purpose of

[1] On Reich's hypothesis, it is of course no accident that swearing mainly concerns the Madonna, as the central activity of the church is in regulating sexual conduct, and sublimating sexual fantasies.

[2] Figures taken from annual reports on the working of the Prisons Department.

titillation as most of *Titbits* features.[1] Saxon dwelt heavily and gloatingly on the unpleasant details of the area, and emphasised how unattractive he found the prostitutes.[2]

The offensive issue of *Titbits* was banned in Malta, but some copies circulated and local opinion was so incensed by them that public comment became necessary. Several newspapers felt that national honour could only be upheld by a vigorous official denial. The *Malta News* thundered on 6 March 1965:

> Last month the English Magazine *Titbits* carried an article which shocks and shakes anyone familiar with Malta and her people. . . . Malta Government officials feel a protest through Malta House in London would not help matters. We take a dim view of Government's attitude. Though it may not be the case, still it makes us worry whether the Government is more concerned with preserving the Anglo-Maltese connection than with fighting back attempts torpedoing Government's own tourist drive and smearing Malta's name in the eyes of people abroad.

The Government Public Relations Officer and Tourist Board Chairman described the article as 'scurrilous' and 'disdainful', but

[1] *Titbits*, February 1965. Eric Saxon reports from Valletta, on 'THE STREET THAT SHAMES HERO ISLAND'. Ostensibly the report is a warning to British tourists to avoid Strait Street in Valletta (which *Titbits* mispells):
> But I say British tourists should steer clear of Malta till the island's government take this advice; Stamp out the vice in a street that is the shame of Malta – Straight Street.
> This is an area of vice and prostitution that ranks with the world's most notorious sin-spots. . . .
> Officially, the problem does not exist. The Gut [Strait Street] is not mentioned in the newspapers, on radio, TV, by parliament or even in polite conversation. . . .
> The Maltese police turn a blind eye to what goes on in The Gut. The only effective control comes from the naval police who intervene when one of their sailors is involved in a fight.

[2] For example, Saxon declares:
> [The Gut] is a dirty, squalid alley that is packed from noon to early morning with prostitutes who sell themselves for the price of a drink. . . .
> A street where teenage British sailors are accosted by women old enough to be their grandmothers. . . .
> Most prostitutes are middle-aged or older. Many of the younger ones are pregnant.
> Their hair is greasy, their faces dirty, their dresses are crumpled.
> Some have been there years, trying to smile through toothless gums. They earn a living because most customers are too drunk to know or care about their looks.

said that no official action was to be taken:[1]

The two officials agreed that this was an overt attempt to smear the island's image, but said a reply would only serve to start a controversy detrimental to Malta's national interest. A spokesman for the Police said the public knew that the Police were keeping a watchful eye on events in Strait Street, and that they were doing their duty well.

The dilemma was obvious. An official and explicit denial of Saxon's allegations would have been a nonsense, as they were basically true. On the other hand a completely passive acceptance of them would have been too painful and offensive, and would have led in certain quarters to demands that Malta should be cleaned up – which was not feasible. The only reasonable reaction in these circumstances is in fact to fudge the issue by stating that the situation, whatever it may be, does not merit public scrutiny. So eyes are averted, and the vague belief entertained that the authorities have matters under satisfactory control.

Public attempts to eliminate vice in Malta

This response of fatalism and withdrawal is characteristic of the Maltese on issues where their minority status in their homeland has inhibited realistic and direct tackling of problems. But it has not been the automatic response, and was adopted only after efforts to stamp out prostitution had been made. It was the failure of such 'real' action which finally confirmed the underlying fatalism of the majority as the most sensible approach to the vice problem and which endorsed the view that all that could be done was to make prostitution as inconspicuous as possible.

The main attempts to clean up Malta seem to have been made at the turn of the nineteenth century and in the first decades of the twentieth. National consciousness was awakening, as definite prospects of domestic sovereignty emerged. The desire to improve the moral climate was closely bound up with this growth in national pride and identity.

Although the measures to clean up Malta appear to have been popular in the sense of receiving public support, it is nevertheless significant that a central role throughout this programme of

[1] *Times of Malta,* 6 March 1965.

reform was played by a man who was in so many respects not a typical Maltese, Gerald Strickland. Strickland was immensely patriotic, and came to power as First Secretary to the Governor in a period of growing national feeling, under a constitution designed to give some expression to it. But he was not himself nationalistic in a narrow sense. His own ethnicity was mixed, as he was the product of intermarriage between English and Maltese aristocratic families; and throughout his life he had strong international connections. In addition to leading the Maltese administration he served in the British colonial service, was an MP in England, and later a member of the House of Lords. He was a rationalist, optimist and radical who believed in the possibility of engineered social progress. In short he was a thoroughly Victorian man of affairs, and it is fitting that his period of greatest internal influence in Malta should have been in the late 1890s, under Joseph Chamberlain's policy of anglicisation of Malta. His greatness lay in managing to be at once Maltese and English; and only an English Maltese would have seriously thought prostitution in Malta could be removed by statute.

Direct efforts to clean up Malta lasted from the 1890s to 1930. This was a period of concern and legislation about vice throughout the western world, related to the growing concern of nation states with international opinion. From about 1880, the Maltese were themselves becoming more and more sensitive to their national image and the deleterious effect of vice upon it. This increasing sensitivity is measured by the steady decline in the numbers of women in Malta recording themselves – or being allowed to record themselves – as prostitutes. The number of 'femmes declassées' in the occupation tables of the 1881 census was 136. In the corresponding tables for 1901, 1911 and 1921 the figures were 97, 86 and 54. At the 1930 census there were none, although four occupants of the Poor House were classified as 'former fallen women'. In later censuses there has been no mention of them at all. As will be shown below, this apparent withering away of vice in Malta is not matched by any drop in business. The sole meaning of the figures is that tarts, enumerators and government statisticians were becoming alive to the threat to Malta's national honour.

This mood received its first real expression in a programme of regulations dealing with the dwellings of prostitutes which

Strickland inaugurated in the 1890s, culminating in the government notice 41 of 1902 just before a resumption of full gubernatorial powers.[1] These regulations were in part aimed at making prostitution less visible, by requiring the girls to keep doors and windows of their dwellings closed and not to loiter near them. But the controls were intended to go beyond the simple containment of vice and clearly marked a step towards the eradication of brothels. A clause in the regulations prohibited altogether the residence of prostitutes in certain streets, and successive amending government notices extended the list of streets considerably. This was not even a matter of keeping the nicer areas clean, because the lists included precincts such as Strait Street in Valletta which were traditional vice centres. In fact a direct attack was being made on the chief areas of vice, and the periodic addition of further streets probably indicates that mopping up operations were needed in adjoining districts as trade moved into permitted areas. The list of prohibited districts was added to piecemeal up to 1928 when Strickland, then newly elected Prime Minister, gave a last tremendous boost to the restrictions by extending the ban to all the streets in the main towns of Malta, and most streets in the remainder.[2]

At the same time as these police regulations were being tightened, statutory measures were extending the criminal law's coverage of the organisation of vice. Under the 1899 Aliens Law, deportation of aliens for living on immoral earnings was expedited; and the departure of Giuseppe Messina from Malta may have been prompted by this. Then in 1918, a year after the return to Maltese affairs of Strickland following his retirement from the colonial service, the first White Slave Ordinance was passed, in line with the 1910 Paris International Convention on white slave trading; this made procuration and the organisation of vice specific statutory offences. More radical still was the 1930 White Slave Ordinance, passed by the caretaker Strickland government during the suspended constitution. This took to their logical conclusion the progressive restrictions on brothels by abolishing completely the concept of a legal brothel. It now became criminal simply to allow premises to be used for prostitution. This ordinance marked the high tide of the vice 'prohibition' era in Malta, and coincided

[1] Published in the *Malta Government Gazette*, 26 February 1902.
[2] Government notice 339 of 1928.

with a general drive against the organisation of prostitution in the Mediterranean area.

But since there was a continued military presence in Malta, this attempt to wipe out vice was doomed to failure. Offences by prostitutes against the police regulations rose during the twenty-five years following their introduction. What is more, these offences were concentrated in the traditional vice areas covered by the main code – according to the 1902 government notice – rather than in secondary districts dealt with in subsequent amendments. So the controls had not even served to relocate the activities of prostitutes.

TABLE 5 *Offences by prostitutes in Malta, 1912–1932*

Administrative year	Offences against regulations respecting public prostitutes: as per Government Notice 41 of 1902	Offences against regulations respecting dwellings of prostitutes: as per Government Notices 49 of 1912, 112 of 1918, 256 of 1918, 67 of 1919, 281 of 1919, 166 of 1923, 339 of 1928
1912–13	268	—
1913–14	362	8
1914–15	393	2
1915–16	473	8
1916–17	675	25
1917–18 – 1919–20 No figures found		
1920–1	2,450	63
1921–2	2,119	112
1922–3	2,299	29
1923–4	3,307	11
1924–5	1,794	4
1925–6	635	—
1926–7	574	—
1927–8	433	—
1928–9	363	61
1929–30	293	—
1930–1	61	—
1931–2	34	—

Source: Annual reports of Police Department, Malta.

From the middle of the 1920s, the numbers of convictions dropped (see Table 5). This may have been due marginally to postwar reductions in the size of the garrison; but the main thing they measure is a shift in the pattern of vice supply. The sustained attack by the police on the traditional modes of prostitution was forcing the trade under cover. Instead of soliciting in streets and doorways, the girls were taking jobs as barmaids and artistes, and using these as camouflage. The number of bars multiplied very rapidly, and many of them employed over a dozen girls.[1]

Rules controlling the licensing of bars and barmaids were reinforced in 1924, with such provisions as that barmaids should not be more numerous than one for every hundred square feet of floor space, and must not loiter at or near the entrance to the bar. But there were difficulties in administering these regulations. The basic problem was of course the large numbers of clients demanding prostitutes; and the duties of the police in implementing controls were in stark conflict with the interests of the garrison. The 1927 Police Department Report made this point perfectly plain:[2]

Barmaids and Music Hall Artistes

One of the most difficult and delicate tasks with which the Police are confronted is the issue of licences to and the control of barmaids and artistes. On the one hand public morality must be upheld and on the other the interest of the various wines and spirits shops, on which so many families are dependent for their livelihood, cannot be altogether disregarded.

The fact must be faced that the Public and the Services will not frequent these shops unless dancing, singing, and similar sort of amusements are provided. . . .
The increase of the Fleet and the attractive salaries offered to these artistes and barmaids have brought about a corresponding increase in the number of females who look to this occupation as a means of earning their livelihood.

[1] There are some striking similarities with the effect of the 1959 Street Offences Act in Soho, with the important differences that in Malta public anxiety was not abated, and morals continued to be offended. In 1925 and 1926 a member of the Senate expressed grave concern at the development, and asked for information on the exact numbers of barmaids, etc.; but the Nationalist government did not release any figures. See H. B. Forma, 'Immorality – A conscientious appreciation of the past and present attitude of the Church of Malta'.

[2] Report of the Police Department, 1926–7, p. 3 (para. 13).

The power of the local police in a minority situation was limited. They required the co-operation of military authorities in keeping order among prostitutes' clients, and were obviously in no position to enforce regulations against the wishes of servicemen.[1] It was not possible both to restrict the soliciting of prostitutes in public *and* to hold back the boom in bars and floors shows.

Strickland however considered that it was, for in 1929 he introduced further licensing regulations which gave police additional powers to cancel licences of barmaids and artistes whom they considered had violated public morality, propriety or decency, and to disqualify women from holding a barmaid's licence within six months of being registered on the roll of prostitutes.[2] Although clearly intended to be restrictive, these new measures probably paved the way for a new system of police supervision of prostitution. The White Slave Ordinance of the following year abolished legal brothels, so that existing police registers of prostitutes and their dwellings were made redundant. But by this time the vice trade had become fully established in the bars and music halls. This was less objectionable than overt vice in the streets, and the new barmaid and artiste licensing system offered a perfect basis for police supervision of the new style of business. Police control could be much more discreet than formerly, as there was plenty of room for administrative, invisible influence; and those offences which did come to court could be aggregated with other 'licensing' cases. So offences by prostitutes became undetectable in published police statistics. Although the police could not eliminate prostitution, they were now better placed for directing the business and confining it within certain areas – while giving the impression in public that the vice problem had been solved by the 1930 Act.

This new pattern of discreet and indirect public control was an altogether more realistic and appropriate solution to the problem. National honour was sustained by the outlawing of more flagrant offences, and by cloaking the remainder with public reticence or equivocal denial. The Nationalist government

---

[1] One MP who took part in the debate on the Street Offences Bill had served in Malta as officer responsible for keeping order among clients. His own view was that removing prostitution from the streets and organising it in some way had much to be said for it. See *Hansard,* vol. 604, col. 535, speech of Lt.-Cl. Cordeaux.

[2] Government Notice 392 of 1929.

which succeeded Strickland in 1933 embodied the traditional fatalistic responses of the church and establishment, and under it the transition to this new system was eased and speedily completed. From that year onwards no offences committed specifically by prostitutes have figured in the annual police reports. Also some formal relaxations were immediately made to allow business to expand within police discretion; the minimum age for holding a barmaid's licence was lowered from 18 to 16, and the White Slave ordinances amended to reduce the maximum sentence for importuning.

The major concern of administrations since Strickland has thus shifted from cleaning up vice to covering it up.[1] Prostitution has been contained within three precincts where it is afforded implicit toleration by the police. During the 1930s the police were quite active against organisers of brothels, but they soon relaxed on this front also. Apart from a flurry of prosecutions following the Messinas' exposure in Britain, convictions for living on immoral earnings and organising prostitutes have become almost negligible.[2]

During the period of attempted prohibition, vice crimes made up quite a large proportion of the total. For example, at the 1921 census, nineteen men enumerated in the prison had been convicted of living on immoral earnings – not counting those jailed for corruption of minors and daughters etc., who may also have been involved in vice. This category was exceeded in size only by that of property offenders. Similarly in the 1930 census, twenty-two out of 140 men in prison – again the second largest group – had been convicted of 'crimes against morals', most of which were vice offences. The proportion has dropped since that period.

In retrospect it might be tempting to regard this whole episode as little more than a face-saving operation, which was only ever intended to improve appearances. As there was little public debate on the issues it is difficult to reconstruct the politics of the business. But from the content and ordering of the legislation it does seem likely that some people, Strickland foremost, hoped

[1] Symptomatic of this mood, was legislation in 1933 by the new government, which extended the meaning of 'immoral act' to include gestures. Interest was fast moving back from the content of reality to its form.
[2] Available figures are shown in Table A.11 in Appendix A.

materially to reduce the volume of actual vice. This was however probably never the objective of more than a powerful minority, and the actual programme of public action most likely rested on an alliance of interests between a few committed abolitionists and a less ambitious majority hoping merely to make vice less visible. For as long as the aim was to remove blatant brothels, action would serve both aims equally. But when the trade had moved off the streets, the interests of the abolitionists and the rest diverged. If Strickland had remained in office he might have continued to try to keep the bars clean. But he did not – and his failure to do so was perhaps indicative of his increasing isolation. The Nationalist government which took over from his caretaker administration did the opposite and eased restrictions on bars. Having waited until events had confirmed the view that eradication was not feasible, the Maltese establishment moved in to stabilise and make the best of the situation.

Abolitionists in Malta since Strickland have been more realistic about the relation of prostitution to Malta's minority position. The Labour Party, which emerged after the war as a properly radical movement, recognises that political and economic independence are essential first steps in the reduction of vice in Malta. This is one of the reasons why the party has been in favour of a complete break with Britain, even though its members are culturally pro-British. It does not consider that an economy based on tourism offers a much better prospect than the garrison, as it still places Maltese people in a servile role. When in office the MLP has tried to set up an industrial basis for the Maltese economy, to rid the island permanently of sexual exploitation by foreign masters.[1] No purely legislative, internal solution has ever been attempted by them.

[1] Forma (see note 1, p. 115) estimated in 1967 that there were still 1,000 prostitutes in Valletta. Tourism might change the pattern of vice by promoting a better class of tart; but the relationship is the same. Even the Labour Party has found its hands rather tied when it comes to tackling this issue. On return to power in June 1971, Dom Mintoff set out again to create a non-servile foundation for the Maltese economy. By January 1972 however he found himself, in the Rome discussions with Nato, being asked to consider the provision of 'recreational facilities' in Malta for the US sixth fleet, as part of the proposed package deal. The final terms of the March agreement do not include formal reference to this, so that the sexual decolonisation of Malta can perhaps be regarded as now under way. Mintoff apparently hopes to find a completely alternative role for Malta in the world by the 1980s, when the new arrangement terminates.

Sex in the Maltese service economy

Sexual exploitation of Maltese women by outsiders is a matter of some antiquity, for privileged access to them has probably always constituted an element of the 'personal services' provided by the local population for alien rulers there. There may not always however have been the same tension between moral principles and behaviour; in fact it seems quite likely that this did not develop until the British period of sovereignty and occupation.[1] Under the Knights sexual exploitation was a factor in the relationship between rulers and ruled, but it does not seem to have been treated then as a terribly disgraceful state of affairs requiring a national conspiracy of silence. Forma has collected the following evidence on this matter:[2]

> Doublet, the Secretary of the last Grand Master, wrote as follows in his Memoirs: 'The Knights made no secret of keeping mistresses, generally married women and mothers of a family, a practice which became so general that neither age, nor ministers of the Gospel, dissolute like the rest, blushed at the fact.'

> S. T. Coleridge, sometime Secretary of Sir Alexander Ball, had this to say on the same subject: 'Every Knight attached himself to some family as their patron and friend, and to him the honour of a sister or a daughter was sacrificed as a matter of course. But why should I disguise the truth? Alas, in nine instances out of ten, this patron was the common paramour of every female in the family.'

> Lt Anderson of the 40th Regt, who was stationed in Malta for a year in 1800–1, made the following note in his journal, subsequently published: 'Though all ranks of people are devotees, and minutely attentive to the church's ordinances,

[1] It was fitting that the taunting article in *Titbits* should have appeared under a name like Eric Saxon. Although Malta had gained political independence a few months earlier, many Maltese reading the article must have realised that it would be some time before they would stop having their noses ground in the dust.

[2] H. B. Forma, op. cit., p. 7. Similar evaluations of the Knights circulated in Britain at the time. An article in the *Penny Magazine,* 29 June 1839 (p. 241), comments that: 'Corruption in the administration of the law (under the Knights) spread its taint over the morals of the people; and it was scarcely considered disgraceful to be the Mistress of a Knight.'

E

yet chastity does not appear to maintain its due rank among their virtues. Certainly it is not to be found in the Island. While Prostitution, from the familiar and open manner in which it is carried on both by married as well as single women, and with the knowledge of their husbands and relatives, is not, unless attended with some particular degree of enormity, considered as a crime.'

To complete this picture of celibate depravity and its effects on the morals of the people of Malta I need only mention the 'edict against Co-habitation of Women with Priests' issued by Bishop Labini in 1780, a bare month after he had landed for the first time in Malta to take charge of his diocese; and which was followed by a stronger edict on the same subject four years later. It is interesting to note that none of Bishop Labini's predecessors had ever taken the slightest notice of this immoral scandal; nor have any of his successors.

Unfortunately there does not seem to be a direct record of what the Maltese themselves thought about this aspect of the Knights' hegemony at the time, and foreign observers may not have been sensitive to finer local feelings. The later Knights were an autocratic bunch, and the Maltese could have had little option but to make the best of their lot. But although this evidence is far from conclusive, it does suggest that the relationship was accepted without great truculence, and that the degree of moral opprobrium attaching to sexual compliance was not great.

A further reason for accepting this evidence is that it fits in with a hypothetical reconstruction, based on consideration of the nature of respective populations, of how replacement of the Knights by the British would have changed the pattern of sexual servicing. The numbers of British residents soon became much greater than the Knights had been, both in absolute terms and in relation to the size of the growing domestic population. Furthermore this presence was more plebeian. As the garrison blossomed, it would have created a great additional demand for cheap prostitutes; while at the same time middle-class Maltese families were being freed from the requirement of sexual tribute. For, unlike the celibate Knights, the British rulers brought with them wives to serve their needs; or if they were single were in a position to take Maltese girls as legitimate brides. As respectable Maltese families latched on to the possibilities of honourable marriages, the supply of well-born mistresses would have dwindled. Mixed marriages became common during the British period, and many of the chief Maltese families forged useful alliances in this way. The returns were much more long-term than the patronage of a bachelor Knight.

The element of exploitation in this intermarriage would have been comparatively small, especially as the chronic balance of male emigration left a residue of women. In fact it is arguable that as such marriages became mutually acceptable, the boot was transferred to the other foot, and that in some cases it was the British who were placed at a handicap.

A divorce case completed in London in 1965, involving an Englishman who had been in Malta and a Maltese girl, illustrates the sort of thing that could happen. In 1952, at the age of 21, the man in question had taken out a Maltese girl a number of times on 'completely harmless social occasions'.[1] Some months later he was called to a police station and charged with defiling a minor. He immediately went to a solicitor and asserted his complete innocence. In the words of the legal report: 'The solicitor's advice was cynical in the extreme. It was to the effect that this sort of charge for this sort of act was a common occurrence. British serving personnel who were guilty usually escaped before being brought to book. Consequently he had little chance of getting off.' So he was advised to marry the girl, or face the prospect of a long period of imprisonment. He saw the police inspector, who sent him to a parish priest who apparently had been fully briefed about the case. He was married by the priest on the same day, and the girl's father withdrew the complaint. There was no co-habitation and the husband soon afterwards returned to England and remained there. In 1965 he was granted a divorce in England on grounds of fraud and duress.

The possibility of marriage with members of the ruling group raised the status of Maltese girls, and a polarisation would have taken place during the nineteenth century in the types of sexual relations between them and British men. At one end of the social

[1] The formulation accepted by the court. See *The Times* law report, 20 February 1965.

scale, respectable Maltese families were forging links of inter-marriage entailing relative equality; while at the other, the numbers of prostitutes swelled to keep pace with the expanding garrison. So as the middle classes became less servile, the masses were made more so. This behavioural polarisation would have fitted in quite well with the dual sexual morality of Victorian England, so that there may have been definite confluence of British values with the pattern of sexual servicing.

This divergence in types of sexual relations with the rulers would also be consistent with a developing tension between moral expectations and visible social realities. The sectors of the Maltese community which led public opinion, the middle and upper classes, were liberated from sexual compromise and forced immorality, and were now in a position to support with clear conscience the religious value of chastity, and to insist that the clergy observe it themselves. So a nationalistic moral revival was possible – and would have been furnished with ample fuel by the worsening prostitution. As the sensibilities of leading citizens became clearer and finer, the vice predicament would have been an ever greater embarrassment, and the urge to reform more insistent.

Under British rule the Maltese had grown more aware of themselves as a national entity. This was related to wider move-ments of ideas in Italy and the rest of Europe; but as shown earlier, it was also closely bound up with the emergence of an independent and national church, as the repository of group consensuality. The problem of vice and sexual servility of the Maltese would have contributed to this development of the church as the chief focus of national feeling, as the dependence and minority status of Malta was experienced most directly as a *moral* difficulty which ultimately only the church could do any-thing about. As shown above, outrage at the existence of wide-spread vice in the island could not find any satisfactory expression in rational political action, and it is the approach adopted by the church which has provided the only tolerable collective response.

The retreatist reaction of the church serves the needs of respect-able Maltese quite well. Unpleasant and intractable reality is banished, and as far as public utterances of clergy are concerned, vice might not exist. Consolation for minority status is provided in religious fantasy. Churches exist in great profusion and splendour in the island, as manifestations of a dimension of nature far more durable and perfect than the secular world. Within their heavy walls the problem of vice cannot penetrate. This containment of evil is, however, never easy. Immorality is a constant threat to the fabric of decent family life in the real world. Severe sexual restraints are necessary to protect the value of chastity, and mutual vigilance must be unremitting. However some sort of resolution of the dilemma is achieved, and most Maltese are able to keep their own noses clean and to maintain a reasonable national dignity.

Sexual frustration and emigration

At a public, institutional level the denial of vice and the channelling of concern into fanatical religious devotion may be a useful means of resolving the stark discrepancy between values and reality, but at a personal level it often compounds emotional difficulties over sex. The Maltese population cannot be physically sealed off from contact with prostitution. Economic pressures force many into direct participation, and in a small and intimate island these cannot be completely insulated from the rest.

The church itself is caught in an impossible position. Given its moral objectives, and the duty to pursue them, it cannot stand amiably by while its children are drawn into mortal sin. But nor is there much that can be done to stop them. The exercise of fierce prohibitions cannot prevent some girls becoming prostitutes. And the smaller the number of prostitutes, the larger their material rewards, and the greater the temptation for others to join them. So prohibition and temptation escalate together. Similarly, the more rigorously and explicitly that sexual restraints are urged, the more the church's denials or reticence about the vice problem are belied. Whatever measures the church employs to limit vice, the more conscious of sex its flock will become.

The church would like to be able to claim that as a result of its efforts, few *Maltese* people are involved in vice. Devout Maltese, if really pressed on the question, will say that perhaps prostitution does occur, but that it is performed by foreign girls, mainly Italian, who came there expressly to ply that trade. It is true that some foreign girls are concerned; but this can only be a small minority of the total. In the 1881 census for example, of the 136 women who were listed as prostitutes, 20 were Italian, one was Greek and four non-Maltese British. The rest were Maltese. The same is probably true of the people who organise vice.

Religious and moral restraints help stimulate sexual interest and temptation of a general kind, not just in relation to vice. Maltese men are in a particularly invidious position here, as the pattern of sexual servicing requires them to exercise self-abnegation in order that British men can indulge themselves. For while Maltese boys and men have been subject to the strictest regulation of sexual behaviour, British residents have not merely been free to act as they wished, but have done so with the Maltese girls whose services ought properly to be at the disposal of Maltese manhood. If morality is based on jealousy, then the fierce sexual morality of the Maltese is grounded in very great jealousy indeed; and the cause of fanatical chastity is served well by the profligate example of the garrison. If you personally have got to accept harsh relative deprivation, then there is a great incentive to make a virtue of it and force it on your neighbour too.[1]

The sexual desires of men in Malta are thus inflamed by the very restraints demanded by religious and public opinion; and outside marriage there are few opportunities to satisfy them.[2] Although the church is unable to prevent vice, its teachings and sanctions do hold most people back from unapproved sexual activity. Priests wield secular as well as moral influence; and because of the small size of Malta there is no place in the island which provides relief from their pressures. Open country is not very extensive, and the individual is never far out of sight of a church or religious symbol. Built-up areas are not large or dense enough for moral fugitives to find anonymity. And everywhere the interests of the clergy are mediated and supported by the jealousies and mutual suspicions of their flock. There is a pervasive and comprehensive web of moral constraints which keeps most Maltese chaste. The result is a good deal of frustration and sexual

[1] Recruitment to the priesthood may be served by this, as celibacy does at least offer a consistent – however arduous – solution to this.
[2] The very large size of families in Malta, and religious approval of high fertility (see note 1 on p. 108) suggests that this leads to high levels of sexual interest and activity *within* marriage.

neurosis. Even middle-aged, respectable men in Malta will giggle like schoolboys when talking about matters with a sexual reference; and many of the mannerisms which Maltese attribute to their Mediterranean 'temperament' may be manifestations of tension created by this high level of frustration.

The people who suffer most in this business are young, unmarried men; for it is when their sexual capacity and needs are greatest that their chances to perform are most limited. Bachelors are the sector of the population most weakly integrated into the traditional social structure, and in which most disorder or potential deviance is located. Married men with families find it easier to get jobs; so unmarried men are more often unemployed. This compounds their sexual frustration, for until they can get work it is difficult to get married. So there is a vicious circle operating to create a pool of young dissidents, whose transition from adolescence to adulthood may be prolonged or interrupted.

It is bachelors such as these who have made up the bulk of emigrants from Malta, for emigration can resolve for them difficulties insuperable within Malta. It provides an escape from the suffocating controls, and a chance to taste sex. A desire for sexual adventure is common among emigrants; and for those imbued with a sense of national pride, there is the additional motivation that the only way to redress the exploitation of Maltese womanhood in Malta is by extensive conquests abroad.[1]

This internal situation in Malta is a function of the external relationship with Britain, and is changing with it. Since Independence and the partial rundown of the garrison, these social patterns evolved during British rule have started to dissolve. The mass market for prostitutes is declining, and in so far as tourists have stepped in to fill the gap, their demands are for a different type of service.[2] The new market is smaller and more refined in quality, and less constant through the year. There is less work for the old professional, and more for part-timers. The growing number of civilian British settlers has also begun to influence moral standards, as they mingle more closely with the indigenous – including rural – population. The Louvain study published in

[1] Especially of course in Britain itself, homeland of the rulers, in which Maltese men are able to act out a certain 'Black Apollo' role. See Roger Bastide 'Dusky Venus, Black Apollo'.
[2] Eric Saxon may have been making this point obliquely. See note 2, p. 110.

1960 found that the rising contacts with non-Maltese, plus an improved bus-service in the islands which made it easier to get into Valletta from the villages, seemed already to be leading towards a decline in moral and religious certainties.[1] And during the 1960s the church in Malta has shown increasing concern about a general relaxation of moral standards.

From the point of view of young men, this means that living in Malta may gradually become less arduous than it has been. The steady drop in emigration in recent years, which has occurred in spite of continued unemployment, may in part be related to this. For as life in Malta becomes less oppressive and frustrating it will be easier to get through young adulthood there. As will be argued below, this relationship can also be looked at the other way round. As emigration is reduced, life in Malta *must* become less oppressive, in order to accommodate the dispositions of people living there. A temporary loosening of controls and restraints took place during the chaos of the last war, when emigration was impossible. A more fundamental liberalisation may have been gathering momentum over the last decade.

Emigration, culture and counter-culture

A corollary of the fact that emigration draws off many deviants or potential deviants from Maltese society, is that the existing social order in Malta has required emigration, to provide the safety-valve for maintenance of the tightly-constrained way of life in the island. It also follows that few migrants leave with a desire to re-create somewhere else the traditional forms of Maltese social organisation, and that there is a strong tendency in Maltese settlements outside of the homeland towards the development of anti-authoritarian 'counter-cultures' instead. The café society of Maltese in Britain can be seen as one expression of this general tendency.

The operation of emigration as a safety-valve is firmly ingrained in Maltese institutions. Many deviants and discontents see it as a means of salvation – or at any rate of getting away from the paralysing tension which grips the island; and a wide range of social pressures acting on them support these sentiments and

[1] Op. cit. (see note 1 on p. 108), pp. 140–50.

prompt their early withdrawal. One important factor here is that emigration is represented as an honourable act. Because of the ever-threatening problem of over-population, and the difficulty of regulating births, the decision to leave is defined publicly as a noble and patriotic sacrifice. This may give a special incentive to a misfit or deviant, as it helps absolve him in local eyes and transform him, after his departure, into rather a good fellow. If he stays at home he is under constant pressure to conform. By going to sea or settling abroad he can at a single stroke evade these sanctions and achieve a modicum of respectability.

This process is further assisted by the fact that behaviour of Maltese overseas is reported selectively in the Maltese press. Misdemeanours outside of Malta are not likely to be publicised. The conspiracy of silence in Malta about the actual behaviour of colonists has helped keep deviance invisible to the local population, and has played a part in the maintenance of domestic social order, by bolstering the reputations of emigrants in their native communities. Should someone go badly wrong overseas, and be deported back to Malta by an alien government, he would still suffer less of a stigma than if he had stayed in Malta and sinned there. For everyone knew that foreign jurisdictions were malevolent towards Maltese, and that life under them was more onerous than life in Malta. So overseas offenders might be received back into the fold with reasonable good will.

The use of emigration as a covert mechanism of social control is effective at various levels, and at times seems to have been used as a formal tool of administrative policy. For example, according to Price (pp. 70–1), in the first part of the nineteenth century the government of Malta:

> tended to encourage its less law-abiding citizens to make their homes overseas. Certain criminals, for instance, might receive free pardons so long as they remained outside of Malta, while others would obtain new passports for their old homes abroad, even though they had just been sent back to Valletta by one of the Consuls for breach of local law. This procedure, together with the influx of Maltese criminals fleeing punishment in Valletta, greatly angered various Mediterranean governments. . . . Quite clearly the friction arose from an insoluble clash of interests between Malta and

127

E*

its neighbours – each trying to foist on to the others its lawless Maltese inhabitants. Certainly this friction did nothing to slow down the rapid 'coming and going' of Maltese migrants during these years.

Following changes in consular procedures and powers in the mid-nineteenth century, the formal use of this mechanism diminished. But the Maltese authorities have continued to smooth the exodus of known criminals, for example, by judiciously over-looking the records of men applying for passports. This seems to have continued up to the present day. Several men interviewed in the 1967 enquiry either knew of recent cases in which people convicted in Malta had been given clean records by the police when putting themselves forward for jobs overseas or for passage assistance, or in which charges had been dropped against men when they agreed to emigrate, or they fell in this category them-selves. It seems quite likely – although it would be difficult to document – that emigration officials have frequently connived with the police in expediting the removal of offenders.

These cases are themselves greatly outweighed in volume by the less direct processes which prompt potential deviants to leave Malta. The dominant mode of emigration from Malta has evolved in relation to the needs and motivation of such people; and the casual and individualistic character of Maltese emigration is a direct consequence of the safety-valve function that it perform-ed. Migration has traditionally been a personal adventure and escape. Official organisation or overt control of migration would easily upset this balance of forces in which unsuitable people are encouraged to leave and receive approbation for doing so. Discreet and indirect underpinning of this type of migration was, however, possible through the mechanism of a generous re-patriation system. The best way to assist and encourage casual and informal migration was to ensure that no Maltese going abroad felt that he would be unable to come back if he wanted to.[1] During the nineteenth century relief and repatriation payments made up the major public contribution to migration, and even under the increasingly organised pattern of twentieth-century

---

[1] Except of course for locally convicted criminals whose departure was in lieu of imprisonment.

movements these have still formed a sizeable chunk of the work
and expenditure of the Department of Emigration.

The system of unrestricted repatriation was criticised outside
Malta, and was only tolerated by Imperial authorities because of
the small size of Malta and the relatively low cost. For example,
the Committee on Distressed Colonial and Indian Subjects in
1910 observed:[1]

> The case of Malta is a striking instance of the danger just
> alluded to. The Government of Malta is willing to bear the
> cost of repatriating almost any distressed person who proves
> that he is Maltese. And the cases of distress are undoubtedly
> more frequent from that Colony, having regard to its size,
> than from any other British Colony. They come, as Mr
> Baynes told us, 'with the (practically) certain knowledge that
> they would be provided with a free passage back to Malta
> whenever they felt inclined'.

The committee noted with disapproval that few of the
repatriated Maltese were bona fide seamen or migrants. Most
were stowaways who wanted to see the world, and who knew
that they could get a free passage home if need be, since it was a
matter of government policy in Malta that no Maltese should
ever be prevented from returning by lack of money.[2]

This policy entailed friction between the Malta government and
British consuls in the Mediterranean, and was the topic of much
official correspondence. The consul at Alexandria – from whence
over a hundred Maltese 'adventurers', 'stowaways' and 'vaga-
bonds', as they were variously called, were shipped back to
Malta annually – considered the Maltese a great nuisance and
proposed letting the Egyptian police keep them.[3]

But the system was in fact probably efficient at giving Maltese
youngsters a chance to let off steam on someone else's doorstep.
By the time they turned up in Malta again, they would have been
readier to settle down as responsible citizens. Their experience of
the world, if couched in suitable terms, would help them compete
with raw young men who had not been away, in finding work

---

[1] Command paper 5133, April 1910, para. 100.

[2] Command paper 5144 (minutes of evidence), April 1910, para. 763.

[3] Correspondence relating to the Maintenance and Repatriation of Distressed
Maltese Abroad, 1913 (Colonial Office; Mediterranean Pamphlet 85).

and wives. So for many high-spirited Maltese a spell of overseas wandering would have actually helped them over the most difficult phase of maturation.

This style of migration, if it can be called that, had its cost; for as the colonies of Maltese consisted mainly of banished criminals and young adventurers, they were often extremely refractory and lawless communities. Price (pp. 69–70) quotes Sir Thomas Reade, consul at Sfax in the 1830s, to this effect:

They are insolent in the highest degree to their own authorities, and although I have used the utmost exertions to keep them in some sort of order, they set me at defiance; in many instances they are aware that I have no power over them except to send them away from the country, for which they care little or nothing. . . . They have a very bad reputation and, if any crimes are committed, they are immediately suspected and generally accused of them.

Consular problems were severe at this time; the strengthening of their powers in the 1840s and then again in the 1860s reduced the disorder somewhat, but there seems to have been a strong tendency towards disorganisation among Maltese in the Mediterranean right up to the First World War when migration to these settlements more or less ceased.

Since this period Britain has inherited this tradition. As barriers to free movement were erected in more and more of the countries which had previously received Maltese, an ever larger proportion of the casual movements from Malta were in the direction of the United Kingdom. Before the first Commonwealth Immigrants Act there was no power to deport Maltese convicted of offences here, and so Britain was a natural haven for those rejected or deported from other countries and unwilling or unable to return to Malta. This build-up of dissident or deviant Maltese in Britain was cumulative, as respectable families would not come here, or would go back to Malta quickly when they realised the nature of the settlement, which eventually emerged as the chief centre for the culture of revolt of emigré Maltese. The actual form taken by Maltese café society in this country was shaped by local conditions, but its central characteristics of anti-clericalism and individualism were products of social life and tensions in Malta itself.[1]

Sexual adventurism has been an important element in this counter-culture, though it may not have been equally so through-out the whole of the last century. If it is true, as suggested earlier, that sexual exploitation, and consequent rigour in domestic moral controls, sharpened together over the course of the nineteenth century, then this aspect of the migration escape would have been less important in the early years. There is in fact not much evidence of sexual deviance among colonists in the Mediterranean; but this may have been because of the legality or tolerance of vice in the North African ports. There is slight evidence – not counting the ambiguous instance of the Messinas – of such activity in this century. The most recent incident was in 1967 when some men were sentenced to 15 years in prison at Constantine for organising a network of prostitution and currency smuggling – in what was described in *The Times* as the most important civil case in Algeria since Independence. One of the men had a Maltese name, and this could indicate some involvement in vice in this area.[2]

Even in Australia, where Maltese migration has been more organised and family-based, there are indications of vice. For example when in May 1968 the will was read of Joe Borg, an animal-loving Maltese blown up in a gang war in Sydney, he was discovered to have left twenty-six brothels to the local RSPCA.[3] The case found its way into papers in Britain only because of the picturesque dilemma this presented to the charity. Two rival Maltese were later charged with his murder, and it seems likely that Maltese vice operations in Australia are also quite well established.

When it is placed alongside these other instances, the sexual deviance of Maltese in Britain seems less likely to be due to purely local or haphazard determinants. The form of criminality may be more dramatic than elsewhere, but there does seem to be some

[1] In an analysis of the criminality of immigrants in Britain, Bottoms has urged that the effect of different cultural patterns needs to be examined. A. E. Bottoms, 'Delinquency among Immigrants'. In this case though the significant fact is that Maltese culture is *not* reproduced in London, not that it *is*.

[2] *The Times*, 26 February 1967.

[3] *The Times*, 2 June 1968.

general disposition towards sexual disorganisation related to the escapist mode and conditions of migration.

Conflicting objectives of Maltese emigration policies

During the period of British rule emigration clearly served two quite separate types of objective. Officially it provided an important – though overrated – demographic outlet for a dense and economically vulnerable population. In addition to this it served as a moral safety-valve, a more or less veiled instrument of social control, relieving some of the tensions contained in the tiny island.

In the short term these different functions were eminently compatible. The demographic exigencies provided a useful face-saving cover for the departure of deviants, and the use of emigration as a tool of social control contributed to the demographic easement. The snag of course is that an accumulation overseas of criminals and the rebellious young will soon tarnish the image of the donor country and put in jeopardy its longer term emigration and settlement prospects. Receiving communities will raise barriers to entry; responsible migrants with ideas of settling down permanently will have doubts; and attempts at home to promote and organise migration will founder in a muddle of conflicting reports and prognostications. Price observes that this happened in the Maltese settlements in the Mediterranean, but that because of the public conspiracy of silence which surrounded the behaviour of Maltese overseas, it failed to receive serious attention from official authorities:

> It was this wholesale disrespect of law and order which, when combined with the mass arrival of Maltese paupers, led various Mediterranean governments to restrict the entry of any Maltese – and other Europeans – unable to give surety for good behaviour (p. 69).

Crime and mendicancy provide other examples of this tendency to ignore the realities of settlement abroad. Events in Africa and the Levant, in Cephalonia and Grenada, showed plainly that the readiness of some Maltese labourers to revert to violence, theft or beggary, was a factor of practical importance. Not only did it tempt colonists to abandon pioneering endeavour long before difficulties became acute; it helped both to keep the Maltese population overseas in a constant state of movement, and to provoke various public authorities to discourage or prohibit immigration. Yet the discussions and writings of Maltese interested in migration, both then and in later years, are almost devoid of reference to the matter. . . . Those concerned to make migration succeed might well have pondered the disadvantages of the banishment system or been more careful when selecting volunteers for organised ventures. Too much hung on the outcome of these expeditions for there to be much room for convicted thieves and troublemakers (p. 88).

These difficulties were a major factor preventing the development of *stable* Maltese colonies, and help to explain the continuing high migration return rate up to the First World War. This tendency towards disorganisation may even have played some part in confirming the definition of Maltese as non-British, with related quota restrictions, by the Dominions between the wars. Casolani (p. 46) almost conceded this point in 1930:

It has been a subject of surprise often . . . that . . . in most of the British Dominions, the Maltese migrant is regarded as an alien. In theory, as a British subject of white European race, . . . the native of Malta should enjoy free access. . . . In effect he does not. . . . The fault lies in a combination of circumstances, chiefly a lack of appreciation of our position within the Empire by the bureaucracy of the Dominions, and to the ruinous and haphazard emigration of the past which permitted masses of Maltese undesirables and illiterates to find their way into the British Dominions.

As long as some free migration outlets remained, there was no absolute need for these different objectives to be reconciled. A sort of slash and burn approach was adequate. But when the prospect of a curtailment of all migration arose, attempts were quickly made to rationalise the emigration system. Thus the first real movement to control migration was precipitated by the events at the end of the First World War. There was acute unemployment in Malta, but restrictions in migrant-receiving countries were mounting. The problem was so great that informed opinion moved behind the idea that massive, permanent and above all organised emigration had now become essential. An office was set up to deal with the matter, with Casolani as its head.

Casolani believed that unless migration was closely controlled, there were bound to be reactions against Maltese. So the first task of the office was to eradicate the results of past negligence and repair the image of Maltese in receiving countries (p. 16):

> In this way the Organisation came into being whose aim and purpose were, and are, to guide, control and instruct, and to test, and ruthlessly turn down, whenever expedient, such candidates as offer themselves for emigration . . . even now, after the lapse of ten years, there are still those who fail to realise that this is done in the national interest also, in so far as lapses from the Immigration Laws and Regulations, or the arrival in other countries of sub-standard men, must infallibly diminish the credit of the Maltese and jeopardize, if not destroy, the Maltese emigration movement altogether.

His programme for the improvement and control of emigration had two prongs. It was essential to select and train migrants. But it was also important to see that whenever feasible priests should accompany the parties, to serve as a moral backbone around which a decent community could mould itself. Not to make such provision was 'gambling with the moral welfare of the Maltese settlers, who, under the over-powering impact of their materialistic surroundings must, sooner or later, give way, losing both their morals and their Faith' (p. 37).

Among people who recognised that a problem of disorder existed in Maltese colonies, it was understood that the influence of priests could be absolutely critical. Looking back, Price (p. 71) found that they had played a potent role in reducing disorganisation in the nineteenth-century settlements:

> In short, those who asserted that Maltese emigration without native priests was a disorderly and undesirable phenomenon had a good deal of evidence to back their contention; the Maltese characteristics of quietness and sobriety needed, it would seem, pastoral supervision and care if they were to be maintained in settlements overseas.

Casolani, in his inimitable bombast, gives a more recent illustration of this power (p. 36):

> To quote one instance, that of the Abbe Angelo Camilleri, a humble Gozitan missionary, who, in 1927, volunteered to go to the South of France – unconditionally. Here thousands of Maltese are settled, and from a derelict and religiously forsaken colony, by his tact and his tireless industry and perseverence, his religious zeal and missionary spirit, and the compelling influence he established with the Civil and Ecclesiastical Authorities, he succeeded in forming, out of a disorganised crowd of people, a well disciplined Maltese parish with its own Maltese Church; he eliminated distress among the colony and reduced to a minimum repatriations at Government expense; daily, he obtains, ashore and afloat, employment for the settlers, concessions and benefits in every direction. Above all he has raised the moral and the social tone of the Maltese settlement which is now an example to others and respected by all. That is a labour of love and a road to follow. There is no limit to the mission of a willing, self-sacrificing and self-respecting and patriotic Priest.

Although priests abound in Malta, their supply has not been unlimited, and not all colonies of Maltese could be furnished with them. In practice they have been deployed in such a way as to maximise the migration possibilities. Price shows that in the later nineteenth century they were sent to help reform and stabilise settlements in danger of inviting local reprisals – in the form of migration restrictions – or to accompany major organised parties of settlers. With the advent of controlled and large-scale migration to the Dominions the latter pattern has grown in importance, and missions have for example played a crucial supporting role in the postwar family migration of Maltese to Australia.

The growth of organised emigration over the last half-century, in pursuit of solidly demographic objectives, has gradually but inexorably undermined the moral safety-valve function of migration, thereby placing in jeopardy the social order of the homeland. The respectable Maltese colonies which Casolani regarded as so desirable are facsimilies of traditional Maltese society, and if that was all that emigration offered the deviants and adventurers they might as well stay at home.

In fact in order for the second function of emigration to be fulfilled there is a need for some settlements which are *not* organised around a church. The problem is that it is exactly these gatherings of rebellious Maltese which have provoked governments into erecting controls against Maltese, and these restrictions which have furnished Maltese priests with their most powerful weapons against recalcitrant countrymen in their settlements. Priests are most readily accepted as leaders of the community where the local, secular authorities are hostile and threatening to expel migrants. Submission to the authority of a priest is a traditional price to pay for security – and only if there are other places easily accessible is there good reason to refuse to pay it.

While areas of free entry remained open to the Maltese, the fact that some settlements were becoming orderly and respectable did not have any real implication for domestic order in Malta. But this escape-route has progressively narrowed, with Britain as the last main refuge for the dissident element. As other settlements grew more orderly and organised, and bore the brunt of Malta's excess population, that in Britain probably became increasingly specialised as the haven for high-spirited young men and for criminals.

The imposition of immigration controls by the United Kingdom has finally sealed the safety-valve, with far-reaching consequences in Malta as well as London. Now that casual movements are not possible, it is more difficult for young Maltese to come here to let off steam and enjoy an adolescent adventure; and as a result more wild oats are being sown in Malta itself. An additional jolt to the traditional social order has been brought about by the return of criminal migrants to Malta as a result of deportation from Britain. Several vice offenders have taken girls back with them to Malta, and set up in the expanding and diversifying entertainment business which the burgeoning of tourism has encouraged. Their labours are surely a factor in the liberalisation now taking place in the island.

The other side of this coin is that the Maltese settlement in London has started to become more like other Maltese colonies. Some respondents in the London sample believed that the Maltese police were still helping Maltese criminals to come here; but migration restrictions and provisions for deportation mean that they have not been able to congregate so easily as they did formerly.

Because of the hard core of old offenders who cannot be deported, London is still a centre for the expatriate counter-culture; but it cannot recruit so many new members and is already fading away. Now that the safety-valve has been closed and a new social order developing in Malta, the need for this type of counter-culture has rapidly dwindled anyway. If further migration to Britain does take place it is likely to have a rather different character.

Recruitment of Maltese to a deviant sub-culture in Britain

The desire of Maltese emigrants for adventures has been an important factor predisposing them to deviance here. And although the channelling of their behaviour into specifically illegal activities is closely related to their weak position – as immigrants – in the opportunity structure, the distinctive form taken by their deviance suggests that on balance, and by comparison with similarly placed minority groups, many Maltese have found these activities reasonably consistent with their initial motives.

The first contacts which many Maltese had with people in this country were in dockland society, and it might be argued that selective association with members of marginal, poorly regulated sectors of society has been a significant determinant of subsequent Maltese behaviour here. Maltese crime in London can be linked historically with that in Cardiff and other ports, and the incorporation of Maltese to criminal society was clearly mediated by prior settlement in these marginal areas.

Purely ecological or sub-cultural hypotheses do not however explain why the reaction of Maltese to these contacts was so much more positive than that of other seamen in an objectively similar position. A high proportion of Maltese seafarers actually settled in British ports, instead of remaining at sea.[1] Also these Maltese adopted a very specialised role *within* dockland society. Vice is a normal feature of port life, as seafarers have sexual needs which local populations are not usually willing to accommodate openly in respectable parts of town. But the interest of most seamen is transitory – for the satisfaction of immediate personal needs. Maltese seem to go beyond this and become middle-men in the

---

[1] The number of active seamen seems small in relation to the size of the port settlements, by comparison with some other nationalities. And why should so many have settled in notoriously disorganised ports like Cardiff, and so few in places like Bristol?

provision of prostitutes. In a general situation where there is a great demand for girls, the Maltese seem ready to adopt a specialised role of servicing this demand. Little refers to this in the context of Cardiff, and the same thing seems to have happened in London during the war, when the demand for prostitutes grew in Stepney as a consequence of the difficulties of coloured seamen and servicemen in getting supplies through ordinary channels. In a slightly different context, David Downes has suggested that the Maltese in Spitalfields may recently have taken an analogous servicing role in relation to the male-dominated Pakistani community.[1]

One hypothesis which could account for this specialisation of function is that, as a result of the British occupation of Malta, the English public held a stereotype of the Maltese as practised in organising girls – even before the Messinas' exposure. This would lead to role expectations which could have the consequence of recreating in Britain the type of sexual-servicing relationship which the British have enjoyed in Malta itself. Thus Maltese in this country would be encouraged to run cafés, to which prostitutes and clients alike would be attracted by the expectation of business, with the result that vice would soon become foisted upon the establishments, and the label quickly confirmed.

This is conceivable, but it is unlikely to be a major factor. It is true that public opinion defines Maltese as suitable for employment in restaurants,[2] but this is also true of other immigrant groups. There is no evidence of the existence of a Maltese vice image prior to settlement – though more extensive library work would be needed before this could be confidently asserted. An enquiry carried out among non-Maltese people in London in 1969 showed that those who had no personal contact with Maltese in Britain did not know much about the reputation of Maltese for vice. So it would appear that Maltese settlers carry their image along with them – or receptivity to it – and do not find it established before their arrival.[3]

[1] David Downes, *The Delinquent Solution*, p. 219.

[2] Many Maltese are recruited to the navy as stewards (see Table A.8 in Appendix A); and nearly half of 1967 respondents in London had been employed in some sort of catering job since arrival, while only a few had this sort of job in Malta beforehand.

[3] See the following chapter and Appendix F for more detailed analysis of the findings.

On the labelling hypothesis, the types of people most prone to entertain and propagate a Maltese vice image would be the sailors and servicemen who had used the facilities in Malta. The study in 1969 also showed though that people who had visited or served in Malta knew less about the Maltese reputation than those who met Maltese in London. It is possible that, to widely-travelled men, every port or garrison in the world appears as a brothel, so that they would in fact be the persons *least* inclined to consider vice in Malta as an intrinsically Maltese phenomenon. So it probably cannot be contended that the specialised role adopted by Maltese in dockland society is a response to a sea-borne image. People in Britain with first-hand experience of Malta seem to be the least likely to have notions about cultural determination of this sort of behaviour.

In one sense the labelling hypothesis would be redundant even if the existence of a prior stereotype were established. On the evidence presented in this chapter it could be expected that regardless of local images about them, Maltese migrants would have a leaning towards sexual pursuits which would put them at risk of being caught up in prostitution. Any image to this effect would therefore be a reflection of reality – not an independent determinant.[1] Local labelling might smooth the process, but it would not materially affect its direction. For only where an image results in behaviour against the inclinations of its objects can labelling be regarded as having had a critical effect.

The main explanation for the specialised role of Maltese in dockland vice must surely be that this environment provided a congenial soil in which Maltese counter-culture, with its emphasis on sexual exploits, could take root. There is great freedom in dock areas, police being prepared to allow residents a certain autonomy so long as they do not disturb people outside. Sexual behaviour there is relatively uncluttered by moral prohibitions, and to young, frustrated Maltese it must have seemed like the promised land.

This dockland society is perhaps not really part of a proper criminal sub-culture. The delinquencies of its members are mostly petty and disorganised; and the way of life would be congruent with the needs and aspirations of liberated Maltese youngsters

---

[1] An image which saw vice as *culturally* determined would be inaccurate and unjust though.

rather than confirmed, exiled criminals.[1] But, although little full-blown criminal activity may have taken place in this café-society, it certainly served as a stage in the recruitment to more serious crime in this country. An important factor in this was the affinity between Maltese men and English prostitutes.

Like the Maltese, prostitutes are commonly in revolt against an oppressive background – often Catholic. Many are runaway girls, in the way Maltese may be runaway boys; and their attitudes to authority, religion and having a good time are very similar. Maltese men also seem to be attractive to prostitutes. They are small, charming and knew how to be ornate at a time when most Englishmen were still dull and drab. In many respects they are ideal companions for girls in revolt against conventional sexual and marital values. It has frequently been put forward that most prostitutes are girls unwilling to put up with the dependence normally expected of women. The life of a prostitute compensates doubly for this; the girl can be not merely independent, but can herself support males.[2] Her desire to dominate men is supported by the law which assumes that it is the woman who requires public protection; so she can shop her ponce whenever she likes, and he has no legal recourse. He is a sort of pet. A well-off prostitute can take pride in dressing her man nicely, and showing that she can look after him better than other girls can.

All this would have been congruent with the sexual fantasies which brought young Maltese to these shores; and since they were themselves attractive to the girls they were taken up quite readily as companions. Rolph (op. cit.) reported in the 1950s that the prostitutes in London who had Maltese ponces were in general pleased with them.

Through this mutual attraction and affinity with prostitutes, the Maltese in dockland society would have created a specialised social niche for themselves by which they were eventually drawn

[1] Some Maltese see a connection between Strickland's attack on vice in Malta, and its appearance in Britain, and argue that hardened vice-racketeers were driven into exile here. There is no evidence that the early offenders were experienced in vice in Malta – and it is unlikely that there were really many exiles at this time. Certainly the mass of offenders have had no prior experience before arrival, and there is no need to hypothesise an exporting of skills from Malta to explain their behaviour in Britain.

[2] See for example Harold Greenwald, *The Call Girl;* John M. Murtagh and Sara Harris, *Cast the First Stone;* and the analysis of C. H. Rolph in *Women of the Streets.*

into more systematic crime. The precipitating event in this was probably the Second World War. Up to that point there were several small foci of Maltese counter-culture in ports around Britain, with a group of cafés, operating more or less as brothels, as the hub of ethnic association in each locality. The advent of war upset this balance. On the one hand provincial ports suffered from the decline of coastal shipping as trade became centralised through London. On the other, in London itself the evacuation of families and the build-up of servicemen raised the demand for prostitutes above the level which existing suppliers could meet. Provincial Maltese may have been drawn into the life of Soho in various ways. In some instances they might simply have accompanied their girls in following business. But the rapid expansion of the market would also have provided them with opportunities to use their experience to organise and promote the flow of girls to London. The 1947 protection money case illustrates the sort of arrangement that could develop for this purpose. Provincial Maltese centres would serve as recruitment agencies for girls who would then be brought to London; and, since they were scarce and valuable, there would have been every incentive to the formation of gangs to protect them from other organisations and from the temptation to return to other occupations.

The Maltese were of course not the only men doing this; but for their numbers they seem to have been busy. It is important to remember also that there would not have been great competition from English men, in spite of the profitability of business. This is because vice offences constitute the lowest status criminal activity.[1] Ponces and pimps are despised as much by other criminals as by the police – and on largely the same grounds. These grounds are not moral in the narrow sense, although simple moral disapproval is present. The main consideration is that poncing is felt to violate a basic principle in our culture, that men should not be supported by the labour of women. Just rewards, in criminal society as much as in conventional, are those achieved by men with drive and initiative and ability. Poncing is an offence of supine passivity, fit only for incompetent and unskilled parasites. The ponce is despised as the woman's object – the kept man. And even if he is well recompensed, he will still be

[1] C. H. Rolph (Introduction).

treated by other criminals as belonging to the bottom of the pile.

This is an additional reason why such crimes, in western societies at any rate, are characteristically committed by immigrants and other outsiders. It is a typically pariah activity, necessary but beneath contempt. Just as immigrants move on to the labour market at the bottom of a status hierarchy, so too in crime vice is the first area to be abandoned to newcomers. This would be true even if immigrants had no special leaning towards sexual deviance. Wartime London experienced a labour shortage in the underworld, as in other sectors of the economy. Rationing controls and the presence of servicemen created a whole range of illegal possibilities; and the speed with which Maltese were drawn into Soho suggests that local people were too busy with other opportunities to compete for the role.

Once established, the café society in London became the hub of the Maltese counter-culture; and new migrants arriving in Britain since the war have been recruited more directly into the underworld through it, and have increasingly participated in serious crimes soon after arrival.[1] The older dockland settlements which represented a half-way stage to entry into the criminal sub-culture have now largely withered away.

The effect of relationships within the ethnic community

Café society has contributed in various ways to Maltese criminality in Britain. It has helped draw Maltese into the criminal sub-culture of the host society, and at the same time its own internal relationships and ethos have exacerbated tendencies to personal disorganisation. Instead of protecting members against wider society, this form of intra-ethnic association has made them even more vulnerable.

Maltese migrants here have been young, single men unhampered by parents, wives or children, and unresponsive to the ministrations of priests; they are men without a great deal to lose, much to gain, and minimal restrictions on their choice of means. Society in Britain is vast and anonymous by comparison with Malta, and many migrants interviewed said how struck they had been shortly

---

[1] Some Maltese cropped up in the Kray twins proceedings in 1968–9, as the Krays owned a number of establishments in Soho managed and staffed by Maltese; so by moving into London they had become drawn into the serious underworld.

after arrival with a sensation that nobody cared what they got up to.

The profoundly individualistic setting of café society does not generate any values around which a sense of group membership could grow. Its main emphasis is hedonistic, and fellow-countrymen are important to each other principally as an audience to applaud each other's performance. Interests are similar but not common, and compatriots are competitors not real colleagues. The whole mood of café society is suffused with this competitiveness, and the normal relationship between associators is of mutual jealousy thinly concealed beneath a veneer of camaraderie.

Café society fiercely supports egalitarianism. Participants with money are resented intensely, and are expected to share it around by giving loans, losing at cards, and buying goods – often valueless or stolen – from needy fellows. In this sense café society performs a slight redistributive function which tides some migrants over periods of acute financial strain. But this function is limited by the fact that no long-term reward is given to individuals who *can* keep their feet economically. Personal saving is made very difficult, so that continued association of this type soon comes into conflict with the same material ambitions it has helped to stimulate. So there is a sort of centrifugal force within café society itself, impelling those members who can look after themselves to withdraw at the first opportunity.

Powerful jealousies are aroused by girl-friends. These cannot be – at any rate, they are not – shared round like money. But they can be seduced or enticed and often are. Fights over girls are an abiding source of trouble amongst young Maltese, and the court record analysis revealed a small but steady trickle of manslaughter and serious wounding cases arising from them. The initial interest of migrants in girls is usually entirely sexual, and in so far as liaisons tend to be with prostitutes this is due to their accessibility and special affinities with Maltese, not to calculations of economic gain on the part of migrants. The materialism and cynicism of café society does seem to encourage a more exploitative style of poncing, by creating a greater interest in money for its own sake. Poncing offers easy money for small effort, and girls may become seen as sources of income instead of simple sexual pleasure.

So the values expressed in the counter-culture are disruptive of group life. In the context of villages in Malta, talk about freedom and enjoying the good life excites a comradely feeling among young men. In the thinner air of London, these sentiments explode into a rampant selfishness inimical to any form of social order.

This state of disorganisation is cumulative. Mutual jealousies and suspicions are stronger than ethnic loyalty or dislike of the police. So when conflicts occur the police are not excluded, and may even be used to settle scores with enemies within the group. Several respondents with criminal records alleged, convincingly, that other Maltese had framed them, by hiding stolen property or a gun in their rooms and then calling in the police. Also, some of those who admitted actual crimes claimed that the instigation of prosecution arose out of information given to the police by a rival Maltese. Many of the assault cases analysed in the court record study were related to grassing or threats to grass; and a surprisingly large number of them were brought privately by other Maltese, and not by the police at all.[1]

So quite a lot of the crime of Maltese only becomes visible because of the disorganised nature of the group. Solidary communities or those containing some accepted authority figures, would not need to use the police to settle internal issues, and would on the contrary cover up as much deviant behaviour inside the group as possible.[2] Maltese criminality is magnified by being brought out into the open in this way, since it invites public and police attention, which in turn increases the temptation to frame or grass, eases its execution, and multiplies the occasions for reprisals. The lack of group solidarity is a vicious circle, and boosts the ostensible crime rate several times over.

Membership of so divided an ethnic community fails to confer those benefits generally attributed to continued association with compatriots in a migrant colony. There is little comfort to be drawn from sharing and celebrating social values, as traditional principles are derided and those which the group does share

[1] A high proportion of the privately brought charges were withdrawn before a conviction was secured; so it is possible that in many cases they may themselves have been malicious fabrications. In the court record analysis, only those resulting in convictions were counted in the tabulations.

[2] It seems to be a well-documented fact that for a variety of reasons a weakly-articulated immigrant community will have more visible criminality. See below (in Chapter V) and T. C. N. Gibbens and R. H. Ahrenfeldt (eds), *Cultural Factors in Delinquency*.

provoke conflict. Nor is there much genuine mutual aid, because the anti-authoritarian values of freedom and individualism preclude any real concern for each other. The community of café society does not protect individuals; on balance it clearly endangers them. And the people most in need of sympathetic support – newcomers with limited understanding of local circumstances – are those who can suffer most sharply. Many young men arrive from Malta expecting village friendships and family loyalties to stand them in good stead on arrival. Happy in the certainty of goodwill, they make their way to cafés where they have been advised they may find an uncle or cousin or old friend. Very often they are profoundly disappointed by their reception. Several men recalled that a friend or relative had offered to look after the money or valuables they had brought with them – and had at once spent or made off with them. A café-owner or some other patron would feed and support the newcomer for a while, and then cash the moral debt by persuading the youngster into undertaking some unpleasant task. In such a way are many touts recruited for the front line in Soho, or young migrants co-opted on to housebreaking parties.

The majority of men active in café society in London appreciate its brittleness and underlying anarchy, and the closer the hub of Maltese socialising is approached, the fewer Maltese are found who consider the concept of community applicable to them.[1] As habitués of café society acquire secure jobs and marry, they usually withdraw from regular involvement. There is a hard core of old-timers in it – mainly men who have not been very successful as settlers, plus a few 'boss' figures who have managed to turn the existence of café society to their personal advantage. Both these types are more dependent on compatriots than are other migrants.

One of the most important factors making a Maltese man dependent on café society is a criminal record, and most of the London sample who had been convicted of serious offences were still frequenting Maltese clubs at the time of the survey. The characteristics of these offenders, summarised statistically in Table D.2 in Appendix D, are in fact similar in overall profile to

[1] See Table D.3 in Appendix D.

those of café society respondents in general, apart from a greater proportion of old-timers.[1]

The dependence of serious criminals on café society was indicated by the high proportion of unemployed and the tendency to hold jobs *within* the clubs; many of them had been tied to particular employers for several years. Not all were dependent in the sense of being economically subordinate. The serious offenders included a number of financially comfortable individuals who owned businesses – in a few cases quite profitable ventures. So there were a fair number of non-manual workers as well as others.

Superficially the marriage pattern of serious offenders was close to that of café society as a whole, but their greater dependence on this type of group was reflected in the fact that many of them had spent a long bachelorhood in Britain before finding a wife. Similarly there was a connection between criminality and service in the merchant navy after arrival, which would have been an important factor delaying adoption of an orderly and settled social life.

Although these serious offenders were dependent on café society, and had often remained within it for a long time, this does not alter the essential fact that this type of association was not really suitable as a basis for an ethnic community. Most of those who stayed in it did so because of no available alternative, and many old-timers were thoroughly disillusioned with club life. Some had reached a point of apathy, but more seethed with resentment against their successful compatriots.

The longer the time spent in café society, the greater the lie given to its principle of egalitarianism. Youngsters and newcomers may genuinely believe that café society is for everyone; but those Maltese who stay long in such company discover the hollowness of this cardinal principle, as they become thrown more and more into hierarchical relations with countrymen in consequence of the continual conflicts taking place. Unlucky or weak people become increasingly dependent on stronger and more successful colleagues. Some of the most powerful and hated men owed their positions to having been able to arrange for other people to take the rap for their own offences. Unfortunate and un-

---

[1] The real bias may be less than suggested, as the 1967 sample under-represents currently active young criminals. This does not alter the fact that old lags form the hard-core of café society.

enterprising men are given the risky jobs as front-men for others – for example as licence-holder for a club about to be raided, as touts and bodyguards, or as fences for stolen property. The more convictions they accumulate, the less able they are to break out of the vicious circle tying them to café society. As a few men grow richer and more powerful, the majority are broken more completely.

But even these so-called 'bosses' are insecure. The more successful he becomes, the more despotic he needs to be in order to avoid reprisals from compatriots bearing him a grudge. More than one leading Maltese in Soho may direct operations from the security of yachts in the Mediterranean. But if this is true, few could run to it. The injury and even death rate among leading criminals has been high, and the power structure in café society correspondingly fragile. There appears to have been only limited development of disciplined criminal associations, and the groupings that have occurred between Maltese at various times seem to have been forced by especially powerful market pressures, more than by any willingness or capacity of Maltese to forge stable alliances amongst themselves.

This assessment must be regarded as tentative. If there were highly organised Maltese criminal networks in business, they would hardly be likely to be easily detectable. There would be little point to them unless they helped evade prosecution, either through promoting general efficiency or by buying off the police. So mere absence of evidence can never be conclusive proof that they do not exist.

However the manifest character of visible Maltese criminality argues against the existence of successful organisations of this kind among Maltese. The individualistic and vindictive style of known Maltese criminals is incompatible with the secretive, professional associations which are sometimes found within ethnic minorities. This is not to say that Maltese never become involved in organised gangs: clearly this would be a reckless generalisation, and patently false besides, as some were employed in the Messina network – itself a most un-Maltese type of set-up. Even so, it may be pertinent to observe that it was only after the arrival in London of disorganised Maltese criminals that the public got wind of this organisation, and evidence leaked out on which convictions could be made!

All that is being claimed here is that on the material available, the existence of organised Maltese associations – in particular of vice rings in the West End or linking London with operations in Malta or on the Continent – is doubtful, and also unnecessary to explain overt Maltese criminality. Maltese crime is not the occupation of a solidary grouping, like a Tong society or Mafia brotherhood, forged in adversity or anarchy in the native country and then transferred *en bloc* to the underground of the country of settlement; it is grounded in orderless reaction to an extremely authoritarian, almost totalitarian social system. This reaction has determined the nature of emigration, and is also deeply antipathetic to the formation of cohesive groupings of any sort in the emigrant colony.

The settling-down process

A corollary of the fact that participation in café society leads to crime is that a Maltese man who wishes to change to a more orderly way of life needs to withdraw from it. Generally speaking there are three ways in which this might be done.

Firstly a migrant can return to Malta or go on to another settlement. After a few years letting off steam in Britain, many young Maltese do discover that they are ready to go home, and the persistently high return migration rate is some measure of this process.

An alternative procedure would be to withdraw from café society to the traditional community based on the Catholic Mission. As already pointed out, though, up to the present the Maltese priests have failed to present an acceptable version of this culture in London. If they could operate as local patrons, by commanding access to good jobs, or even by deploying a reserve of nubile Maltese girls,[1] their appeal would be greater. But they have not yet proved any capacity to attract ordinary migrants.

As Maltese in Britain have not experienced severe difficulties in finding jobs and local wives, most migrants who stay have chosen the third means of withdrawal from café society, by

[1] This is not so fanciful as it may sound. The Catholic Emigrants Commission sponsors a migration programme for single girls to Australia, to help redress the sexual imbalance of the regular migratory flow. Intra-ethnic marriages have accordingly increased there, and the influence of priests is served by this.

becoming ethnically uninvolved altogether. This process often entails a fair degree of personal incorporation into local British society. Intermarriage is very significant here. A Maltese who takes an English bride is not just finding an orderly solution to sexual frustration; in many instances he is also creating long-term alliances and a stake in the local community, which will assist his settlement in a whole range of matters. English fathers-and-brothers-in-law frequently help migrants obtain more lucrative and respectable jobs. Some respondents' affines had adopted them almost as sons, and had sponsored them financially in opening up in business; and in some cases had helped prevent their imprisonment or deportation by acting in court as guarantors of their future good behaviour. So in various ways the relationships forged through marriage outside of the ethnic group have provided exactly the type of support which the Maltese community itself fails to offer.

Not all Maltese who take English wives benefit equally. Young men who marry too soon, before feeling a real need for stability and security, may find themselves trapped by it and seek further escape in compulsive infidelity or desertion. A number of abandoned or disgruntled English wives turned up in the course of the 1967 enquiry, whose husbands had slipped back irretrievably into disorganised lives. Similarly there is not much to be gained from marrying girls who are themselves not willing to settle down. Some Maltese marry prostitutes who go on working afterwards against their husbands' wishes. These marriages are often very unsatisfactory, as the wife can shop him whenever she wants to hurt him. So as a result of their match, these men may end up with a string of convictions, and be all the more dependent on café society.

In addition to these actual dangers, there is the fact that sponsorship from in-laws is not invariably forthcoming. If wives are themselves runaway girls, and perhaps permanently disowned by their families, marriage to them imparts little status in local society and is not very advantageous. Nevertheless it does serve to temper individualism, and responsibilities to wife and children are stabilising influences in themselves, irrespective of their wider social context. Many Maltese are happy to lead fairly privatised family lives, and this is sufficient to draw them out of café society.

A Maltese wife inhibits recourse to café society, and an English wife facilitates withdrawal from it. So marriage is altogether a potent factor saving a Maltese migrant from disorganised ways. This shows how important a network of close personal relations is in maintaining order amongst Maltese. These relations set boundaries to individualistic aspirations, and provide some basic satisfactions and shared values around which a meaningful and integrated life can be constructed. Such relations are perhaps more important sources of order for Maltese than for some other people, because the social control system in Malta itself relies heavily on externalised sanctions of mutual personal restraint.

Social disorder among members of ethnic minorities which attempt to reproduce a traditional style of life in the migrant colony can usefully be regarded in part as the outcome of conflict between different cultures, and can be expected to occur typically a generation or two after arrival, when children brought up within a cultural minority may reject parental and ethnic group authority, yet at the same time have difficulties in adjusting themselves or becoming accepted in wider society.

The Maltese in London exhibit a very different case, in which deviance relates more to the breaking *by* migration of the networks of personal relations which sustain social order. Maltese migrants are already in a state of adolescent rebellion when they leave Malta, and become liberated from the framework of personal constraints just at the moment when they feel them to be most burdensome. There are no real authority figures in the settlement, and so the delinquency of Maltese takes place almost immediately after arrival. The element of culture-conflict is minimal, mainly because of the absence of effective, traditional authority figures, and most migrants who settle here happily accept English society as they find it, and readily adopt English identity. Their children are almost wholly English, and the 'second-generation' problem is avoided.[1]

The fact that the order-sustaining relationships of settled Maltese are in the local community rather than within the ethnic

[1] The Irish in Britain are similar to the Maltese in this respect, and for essentially the same reasons. John Lambert, for example, in his study in Birmingham, reported that Irish criminality in that city differed from that of other immigrants by occurring most commonly among the first generation, and among adults. Their situation is however less extreme than that of the Maltese. John Lambert, *Crime, Police and Race Relations: a study in Birmingham*, pp. 125-7.

group has serious implications for the potentiality of ethnic organisation and the nature of the ethnic community. The more mature, responsible Maltese are those who have disappeared from ethnic participation; so the collectivity is unable to benefit from their experience and leadership, and the level of most ethnic socialising is stuck at an adolescent stage of revolt and disorder. The adjustment and personal assimilation of most Maltese to local society is concentrated into such a short time-span, that the individuals who remain reliant on the ethnic group have only others like themselves to lean on. Consequently those Maltese who do not manage to find orderly lives, fail most visibly and dismally, and the collective or categorical integration of the 'Maltese community' has been much more problematic than the assimilation of individuals. There is a vicious circle in all this which has continually, and perhaps even progressively, weakened the solidarity of the ethnic group.

V

CRIME IN A MINORITY SITUATION: THE IMPUTATION OF COLLECTIVE RESPONSIBILITY

Collective responsibility and social control

Even if the poor public image of the Maltese has not been a primary cause of their criminality in London, it has certainly reinforced deviant tendencies. This process seems to have been so critical that quite a detailed analysis is called for, both of the underlying general principles and of their manifestation in this particular instance.

The crux of the matter is that a substantial sector of British public opinion seems to regard the whole Maltese community as having a collective responsibility for the visible delicts of its members, with the result that all Maltese in Britain are treated as accountable for each other. The obsession that many Maltese in Britain have with their bad name only becomes comprehensible when the implications of this are appreciated.

Early interviews with Maltese in London soon revealed that they felt they were being judged as a collectivity for the actions of individual compatriots, and that this fact dominated their relationships both inside and outside the ethnic group. In the beginning it seemed probable that, since the Maltese were so touchy about their reputation, they were imagining the whole thing. So a few unstructured interviews were conducted with non-Maltese people living in the same localities as 1967 Maltese respondents, to see how far outsiders really were inclined to judge the Maltese as a group. This was followed up by a larger and formalised postal enquiry in 1969, to test and put in perspective the findings of these pilot interviews. Some caution is needed in the interpretation of the findings of this study, but the results did generally confirm the impressions formed during interviewing, and provided some measure of the distribution of these responses.[1]

The central finding of the postal enquiry was that only a quarter of the respondents rejected the suggestion that the Maltese community might have a group responsibility for controlling its members' behaviour. A similar proportion strongly endorsed the idea, a third considered that the group had some communal liability, and the remainder were unsure. Those respondents who knew some Maltese personally in London were more likely than others to subscribe to this imputation of collective responsibility – or 'group blame' for short; but only a small number did have this sort of personal contact. Most of those who supported the notion of collective responsibility presumably did so as a result of opinions they held about the nature and position of ethnic minorities in general.

TABLE 6 *Relations between views about group blame and personal contact with Maltese in London (indicators of association)**

Type of contact with London Maltese	Definite collective responsibility	Group blame views Some collective responsibility	No c.r.	Not sure	n	p
Maltese neighbours and personal friends	1·5	1·0	0·7	0·8	27	
Some Maltese met through work	1·4	1·0	1·1	0·4	39	0·2
No personal contact	0·8	1·0	1·0	1·2	154	
n	54	67	57	42	220	

Source: 1969 survey, questions 2 × 15.

* For an explanation of this index see the note preceding Table D.1 in Appendix D.

The results of this 1969 investigation showed that these views on 'group blame' were closely interdependent with a number of other ideas about the group which also seemed to be of a generalised, categorical nature. Firstly it was bound up with the conceptualisation of London Maltese as a 'close-knit' community.

[1] The design of the investigation, and its problems are discussed in Appendix F.

Responses on this particular issue were remarkably positive. Although so few respondents had any personal experience of Maltese people, the majority were not inhibited from making a categorical assumption of solidarity and only 5 per cent of respondents thought that the Maltese were not a cohesive group. This belief in group solidarity was quite definitely related to the imputation to the group of collective liability.[1]

The conceptual link between group blame and the assumption of group solidarity was the notion that sanctions and mutual controls operated inside the community. Most respondents considered that members of the Maltese community would be able to influence each other's actions; and some believed that the group could punish members if it wanted to. Those who felt that the ethnic group could *not* exert these internal controls were hesitant about supporting the proposition of collective responsibility. Furthermore most people also thought that if criminal activity by individuals created problems for the whole community, then it was directly in the interest of law-abiding Maltese to exercise those sanctions assumed to be available to them. This last point suggests that, once assumed, the idea of the collective responsibility may be self-reinforcing; for if mutual controls within it are seen as both possible and rational, then the most plausible explanation for any failure by a group to impose restraints on members is its complicity in their crime – thereby compounding any original liability.

Group blame as an instrument of indirect social control

When collective liability is imputed to a group it would appear to be in the expectation of augmenting society's control over the individual members of that group, by mobilising its internal loyalties and relationships. Broadly speaking there are two considerations underlying this policy of indirect control of individuals. Firstly there is the hostage principle. Most people have close personal relationships with others, whose well-being is of concern to them; and they are more likely to conform to a required mode of behaviour if they know that these other individuals are in risk

[1] For a statistical representation of these relationships, see Table F. 1 in Appendix F.

of punishment, in addition to themselves, should they fail. The more widely that this liability is spread among other people, the greater the probability that someone would in fact receive punishment. Not everyone could hope to escape it; and the more people who can be punished for an act, the greater the sum of punishment.

This leads into the second principle – the amplifier effect of collective responsibility. Where the fear of punishment or reprisals is spread and magnified amongst a group of people, many additional influences and sanctions are stimulated against a potential offender, to warn and deter, or even to detect and punish him. The internal group relations can augment as well as transmit sanctions or threats originating beyond them; so not only is the probability increased of punishment being meted out to *someone*; it also becomes more likely that the actual 'offender' himself will eventually receive some of it. In theory therefore collective liability can raise the deterrent value of punishment by increasing both the probability and, curiously, the precision of sanctions.[1]

The 1969 enquiry does give some indirect evidence of a relationship between the imputing of group liability to the Maltese, and a general concern with upholding social control. A definite leaning towards group blame responses was discernible in those who had the greatest stake in the existing social order, and who would be expected to have had the strongest desire to maintain conformity. This relationship does not show up in simple cross-tabulations of views of group blame with personal character-istics of respondents, because of the complicating effect of contact with Maltese people. As already shown, people in personal contact with Maltese in London were more likely than others to be group blamers. This was presumably due to a greater awareness of the existence and nature of Maltese criminality, for those respondents who knew Maltese people personally in London were both more inclined to know of, and to accept, the Maltese

---

[1] Collective responsibility does not necessarily negate individual responsibility, but channels it *through* group membership. As Sally Moore has put it ' . . . collective responsibility can . . . be a device used by persons outside a collectivity to force the group that has ultimate face-to-face control of individuals to bring pressure on some particular individual. The outsider may be some other group, an individual, or an administrative superior.' Sally F. Moore, 'Legal liability and evolutionary interpretation: some aspects of strict liability, self-help and collective responsibility', in Max Gluckman (ed.), *The Allocation of Responsibility*, 1972.

reputation for vice activities.[1] But direct knowledge of the Maltese and their bad name could only have been a secondary source of a desire to control Maltese behaviour indirectly through the community structure, for most group blamers did *not* know any Maltese personally, and some did not even know of their specific bad name.

In order to unscramble this fundamental, generalised tendency towards group blame from that which may have been stimulated by direct experience of Maltese criminality, it was necessary to separate respondents who did have personal contacts with Maltese from those who did not, and look at each group separately. The detailed results are shown in Table F.3 in Appendix F.[2]

This analysis shows that dogmatic group blame was most common among the conservative elements. Definite affirmation of collective liability was higher among older people, within both contact and no-contact groups. In terms of political allegiance, the highest rates of group blame were registered by supporters of the Tory party, and the lowest by politically apathetic individuals and supporters of minor parties, whose common characteristic was presumably a minimal desire or expectation to actually control other people in society.

Analysis in terms of class revealed a broadly similar pattern, although the influence of personal contacts was different here, in a most suggestive way. The general tendency towards group blame was lowest among unskilled workers – the men who were themselves at the receiving end of most institutions of social control – and highest among non-manual. Contact with Maltese individuals did not affect the views of non-manual respondents, but doubled extent of group blame among skilled workers and trebled it among the unskilled. So, although there was a general

[1] Over half of the total respondents did *not* admit knowledge of the Maltese bad name. Public currency of this reputation had declined quite a lot during the 1960s, since its peak around the time of the Street Offences Act. However, most of the people who knew some Maltese also were acquainted with the reputation – and contact with Maltese people was probably an important sensitising factor. (Conversely, from the point of view of Maltese, *most* of the non-Maltese people they met regularly knew the reputation, so that in effect they experienced it as having universal circulation.)

[2] The numbers in some cells are rather small at this stage of specification, but the trends are pretty consistent throughout this set of breakdowns, and this helps offset the low level of statistical significance of any part of the table considered in isolation.

reflex towards these indirect mechanisms of social control in the middle classes, by far the largest reservoir of it for deployment against minority groups was to be found in the working class. The easy-going attitudes associated with being at the bottom of the pile were dramatically changed by contact with immigrants whose behaviour was objectionable, and who could themselves be regarded as socially inferior.

This finding is of some importance, for it suggests that a large section of the population deemed a special mode of social control to be appropriate for controlling the behaviour of members of minority groups. So, although in the first instance it is convenient to see group blame as just a handy mechanism for indirectly improving control over members of collectivities, in reality it means much more. On closer analysis, the imputation of collective responsibility can be seen as analogous to a policy of indirect rule – and in relation to immigrants may even be regarded as an informal continuation of imperial practices, applied to groups actually within the mother country instead of in dependent territories but still assumed to be external and subject to metropolitan society.

It is relevant that respondents in the 1969 survey with military experience, especially ex-regular servicemen who would have been former policemen of the empire, and thus the most conditioned to thinking in terms of controlling colonial peoples through their indigenous power structures, were particularly avid group blamers. Any type of military activity probably trains men to think in terms of group, rather than individual, actions and loyalties, and so to react more positively to the notion that members of minorities are best confronted as collectivities; so even wartime conscripts held slightly stronger views on group liability than respondents with no military experience at all. Although these military men supported the concept of collective responsibility, they were no more aware than average of the Maltese reputation, nor especially inclined to believe it if they did know of it. Few of them had been stationed in Malta, and so they had no extra knowledge about the Maltese. Therefore their views must be regarded as almost purely dogmatic, and applicable to any other minority community.

The implication of group blame – that individual immigrants do not wholly belong to the English community – is a central tenet of Powellism, and it is in such policies that these sentiments towards minorities find their clearest public expression. As Mr Powell stated in a celebrated speech:[1]

> I have never said or implied that immigrants are more pre-disposed to vicious or spiteful behaviour than the indigenous population.... That however is not the point. With the malefactors among our own people we have got to cope; they are our own responsibility and part of our own society. It is something totally different when the same or similar activities are perpetrated by strangers.

Support for the indirect control of Maltese through the Maltese community is thus implicitly a condonation of the exclusion of minorities. The proposition that immigrant groups should look after their own affairs is tantamount to a demand that they should not interfere in *ours:* and the very propriety of group blame assumes a conception of the receiving groups as being outside of society. Many people in Britain, it seems clear, do regard ethnic minorities as outsiders whose destinies and loyalties are self-evidently divergent from those of British people, and whose dependent and inferior standing in Britain goes without saying. Wherever a conflict of interest arises it is axiomatic that public sympathy should be against them, and that a minority group which does control its members will be policing itself on behalf of the British majority, in whose favour order and right are conceived. For example when Maltese men cohabit with English prostitutes, then it is always 'our girls' who must be rescued from moral danger, and never 'their lads' – let alone 'our lads'. And in a centralised state like Britain, the exclusion of minorities in this way effectively means their continued suppression.

Collective responsibility and group domination

The practice of collective responsibility within a formally central-ised state is almost by definition a mark of a majority-minority situation. Collective responsibility increases the number of people at risk of being punished for the behaviour of a specific individual;

[1] Extract from the speech to the Rotary Club of London, at Eastbourne on 16 November 1968, as reported in the *Sunday Times* the next day.

and the total volume of punishment inflicted may be far in excess of what any original offence might appear to warrant.[1] A group will only put up with this if it is powerless to prevent it. So the capacity to enforce joint liability is a clear expression of supremacy, and the informal strategy of internal indirect rule is characteristically employed by a politically dominant group on subordinate and inferior sections of society.

The imposition of collective responsibility is more than just a manifestation of superiority; it may also do much to support and perpetuate the position of the majority employing it. Its effects inevitably go beyond social control, if by this term is meant simply the encouragement of behavioural conformity to moral and legal rules binding on all members of a society. For, quite apart from any special legislation for minorities, or biased jurisdiction, or the fact that the basic rules would favour the majority group anyway, the sheer exercise of collective responsibility necessarily implies the *additional* rule for members of minorities that they must concern themselves with each other's moral or legal conformity. A corollary of the extension of liability for an individual's behaviour to other members of a group is that each individual member is made multiply accountable for the actions of others. All are hostages for each other. And the most law-abiding person lives in danger of designation as a deviant by association or complicity. This is a severe infringement of the personal freedom of group members, and is likely to contribute to the maintenance of minority status.

For even though joint liability be purely informal, it can hinder the full participation by minority group members, as individuals, in wider public affairs. If members of minorities succumb to pressures to concern themselves with regulating the internal affairs of the group, they will almost certainly find themselves handicapped in the competition for economic and political power in the society as a whole. The more time and energy spent worrying about what co-responsible people are up to, the less is left to

[1] Writing of national minorities in Europe between the wars, Macartney notes that 'Frequent acts of violence have occurred, and while the (dominant groups) have been allowed to commit such acts with impunity, a single crime against one of them has been visited upon whole villages of the minority.' C. A. Macartney, *National States and National Minorities*, p. 421.

devote to personal advancement.[1] This restriction of individual initiative in wider society creates some closure of the group which may be very detrimental to its position. A minority which does not contain individuals who are powerful and respected in wider society is all the more vulnerable to discriminatory action. It has little voice in the definition of societal goals, and its loyalty and contribution to the common good can easily be called into question. Any degree of acquiescence in collective responsibility would seem to help prolong this precarious status.

When minority group members try to exercise mutual control in response to group blame, the outcome is more likely to be their domination – that is their immobilisation or partial exclusion from society as a result of the burdens of extended liability – rather than social control in the narrow sense of greater conformity to universal rules. This is because it is not possible to increase the sanctions operating on deviants or potential deviants within the group without creating extra rules for the rest of the members. These further liabilities are, however, no guarantee of improved social control, as regulating procedures within the group may be ineffective. So whereas social control is impossible without domination, the latter may quite easily occur without the former. All that is necessary for domination to be promoted is that members of the group should *try* to exercise internal controls; it makes little difference whether they succeed. Indeed if there is any difference it is arguable that domination is served all the better if internal control is not achieved, as criminality among members of a subordinate group gives the majority a charter for even greater discrimination against it.

Related to this is the fact that group blame has a tendency to attach disproportionately to the most active and prominent members of a group. This is significant, because it is these people who pose the greatest potential challenge to the categorical supremacy of a majority, and it is very much in the latter's interests

---

[1] A minority group may provide a captive market for a businessman, or a platform and supporters for aspirant politicians; but these advantages are finite. In the early stages of a career, or locally, they may assist an individual; but at higher levels they become a burden. 'Ethnic tickets' are usually disastrous at a national level, because once an individual has accepted the premise that there is a prior benefit (or public duty) in relation to fellow-members of a sub-group, especially a minority group, questions will arise about his suitability for higher level representation and leadership.

that such people should be saddled with extra liabilities which will help prevent them from interfering in public affairs. For if the most able and successful members of the minority are morally or legally tied to the least successful, participation in competitive areas of social life becomes for them something of a three-legged race, and the main opportunities will continue to be enjoyed by members of the majority.

These general points can be illustrated by reference to a classic and extreme instance of the use of informal group liability in a system of domination – lynch law in the control of Negroes in the post-bellum southern United States. In formal legal terms Negroes were individually accountable like anyone else. But the law was backed up, especially in rural areas, by customary procedures of *de facto* collective liability implemented through lynching. This was itself formally illegal; but since police were slow to apprehend people suspected of it and courts reluctant to convict and punish them, this was no more than a technicality. In fact the illegality of lynching may have heightened its effectiveness, since its application could be more flexible and responsive to local white feelings, and the Negro community was not officially accorded any right to organise themselves in self-defence.

The rationale which underpinned lynching was that, since the individualistic legal process was inadequate for keeping Negroes docile and in their proper place, direct community action was needed periodically to teach them a lesson. After an alleged outrage by a Negro, or whenever those in the neighbourhood were getting uppity, a gang of whites would capture and kill some Negroes as an example to the rest. There was a random element in the choice of victims, to bring home to Negroes that they were all at risk, and thereby terrify them into earnest restraint of any rebellious colleagues as well as purely personal acquiescence. Randomised punishment also enabled the lynch mob to inflict pain far in excess of any original offence, and underline emphatically the superiority of the whites.

In so far as there was any positive selection of victims, mobs seemed to prefer members of the respectable sector of the Negro community. This has misled some commentators into supposing that lynch law must have been ineffective or even counter-productive. Banton for example treats this aspect of lynching as if it were irrational:[1]

> While Negroes were sometimes responsible for violent crimes, the riots injured the responsible (i.e. law-abiding) elements in the Negro community more than others ... (so that) though lynch mobs were ostensibly concerned with the maintenance of order, in fact they were a major threat to it. Once the mob found that they could break the law to kill one Negro they were disposed to kill others when there was less cause to think the accused guilty of a culpable offence.

This rather misses the point of group blame. Lynchings were not really performed for the criminal Negro classes, who were legally actionable anyway, but for the instruction of respectable Negroes in the fact that the whole community had a duty to control its members. 'Responsible' members of the community were in this sense more accountable than the others to the whites. Writers with personal experience of the South have testified to the effectiveness of this device in mobilising the Negro community to police itself on behalf of the white majority.[2] This policing included suppression of criminal activity against whites, as well as a more general maintenance of docility.

Although the Negro community was not permitted an official organisational structure and privileges, it was informally allowed some purely internal autonomy, in the sense that local officers of the law were indulgent of offences committed between group members. This partial autonomy promoted group solidarity, and made it possible for Negroes to influence each other's behaviour – thereby enabling the group to serve as a medium for transmitting sanctions generated outside of it. The solidarity of the group was not antagonistic to the overall pattern of dominance, since Negroes understood that attempts to improve their collective position *vis-à-vis* the white majority would be counted as provocation. So group leadership was confined to activity *inside* the community, and responsible Negroes, who were the most susceptible to inter-group reprisals, learnt that the best sort of influence to exert was self-abasing restraint of troublemakers. The main energy of the community was diverted inwards to spiritual

[1] Michael Banton, *Race Relations*, p. 141.
[2] See for example A. Davis and B. B. and M. Gardner, *Deep South*.

and hedonistic activities, which were politically submissive and at the same time provided some recreational service for the whites.

The *treadmill of ethnic honour*

Because of its extreme nature, the case of lynch law illustrates the mechanics of imputed collective responsibility very clearly. But it is not entirely typical. The solidarity which enabled the Negro community to serve as a vehicle for sanctions originating externally was to a large extent generated by group blame itself, operating across the colour line, at the instigation of the dominant whites. If American Negroes now think of themselves as an ethnic group with a common historical origin and destiny, this is something that has emerged in the context of this solidarity, not prior to it. Collective responsibility is however more frequently exercised in respect of groups which already define themselves as ethnic units in the world, with traditions of shared adversity or triumph in the past which give them an aspiration for some measure of collective self-determination in the future. Sentiments such as these can easily be turned to advantage by a majority group, to enhance its dominant position; for through the use of group blame people organised into communities can be subjugated much more effectively than a mass of free individuals. A collectivity which welcomes the prospect of self-regulation is, within the framework of a centralised state, already half way to second-class citizenship. Furthermore, as the focus of identity of an ethnic group is by definition in a destiny which is alternative to that of the host state – either in a homeland outside of it, or in a distinct and autonomous nation within – such groups can by their very nature easily be shown to be subversive, so that there is always some justification at hand for discriminatory treatment against them.

It is obvious that a minority group which is racially distinctive is readily subjected to long-term domination, as the possession of physical characteristics greatly facilitates the enforcement of joint liability. But even ethnic groupings which are not particularly distinguishable can be exploited in this way, and over long periods, by more subtle discrimination which plays on members' feelings of group loyalty and collective honour. The 'bad name' which ethnic minorities frequently seem to have, or to be afraid of acquiring, is pivotal to this system of informal group liability, and consists of public attribution to the group of some anti-social characteristics, an attribution which serves both as an actual stain on its honour and status and as a charter for a whole range of petty sanctions against group members.

Collective action to prevent a bad reputation from developing seems to be one of the most typical functions of ethnic associations. Writing of the emergence of political movements among immigrants, Krausz has recently pointed out that 'The early immigrants [in Britain] were content with ameliorating their position by mutual aid, and were concerned with controlling elements which might, through their attitudes, bring disrepute to the minority' (p. 74).

Some of the first immigrant societies in America were formed with this object. For example, the Scots Charitable Society of Boston, founded in 1657, was created in order to maintain the good name of the group by relieving and repatriating destitute countrymen who might put it in jeopardy.[1] Similarly, at the opposite end of the history of settlement in the United States, a primary concern of Syrians arriving in the twentieth century has been to prevent one another from sullying the collective reputation.[2] Notwithstanding the formally 'open' and individualistic nature of American society, this sort of anxiety over the good name of the group has been a potent factor in maintaining the voluntary seclusion of groups which feel themselves vulnerable. As noted by Sellin (pp. 73-4), such groups have gone to considerable lengths to keep dishonourable behaviour from the public eye.

A contrary factor operates to lower recorded crime rates artificially and this must be appraised as well by the investigator. Smith notes that 'outside the grosser crimes, the affairs of the Japanese seldom come before the public eye, because of the unofficial system of regulation within the group. The secretaries of the Japanese Associations have settled many difficulties between members of their own group and those of other races and thus have avoided unfavourable publicity. The Japanese are solicitous in counselling their

---

[1] R. T. Berthoff, *British Immigrants in Industrial America*, p. 165.

[2] Handlin observes in relation to Syrian associations that 'The plan is to have those who have been here some time assist the recent arrivals by lectures and informal talks, and so prevent the mistakes and failures which might bring the Syrians into disrepute', Oscar Handlin, *Immigration as a Factor in American History*, p. 87.

children to commit no act which might tarnish the family name or disgrace their racial group in the eyes of the Americans'. The same situation has been reported by Robinson with regard to the ghettos of New York City. It appears then that where cohesive groups exist which are more or less in conflict with the dominant community group, some of the delinquency within such groups will be hidden, partly perhaps out of disagreement with the value attached to such delinquency by the dominant group, partly because of a belief in self-help, and partly as a defence measure in order not to increase antagonism.

The type of public order which this reflex created can be quite consistent with the interests of a dominant group. So long as disorderly behaviour is largely confined within the minority it is no real problem to them. In fact by helping to confuse the lives of minority group members it will support the existing distribution of power. The American police at this time needed little persuasion to turn a blind eye to crimes committed between members of an ethnic minority, as this lightened their load somewhat, and at the same time conjured up an illusion of efficient maintenance of order.

The degree of sensitivity of an ethnic group to its collective honour is largely a function of its position in the social hierarchy of power. Those groups which display the greatest preoccupation with their good – or rather, bad – name will be those in an inferior or insecure position. A bad name matters to such groups, as it serves to justify even harsher treatment of it by the majority. Status and power tend to be mutually supportive here. Although the withholding of public honour may be experienced by minorities as more hurtful than the acts of discrimination or exclusion which accompany it, these other sanctions flowing from the bad name are probably important in upholding the stigma. The prevailing definitions of what is good and socially useful are those supplied by the groups with the political and economic power to back them up; just as the use of this power to suppress minority groups is only seen as legitimately beneficial to society if these groups can be represented as anti-social.[1]

---

[1] Jews in European society show the other side of this coin. In spite of their economic power, they have yet to fully lose their minority status, because so many of the enterprises which they have been permitted to pursue successfully can be portrayed as detrimental to the overall public interest.

The connection between precarious status and concern with group reputation is shown rather nicely by the flurry of anxiety and activity among British Jews over their good name during the resurgence of European anti-semitism in the 1930s. Freedman, who has documented the case, sees the behaviour of Jews in this period as a typical minority reaction (p. 209):

> When ... Jews fear for the consequences of the criminal behaviour of individual Jews and adopt the cause of easing the strains set up by economic rivalries which seem to fall along the lines dividing Jews from their non-Jewish neighbours, we are clearly in the presence of a typical expression of minority spirit.

The charge of engaging in sharp commercial practices was hardly original, but under pressure of public attacks on them, and with horrific examples being set not far away, the Jews in Britain at this time responded to their reputation by organising internal community controls to minimise behaviour which outsiders might find objectionable. The collective reaction was triggered off in 1936 by references in local fascist oratory to price-cutting by Jewish grocery retailers. The Board of Deputies of British Jews replied immediately to the accusations, affirming that: 'We are concerned at the nature of these allegations, and would gladly do all that we can by way of moral influence to eliminate such practices' (ibid., p. 216).

Shortly after this the Board of Deputies Defence Committee set up a Trades Advisory Council with the double object of maintaining ethical standards amongst Jewish traders, and of amassing evidence to refute the suggestions of price-cutting and black-marketeering. As proclaimed on the cover of its annual reports, this council was to be: 'concerned with the good name of Jewry in the business world, and in its efforts to preserve this it deals impartially with offenders within its ranks and defamers without' (ibid., p. 219).

By 1947 the council had eight thousand members, and was investigating large numbers of cases of questionable ethical conduct. It is not known what sanctions the council wielded, but it claimed to have resolved many hundreds of cases.

One of the most interesting aspects of this is that, because of their fear of reprisals, many Jews accepted a measure of collective responsibility for each other, even though the community no longer believed itself to be a very cohesive grouping. Freedman interprets this as an over-sensitive Jewish reflex; but on the evidence of the 1969 enquiry it seems more likely that vulnerable minorities do actually have joint liability thrust upon them by members of the majority. Freedman argues (pp. 212, 220):

> The uncertain boundaries of modern Anglo-Jewry do not prevent many [Jewish] people from thinking of it as a kind of corporate entity the members of which are responsible for one another. This is to be seen particularly in the field of economic affairs where some Jews assume that the community must take responsibility for the impact made by Jewish businessmen on the wider society in order to preserve the good name of the community and the good will of Gentiles. It may be doubtful whether non-Jews generally think that Jews ought to be held responsible for one another, but some of their generalising prejudices against Jews in economic life seem to stimulate the latter to answer for their fellows. . . . One must not, of course, overlook the probability that the image in some Jewish minds of a minority constantly under the critical scrutiny of the Gentiles has no close parallel in the minds of the latter.

Preparedness to be brow-beaten into acceptance of collective responsibility is indeed a true mark of minority status. The demonstration of a desire to check the objectionable behaviour of colleagues may result in a reduction of intergroup tension, and Robin Williams recommends it as a means of bringing this about.[1]

---

[1] Robin Williams lists the following measures through which a minority can minimise antagonism towards it:

A vulnerable minority can itself help to reduce hostility and conflict insofar as there is group control over individual members, by:

    a) educating its members to an understanding of the dominant group's reaction to the minority's values and behaviour,

    b) careful study of the behaviours of its own members which are regarded as objectionable by other groups,

    c) minimising conspicuous displays of traits of marked negative-symbol value,

    d) participating as individuals in the wider community activities which are widely regarded as necessary in the common welfare.

(Robin M. Williams, Jr, *The Reduction of Intergroup Tensions*, p. 77, proposition 101.) The difficulty with this programme is that only the last tactic seems likely to effect any improvement in the group's position in society – and it is easily inhibited if too much attention is given to those preceding it.

But it is essentially a capitulatory reaction, a symbolic genuflexion. It is subservient, accepting that the main public duties of group members lie in action within the minority, and it weakens the position of group members in the wider society.

It may not be in the long-term interests of group members to accept responsibility for each other, as this is unlikely to do anything to improve the status of the group. Members of a minority may believe that they can raise their public standing, and vindicate their honour through internal controls. But even if their efforts were to achieve some reduction in certain kinds of behaviour, it remains in the power of a dominant group to define something else as objectionable or subversive. And there need be no end to such demands on the responsible members of the minority. In any case it is unlikely that internal controls can do very much to eradicate such behaviour, since this is often an expression of the subordinate position occupied by group members in the society. So those in the ethnic community who attempt to exert control on behalf of the majority will have been sent chasing each other to no avail;[1] and whether they have been able to influence each other or not, they will have been forced into internal activities instead of improving their real standing in the wider economic and political systems. At the end of the day the group members will still probably hold the pariah jobs.

The prospect of enhancing the status of an ethnic minority through the cultivation of ethnic honour is largely an illusion. Group status depends on factors which internal discipline can do little to change. Mutual social control may reduce pressure from others, but it is irrelevant to the more fundamental problems. Too great a preoccupation with honour will help keep a minority in bondage; the yoke of joint liability, borne voluntarily in the hope of collective liberation from discrimination, in fact increases the burdens of each without improving the position of any.

This style of informal group blame operates rather in the same way as the Hindu concept of ritual purity has done in the subjugation of the lower castes in India. The position of a sub-caste in the status hierarchy is defined by the level of ritual purity it has reached. This purity is a corporate property, and is contingent on the proper performance of duties by all group members. In this

[1] Except perhaps to prevent the situation worsening. Where goodwill of the majority is critical for survival there is probably little choice in the matter.

way the desire of individuals to improve their status becomes channelled into a system of unremitting mutual vigilance. Since the code of duties includes appropriately submissive conduct towards higher castes, the structure of interests which is created by the desire to achieve ritual purity serves as a brake on insubordinate behaviour and thus helps prevent social mobility. Changes in relative group status do take place, but not as the result of these internal controls. They occur because of population movements or developments in the economic structure. For example, as new immigrant groups – or marginal tribes – are incorporated into the system, a sub-caste may be able to foist its more polluting activities on to them, and adopt more honourable occupations. In the same way, the improvement in position of particular ethnic minorities within modern states usually takes place as a result of the arrival of a fresh group. The Irish in Britain for instance owe their currently improved standing to the postwar immigration of new minorities and to re-drawing of the boundaries of the dominant majority, rather to any internally organised purification.[1]

An alternative technique sometimes used by ethnic minorities seeking to rectify a bad name is public denial of the allegations made against them. This may occur alongside internal control measures, as in the instance already examined of the Trades Advisory Council of British Jewry. However, this sort of anti-defamation programme often seems to have a boomerang effect. By creating a public dialogue, the denials publicize further the original calumny; and by drawing attention to the capacity of the ethnic group to mobilise in reaction to adverse comment, they can reinforce belief in the cohesion of the group and sharpen antagonism towards it for its corporate insolence and presumption in refusing to knuckle under.

---

[1] Acceptance of Irish and their incorporation in Britain to the majority group has proceeded in spite of continuing high rates of criminality, and subversive political activity. Lambert for example found in Birmingham that the Irish still contributed disproportionately to most types of crime, but that since the arrival of new and more alien minorities they were no longer stigmatised for this. The local police held favourable attitudes towards them, and made 'no suggestion of brutality or viciousness; Irish roguery is mild and basically honest.' (John Lambert, *Crime, Police and Race Relations: a study in Birmingham*, p. 187.) Compare this representation with the original reception of the Irish as documented in chapter eight of John Jackson's *The Irish in Britain*. Further discussion of the Irish question can be found in Chapter VII.

The disastrous progress of the National Italian-American League to Combat Defamation illustrates the dangers. This association was set up to counter the reputation of Italian-Americans for proclivities towards Mafia-type crime, but in fact probably helped confirm it. Secretive and highly-disciplined crime became established within the Italian community in the United States at a time when police tended not to bother too much about crime *within* ethnic groups. Owing to the cabalistic nature of Mafia or Black Hand associations, their activities remained outside of the control of the Italian community as a whole, although the associations were parasitic on the solidarity of the ethnic group. Most Italians have always condemned these associations, and have blamed police laxity for their entrenchment in America.[1] Spurred by press and public opinion, sections of the community – for example, the White Hand Society – joined with the FBI in attempts to combat them, but without much success because, as the criminals were extremely secretive and highly organised, they were able to infiltrate and sabotage any ethnic associations directed against them. Consequently there has been little the Italian community could do, as a group, to retrieve its honour.

During the 1960s some leading Italian-Americans, encouraged by general progress in civil rights in the country, formed the anti-defamation league in a bid to redress once and for all the bad name of the community. Their main tactic was to reduce adverse publicity by persuading the communications media to drop overt references to the Mafia. But their own activities were themselves necessarily public, and it was not long before outsiders came to regard the organisation as yet another cover for the Mafia, and which was in reality trying to divert public attention away from organised crime. The founder and chairman of the league, Joseph Colombo, was widely reported in the press as being known to the FBI as a leading member of the Cosa Nostra; and many other key figures were also suspect.

The campaign conducted by the league could hardly have had a more deleterious effect on the reputation of the Italian community. National interest in the Mafia was stimulated, and was soon rewarded with the attempted assassination of Colombo at a public rally of the league in 1971. This was attributed by most reporters, and the FBI, to fellow mafiosi who had become alarmed

[1] See R. E. Park and H. A. Miller, *Old World Traits Transplanted,* pp. 248 ff.

at the surge of interest in the Mafia brought about by the anti-defamation movement. The complicity in crime, or at least the stupidity, of member Italians was confirmed by this event, and the ethnic honour of the group has suffered a further setback. Few Americans can now doubt that the Italians are a subversive element in the nation.

Maltese and the pursuit of ethnic honour

The material outlined in Chapter II suggests that Maltese in London do not appear to suffer the same degree of economic discrimination as most other immigrants – though it would perhaps be wise to await the discussion in the following chapter before attaching too much significance to these findings. However, as bearers of a vicious public image they can be expected to find it difficult to improve their social status, and the members of the community could be presumed to have had strong incentives to mobilise themselves in a programme of mutual control.

In a sense there are indirect stimuli to joint protective action inherent in the experience of simple individual stereotyping, even before any account is taken of explicit group blame and the imperatives of ethnic honour.[1] Stereotypes are powerful determinants of marginal social relations. At a psychological level a stereotype is best understood as a categorical device for the relatively effortless ordering of relationships with people who are not known and appreciated as individuals. Stereotypes make possible a wide range of social action where there is little specific information about other social agents; a small number of generalised assumptions serving instead. Mutual stereotyping may hinder the growth of close personal relations, by making it difficult for each party to predict with sensitivity the reactions of the other; and where personal ties do develop, they usually entail substantial modification of prior conceptualisations. So people often think of personal friends as exceptions to a general stereotype about the social category to which those friends belong. This does not, however, reduce the utility of the stereotype, which is not necessarily placed in doubt by a few exceptions.

All people are categorised in this way by others, and are liable

---

[1] This was the explanation given by Freedman for the formation of the Trades Advisory Council by British Jews. See above, quotation referred to on p. 167.

to treatment on the basis of stereotypes which may be highly inappropriate to them personally. This really constitutes a serious problem only for members of minority groups, in an inferior position in society, for whom special treatment means hostile discrimination. In Louis Wirth's words: 'To the individual members [of a minority group] the most onerous circumstance under which they have to labour is that they are treated as members of a category, irrespective of their individual merits' (p. 310).

In the case of the London Maltese, this means that individuals are liable to be treated in the first instance as though they are ponces – which most are not. This might be expected to prompt respectable Maltese to attempt to eradicate vice amongst their countrymen; and most of the non-Maltese respondents in the 1969 enquiry assumed that this would be the normal Maltese reaction.[1]

However, the difficulties created for an individual by stereotyping are in an important sense finite, and the stimulus they provide towards internal group regulation may be less than often supposed. Most non-Maltese respondents who accepted the Maltese reputation considered that it was nevertheless only likely to be true of a minority of Maltese; and their own problem was in fact sorting out those to whom it applied.[2] As the law-abiding Maltese individuals became known personally they could therefore expect to be exempted from the presumption of guilt. Application of the stereotype to them was provisional, and open to correction when their personal character was appreciated. Thus a Maltese man could minimise difficulties arising out of stereotyping, by cultivating a protective network of close personal relationships within which he was known to be decent and respectable. And as his contacts expanded, the more secure his personal standing would be.

Group blame presents an altogether more intractable problem than this simple individual stereotyping. All Maltese, regardless of blameless personal record, can be seen as necessarily sharing in the collective guilt for crimes of their compatriots. This treatment as member of a *group* cannot be escaped in the same way as treatment as member of a *category*, simply through publication of one's own unique disposition. Whatever an individual's personal

---

[1] See responses to questions 7 and 8 of schedule; given in Appendix F.
[2] See question 11, 1969 enquiry schedule; given in Appendix F.

characteristics and image, and however virtuous he may be himself, nothing can alter the fact that he is accountable for other people too. As a group member, he is inevitably caught up in the inter-group conflict and reprisals for the offences of his compatriots. This is a more onerous difficulty. In a sense this imputing of collective responsibility is itself a form of stereotyping, at a social rather than personal level, as it makes assumptions about the nature of minority groups, and their position in society, which the groups themselves can do very little to contradict.

So group blame would appear to be a much more potent stimulus than simple individual stereotyping to the generation of internal group controls. As there is no escape from its pressure for any identifiable group members, it focuses the interests of them all on mutual vigilance. A Maltese who is liked personally may still remain a group representative in the eyes of some of his friends; and the 1969 enquiry showed that among non-Maltese who knew Maltese personally there was more than average antagonism towards them collectively.[1] So whereas the avoidance of individual stereotyping may encourage the development of close personal friendships outside of the group, the logic of group blame will tend to undermine them, thereby making stereotyping itself more problematic.

This generalised expectation of enhanced group solidarity and internal regulation does not allow however for the particularly fragile nature of the Maltese community structure; and the actual response of Maltese to the burden of their collective reputation has accordingly been rather different to this.

[1] Respondents in the 1969 enquiry who had Maltese friends contained a larger than average proportion in favour of repatriation of Maltese immigrants; distinctions are made between people *as* individuals, and as group members. See Table F.4 in Appendix F. Similarly Krausz has referred to the problems of a Jew who 'was well satisfied with the genuine friendship his Gentile friends displayed towards him in an organisation in which he was active. But he objected to the fact that he was regarded by his non-Jewish friends as a kind of *special person,* an ambassador of the Jews.' Krausz, op. cit., p. 131.

VI

MALTESE DENIAL OF
COLLECTIVE RESPONSIBILITY

The Maltese bad name hinges on the stereotype of the ponce, who combines an indolent and immoral parasitism with a capacity for violence when his fear or jealousy is aroused. This representation has been given a good mileage in the British press, although its heyday passed some years ago. The stereotype is not extended unconditionally to all Maltese, but any are liable to be confronted with it if not personally known as respectable.

This particular stereotype is one of the most unpleasant that can be applied to members of a minority group, as there is no scope within it for the maintenance of personal honour. By comparison, for example, the image entertained by gentiles of the cunning or mean Jew is far less personally offensive, because it does imply some admirable qualities of intelligence and resourcefulness. Even the most extreme anti-semite may respect supposed Jewish attributes,[1] and anti-semitism plays at least as much on the fear of possible Jewish superiority and the prospect of their acquisition of power and social dominance, as it does on intrinsic disapproval of behaviour attributed to them. Even where stereotypes assume inferiority, as with attitudes towards coloured people, this does not usually imply any moral objection, only a concern that such people should know and keep their proper place.

But the Maltese bad name entails the utmost moral censure. No one is so despicable in the public mind as a ponce – especially when he is an outsider preying on local girls. There is nothing admirable in the content of this image, and even the criminal community joins in the condemnation of such persons.

---

[1] One old and highly anti-semitic lady known to me in East London always insists on being taken to the London Jewish Hospital whenever she is ill, as she considers her chances of survival there much better.

Maltese cannot unfortunately look for consolation to the idea that the stereotype is a blatant falsehood. Certainly the majority of Maltese have nothing to do with poncing, and even among convicted criminals only 15 or perhaps 20 per cent have had vice charges made against them. But Maltese do seem to put themselves at risk of such convictions more frequently than other people, and there is no ostensible cause for this which they could cite in defence of their honour.

Nor can Maltese draw any comfort from an alternative set of values in Maltese culture. Maltese vice in London is not a reflection of the parent culture; it is a reaction against it. In the last resort the sexual dilemma in Malta can and should be blamed on the British garrison, and even perhaps on previous occupations. But this does not seem to make the fact any more palatable to Maltese, because their sensibilities have become so deeply encrusted with sexual guilt that few are able to mention it at all, let alone engage in a cathartic debate about final causes. In Maltese values vice is not merely outrageous; in most circles it is literally unspeakable.

This adds to the shock and shame felt by those Maltese who do not find out about the bad name in Britain until they actually arrive. One sample member recalled that before he had left Malta some friends had made oblique, joking references to the fact that some Maltese in London lived off their women. He had supposed, in his innocence, that this meant that they sent their wives out to work, while they stayed at home with their feet up. It had seemed quite a good solution to the problem of how to earn a living. When he came to London and discovered what it really meant he was unable to believe it at first, and then was so ashamed that he went with a friend to try to find a job in Yorkshire, where he had an aunt – a service-bride – and to where he hoped that the reputation might not have spread. It was some time before he could face returning to London; and when he did so it was because he had come to feel that English moral evaluations were less stringent than Maltese, and that the bad name was therefore not so severe a handicap as he had supposed at first. Migrants with a very strong attachment to Maltese values go back home quickly when the bad name becomes apparent to them; much of the re-migration of families is due to this. Many Maltese who do stay find that it creates continual dilemmas of ethnic-loyalty and self-respect.

Maltese experience of stereotyping in Britain

Maltese are undoubtedly inclined to be over-sensitive to their reputation; but this does not mean that if only they could pull themselves together and forget it their problems would go away. It is not possible for Maltese to ignore the stereotype or dismiss it as erroneous, malicious or unfair; the image serves as a charter for wide-ranging discrimination against them. Most sample members in the main survey had experienced genuine difficulties as a result of it. The commonest problems arose in finding suitable jobs, and in connection with girl-friends and their parents. Most respondents found that they were continually up against snubs and insinuations, and several said they were regularly refused admission to dance-halls, where members of other immigrant groups were let in without question. A large number of men interviewed considered that they had been victimised by the police because they were Maltese.

Most of them seemed to feel that these specific provocations were intrinsically less important than the withholding of honour and respect that they implied. The bread and butter matters of employment, accommodation and so on were relatively easier to bear[1] than the constant teasing and affronts they constantly suffered, particularly at work. Sometimes this teasing may have been intended only as a joke. For example, one young migrant who had only been in London for a few weeks when interviewed said:

> Just now there was a case when a Maltese killed another man in a fight because of a woman. He worked in a kitchen and took a knife and killed the man. That was in all the papers. They tease you about it at work. They say 'Did you read about that Maltese who stabbed his friend?'

In many instances the issue went beyond joking, and a good deal of antagonism was generated. An old-timer with a string of minor convictions, mainly involving brawls, explained how this sort of situation might develop into open hostility.

I been working in Shell about four years ago. I went as

---

[1] The material presented in Chapter II indicates that the Maltese probably fared quite well materially, by comparison with most immigrants. But in many cases, as the argument presented later in this chapter will illustrate, this must have been because they were not recognised as Maltese by other people such as employers.

porter, and they put me frying the chips. A boy there was in the Navy in Malta, and he say to me 'Your sort is no good'. I insult him and he says 'You Maltese, you are living on my wife, who is on streets.' When I heard that the blood go to my head and I insult him. The boss says why do I insult him, and give me my money and I go. I had sack.

In order to survive the continual verbal assaults, Maltese need to be pretty thick-skinned. Those unable to manage soon get bitter and may become quite ill from worry and resentment. The respondent just quoted had developed a heart condition and was in a generally poor state when interviewed. A case was found also in the court record analysis where a Maltese sent to Long Grove suffering from paranoia had obviously been upset by his reception in Britain. The Medical Officer at Brixton, where he had been remanded for examination, commented that he was:[1]

clearly suffering from acute paranoid schizophrenia. He has many paranoid delusions, for example that the neighbours come into his flat at night and 'throw piss' on his face, or that everyone in England is against him because he is Maltese. He shows thought disorder, e.g. 'when you buy bread you find it's full of insults'. He shows affective disruption – laughing and smiling when talking of his imaginary persecutors.

The full medical report from Long Grove added that he was suspicious and hostile. He had come to London from Malta ten years earlier, married and held one job for seven years. His wife had left him a few months before admission, following a number of periods of treatment. At the time of this report he was:[2]

markedly paranoid believing that all English dislike him. He maintains that he smashed the windows as a retaliation against his neighbours who, he feels, victimise him, enter his flat and pour water from the lavatory over him when he is asleep. He states that he broke the glass and that 'the law is glass'.

The old-timers who have remained within café society tend to be least able to accept this reception outside of the community.

[1] Thames Court, Court 1 notebook, 17 September 1913.
[2] Ibid.

Difficult as relations within café society may be, they do not involve frequent humiliation. Most Maltese who stay in this country learn to stand up for themselves, however, and the worst period for them is probably soon after arrival. The majority of interviewees recalled most keenly the insults during the first year or two. After a while it becomes tolerable:[1]

> Some English people blame everybody for the wild ones. When you work in factories you find out – people say things – and many times I pass it off as a joke. As I grow older here though I find it better now. You get used to it as you go along.

This amelioration was generally connected with the development of a good personal reputation. A middle-aged Maltese living in the Stepney heartland of the settlement said: 'I hear them talking about the Maltese where I work. The good ones take the blame with the bad. But they don't include me as I get on all right with them.'

This sort of experience may be common. Members of the 1967 sample demonstrated a remarkable stability in their jobs, and an important consideration in this may have been a desire to stay among people who accepted them.[2] Sometimes the defence was to build up a resistance to insults. Another old-timer said:

> We all get a bad name because of those places [the cafés]. An English bloke at work will say to me – 'You're Maltese; you must have a club down the West End!' I don't say nothing back. I just think to myself – 'You English gave us the chance to do it.' That's what I think.

Occasionally the experience of stereotyping may make a migrant more conscious of his own prejudices, and thus more able to

---

[1] Some of this improvement may be objective, in that the Maltese bad name has declined in severity during the 1960s. There did not seem to be any way of measuring the extent to which actual provocation may have been reduced. But since almost *all* respondents, irrespective of when they arrived in Britain, seemed to feel that their first few years had been the worst, there does seem to be a general process of adjustment on the part of permanent settlers.

[2] Twenty-three per cent of respondents in work had been in their current jobs for ten years or more; and only 32 per cent, including the recent arrivals, had been in theirs for less than two years.

cope with those of other people. One fairly well-established settler, who had opened a small hotel and was constantly meeting people of different nationalities, explained that he had realised that he entertained his own stereotypes about them, some pleasant, others less so. He found them useful in a general way in helping organise his first contacts with strangers:

> When an American rings my bell, I tell myself that I am dealing with a member of the meanest race on earth. He will go to every hotel in the area to find out the prices, select the cheapest and then grumble because there is no lift. Eastern peoples like Greeks and Arabs are very nosey and will want to know all about my business and how much money I make. English country people are very easy to please and will accept whatever you offer. In fact the English in general are so easy-going that they usually won't even bother to ask to see a room before taking it.

But however adept an individual may become at coping with difficulties or provocations arising out of the stereotype, these do still stimulate a desire to punish or exert some control over those compatriots causing all the trouble. This may find relief in fantasy; as one young Maltese recounted:

> A bloke with the same surname as me was in the papers for living off prostitution. The English people next door and at work thought it was me and said things about it. They told me afterwards it was only a joke but I didn't think it was. The bloke is in prison now and I've not seen him again – but I often think about punching him on the nose.

Sometimes attempts to regulate the behaviour of fellow-Maltese are made:

> I try to be good myself but I've still got a bad name because of all the others. I try to stop them making trouble when I can, and the last time I did it worked. I had been drinking with my wife and we saw some Maltese and Irish about to start a fight. I stood between them and said something like 'Can't you see you get us all into trouble?', and they went off.

On the evidence of this study, such initiatives are not very common. The usual solution to stereotyping is the cultivation, and publication,[1] of a good personal reputation.

The experience of direct group blame

A certain amount of group blame is implied indirectly as a by-product of simple stereotyping; but it is also affirmed explicitly and deliberately, and the effect of this on the community seems much greater. In attempting to escape from the ascription of group liability, Maltese are driven into a more complete denial and avoidance of ethnic community life than would otherwise be necessary. The enthusiasm with which established settlers have abandoned their ethnicity is largely due to the fact that this is the easiest individual solution to the difficulties arising out of group blame. Paradoxically, group blame undermines the collective life of the ethnic group.

Many of the insults recalled by interviewees clearly represented attempts by outsiders to induce them to accept some responsibility for their compatriots' conduct. For example, a Maltese who had been in London for over thirty years, and had spent the last twenty of them working his way up in his present firm to a position of seniority, explained that although he no longer regarded himself as Maltese in any sense, his colleagues at work often insisted on treating him as a member of a solidary group and extending blame to him for his countrymen's misdeeds.

> Once you've got a Maltese doing something wrong here it gets published in the papers and the whole community gets blamed for it. In the firm where I am, if something happens in the papers, they all still look at me and say 'Why don't you Maltese leave our girls alone?'

In spite of his own impeccable record, and known good character, he was treated as a representative of the Maltese as a whole. There is no easy let-out in these situations, because

[1] This is not necessarily pursued at an inter-personal level. For example, the following item was printed in the *East London Advertiser* on 21 October 1966:
A Disclaimer
Mr Paul Zammit, of 15 Stutfield Street, Stepney, who has a married brother named Spiro Zammit, aged 29, of Christian Street, asks us to state that neither he nor his brother have any connection with the man of the same surname mentioned in a court case last week.

solidarity is assumed and it is considered the responsibility of law-abiding Maltese, as much as of the criminals themselves, to do something. English friends sometimes asked respectable Maltese, out of pure and unabashed curiosity, *why* they did nothing about all the criminals, and were surprised if offence was taken.

A few respondents found this perplexing.

Whenever a Maltese does some fighting or is with girls in the papers, they say at work 'He is one of them'. I don't like it and I can't understand it. I've been here for twenty years and I've never been in any trouble – but that doesn't seem to make any difference to them.

It is possible that, because the ethnic group is fragmented, Maltese are relatively unreceptive to the concept of collective responsibility so that some of them are unable to understand what is going on, interpreting attempts to impute group blame as irrational or as an incomprehensible mistake. The community is so self-evidently weak in its participants' eyes that some are unable to appreciate that outsiders believe them to be a cohesive group.

None the less, most respondents understood only too clearly when group liability was being suggested, and spent a good deal of energy trying to correct the mistaken premises on which they felt it was based. The defence adopted by most was to deny the existence of a Maltese community.[1] A few interviewees were so completely cut off from other Maltese that they had forgotten, or were unaware of, the weakness of the community, and accepted the assumption made by non-Maltese that there was a cohesive ethnic group. Their defence therefore was that they personally should not be treated as co-responsible with other Maltese, since they were not part of the community. Basically these two defences are the same, in that they try to establish that the individual should not be judged as member of a group, but on his own merits.

These protests at the assumption of membership of a solidary group do not seem to have been effective. The 1969 enquiry among non-Maltese showed that people who knew Maltese personally were in fact *more* prone to regard them as a solidary

[1] The denials of group solidarity recorded in the 1967 investigation were doubtless in part a defensive reflex of this sort.

and co-responsible group. This is perhaps mirrored in the finding of the main 1967 study that it was in the ranks of established Maltese settlers, with most contacts outside of the ethnic group, that there was the greatest despondency about the collective reputation. Some of the personally most successful migrants, who had learned to live with regular teasing, seemed to lose confidence all over again as they gradually began to realise that in spite of their individual achievements they would never be fully accepted in London. Their own good character enabled them to minimise problems arising out of stereotyping; but they remained members of a group with a bad name, and this was a further and in many cases unexpected barrier to complete personal acceptance.

A complication is that the Maltese are not entirely consistent in their denials of group solidarity and responsibility. When under attack, their first defence is denial of community or personal dissociation from it. But if this proves ineffective they may be tempted to try to offset the local reputation of Maltese by referring to the good name of Maltese internationally, and their war record in particular. During the Second World War the civilian population of Malta played a heroic role in resisting Italian attacks on the British garrison, and were collectively awarded the George Cross. Maltese in London are proud of this record, and feel that it outweighs any local misdemeanours. Reference to it is useful in a dispute about the behaviour of Maltese, as it stays within the idiom of group-think and group-judgment. But precisely because of this, it reinforces the presumption of solidarity of the ethnic group by non-Maltese and neutralises attempts at personal dissociation.

Not all Maltese are equally liable to experience imputed collective responsibility. Those who meet it most are the people who are active in formal, visible Maltese associations, and who are apparent as foci of community sentiment and organisation. Office-holders and leaders in the community must be prepared to serve as representatives for the Maltese, and to bear the brunt of external public opinion. This has constituted a disincentive to formal involvement in Maltese associations, and has helped to inhibit their development in London.

This was illustrated by a middle-aged informant who had been prominent in the first years after his arrival here in fostering a social club in the East End in connection with the Maltese Mission.

When he migrated he was intensely patriotic, and he was pleased to find a task awaiting him in the community in Britain. As a result of his leading position, he had been co-opted as Maltese representative to a local committee concerned with the abatement of vice. The role given to him proved to be an impossible one. He was assumed by the rest of the committee to communicate with an organised group in which he exercised some definite influence. But in reality no such influence was possible, and he found himself mobilised on behalf of an amorphous and highly individualistic mass. He ended up thoroughly disillusioned with the Maltese. At the time of the interview he was insisting that he now be regarded as an Englishman. He wanted nothing more to do with being Maltese; and the social club had withered away.

Effects of group blame

In Chapter II, on the structure of the Maltese community in London, it was suggested that it was helpful to think in terms of two main dimensions of weakness in the group. Firstly there is very limited participation by individuals in ethnic activities; and secondly there are competing and neutralising ideas, held by different factions, about the proper cultural and institutional basis for community life. The Maltese bad name, with its direct and indirect implications of group blame, seems to have contributed strongly to both these axes of disorganisation.

At the level of individual participation, group blame has strongly reinforced the incentives for personal dissociation from the group. The failure of most settlers to identify with it and take part in its communal affairs can be seen as a direct result of the strategies adopted by them for minimising the unpleasant consequences of the bad name. This commonly goes much further than the denials of community solidarity or of personal involvement, which have been discussed above. In many cases it reaches the level of positive appropriation of an alternative ethnic identity.

It has been shown in earlier chapters that the Maltese are quite successful, by comparison with other immigrants, in settling as independent individuals in London. What has not yet been made sufficiently explicit is that this success is frequently contingent on their not being identifiable too readily *as* Maltese; and one of the first discoveries to emerge from the 1967 enquiry was that many

G

sample members were in fact known to their neighbours as Italians or Cypriots, or as nothing-in-particular – but certainly not as *Maltese*.[1]

Quite commonly Maltese compromise by using an alternative identity as something to shelter behind until they have established themselves locally as respectable individuals.

> People don't say anything to me, but I know that they are thinking 'He is Maltese – maybe he is one of those in Soho'. I am not like that, and when they know me better they will understand. As it happens I am the Italian type to look at, and many people think I am Italian. When they know me better I may tell them I am Maltese.

This particular respondent had worked out the ruse of using an English surname at work, and taking lessons in spoken Italian so that he could pass as an Anglicised Italian. His excess of guile only seemed to multiply his problems, though, as he had just been discovered to be Maltese in his last job, and had been obliged to change to give himself a fresh start. He was however hopeful that when his Italian improved a bit he could find work as an Italian-to-English translator or interpreter, and get to know some Italian people in London.

Italian is probably the favourite cover for Maltese in London,[2] but it is not assumed lightly. The Italians were the chief enemy for Maltese in the last war, and it is felt to be unpatriotic to change sides in this way. Respondents also realised that their passing was bad for the community as a whole; by their failure to stand up and be counted as Maltese, they were ratifying the poor public image. But self-interest usually overcomes any feelings of guilt, with the result that the only really visible Maltese in London are the disorganised members of café society. One Maltese priest put it: 'Very many Maltese living and working with the English

---

[1] Sample lists for the enquiry consisted of names of men who *might* be Maltese. In the early stages of the interviewing, if a listed person was not in, a neighbour was asked about his ethnicity, so that unnecessary return visits could be cut out. It was soon appreciated that few sample members were known by neighbours as Maltese, and some were angry with me for exposing them. Once this became obvious a more circumspect procedure had to be used.

[2] One very successful Maltese restaurateur in the sample employed Italian waiters to give some substance to his chosen image.

are afraid to say they are Maltese – so the English only hear about the bad ones.'[1]

Even criminal Maltese may have an interest in passing, especially when they want to move into the big-time jobs. Criminal society is itself contemptuous of ponces, so an alternative label is useful. One Maltese was referred to repeatedly during the Kray twins trial as a Greek; and this can hardly have happened unless he had encouraged people to believe it.

Passing is common in the second and third generations. Children born locally prefer to define themselves as English; but occasionally darker pigmentation or a slight accent makes this difficult. Several children of respondents said that they had to call themselves Italians at school; for one thing, parents of prospective girl-friends would not want them going out with Maltese boys.[2]

Some Maltese try to find alternative identities which do not, for conscience sake, amount to renunciation of Malta. Migrants from the island of Gozo for example prefer to think of themselves as Gozitans:

> I used to have problems years ago. When I was looking for a job I wouldn't like myself to be known as Maltese. So I used to say I come from Gozo. Sometimes they'd say that's still Maltese. But now it is all right for me. I have a good job and all the workers have been there a long time, and they respect me.

Hyphenated Maltese are well placed for this sort of dissociation as they have genuine alternative ethnic identities, sometimes a whole pack, to play as necessary. Several of the hyphenates contacted in the course of the main investigation said firmly on

---

[1] A similar point was made by the Maltese High Commissioner during the public debate leading up to the Street Offences Act. He was quoted in an English newspaper as saying 'Many [decent Maltese] disown their Maltese nationality. They will not admit they are Maltese in case the stigma these men have brought on our community attaches itself to them.' Colonel Vella, quoted by Robert Hill in the article 'Passport to Vice', in the *People*, 8 February 1959.

[2] It is not always easy to hold back the truth. An English schoolteacher who took a job in West Ham in 1969 told me that a boy aged eight in her class, whom she had regarded as rather shy, came up to her after school one day when she had been there a few weeks and said to her desperately: 'I've got a secret, Miss, I must tell you. My daddy is Maltese.' One issue raised is whether many Maltese were so completely dissociated from the community that they were missed out from the 1967 investigation. A few respondents had heard of Maltese changing their names and disappearing from view. If many had done this the findings of the enquiry may actually overstate the cohesion and solidarity of the ethnic group.

the doorstep that they were not Maltese but Tunisians, Egyptians or whatever. Their Maltese or part-Maltese ancestry had been important in entitling them to British citizenship; but for most purposes, and now they were in Britain, they elected to identify themselves with their countries of birth, or with a non-Maltese ancestor. Even those hyphenates who do call themselves Maltese know that they are not wholly Maltese – and this gives a starting point for a healthy dissociation from the Maltese reputation. There is moreover some justification for this attitude, as hyphenated Maltese are rarely participants in café society or in the type of activity which sustains the bad name.

Because of this escape-route of easy sectional dissociation, the hyphenates manage to avoid most of the problems that arise out of group blame. Paradoxically, this means that they do not have the same reluctance to support associations bearing a Maltese label. In Chapter II it was suggested that the marginal position of the hyphenates in the community has given them a structural advantage of being outside the major factionalism. It can now be appreciated that their marginal status is also an advantage in the external relations between Maltese and the local population. The greater facility of sectional dissociation enables marginal Maltese to participate in Maltese associations with less personal embarrassment, and to play leading roles in the life of the group without being made answerable for the crimes of ordinary Maltese. It is partly because of this that the hyphenates have been so active in the community.

Undermining of associations

The bad name has had an inhibiting effect on the participation of ordinary migrants in the social life of the community, and has undermined a number of attempts to organise facilities for group members. This has had a severely constrictive effect on collective morale. The most visible sector of the community has always been café society, and established settlers do not want to mix with such people. Among respectable Maltese there is a strong body of opinion which asserts that *any* congregating by Maltese may lead to undesirable consequences. A family man, with a criminal record himself years ago – which he did not admit to – said:

I see Maltese every day but I dodge them. I don't find them in my class. The good Maltese go to America and Canada and Australia. The hard working people go to those other countries. I was going to America myself in 1950, but I hurt my shoulder, and they work too hard in America so I stayed in Britain. I wish I had never come here really. There is no community here because the Maltese know that when you have a lot of Maltese people together you do bad for yourself.

A young hotel owner explained that he would himself like to meet other Maltese – but only if they were the right sort:

Unless Maltese are sure that other Maltese are respectable they wouldn't like to mix with them. A lot of Maltese boys not wanted in Malta have come to London and made trouble here. These types of people stick together and create a bad community. There was no future for them in Malta because the police knew about them. You have to be careful before associating with other Maltese, in case they are not good ones. If there were a good organisation with decent people in it, where the bad ones will not go, then it will catch on.

Many of the men interviewed were afraid to mix with other Maltese in any context. Withdrawn settlers commonly explained their lack of contact with others on such grounds as 'If you go with the bad ones you will soon be the same as them', or 'Put a rotten apple in a barrel of good ones and they will all go bad' – that is, good apples should keep out of barrels. Some men who had adopted orderly lives still remained a little unsure of their own capacity to keep control of themselves if they mixed with disorganised newcomers again; the more cut off they were from other Maltese, the more they came to believe the stereotype of the vicious Maltese, and the more fearful they would be of getting involved.

There are many dangers they point to. A man may become contaminated by having disorderly tendencies brought out by association with wilder individuals. There is also the risk of being identified, in the eyes of neighbours or the police, with the wrong types. If you were seen to be friendly with a criminal Maltese, you might easily find yourself implicated with him in some affair, irrespective of actual participation. It was better to keep out of the way, and to restrict social contacts to one or two known and trusted colleagues. Also there is the danger to one's family of possible violence or blackmail; a married man is more vulnerable than a bachelor. Several respondents saw their voluntary isolation as a necessary precaution for the sake of their families.

I don't want to interfere. I've got a family. Those people are weak in mind and hot blooded. I don't want any trouble. I'm responsible to my daughter. She'll hear about the Maltese soon enough anyway.

If I find somebody in that kind of life I keep away from him. I've got a wife and children to think about. And I don't want to put my name with his with the police.

Fear and disapproval of association with other Maltese extend even to meetings in ostensibly respectable settings; this was one of the main factors bringing about the failure of the social events organised by the Catholic Mission. People were afraid to go along, in case there should be any bad Maltese there to get them into trouble somehow. The sense of danger is increased by the fact that it is difficult to be sure whether a particular person is good or not. Even friends alter so much after coming to London that it is not possible to rely on their being decent people any longer. Close relatives such as brothers often drift apart in London and rarely see each other; and one pair of brothers who were both, independently, selected in the 1967 sample, were each carefully keeping away from the other in the belief that he had become a bad influence.

If it is hard to distinguish good from bad among people that you know, the problem is even greater in respect of those not known previously. In many cases families living a few doors away from each other were found in the enquiry to entertain the wildest mutual suspicions, preventing them from getting to know each other. A polite good morning was all they would risk.

So the effect of the bad name has been to exacerbate the individualistic tendencies of migrants. If there had been thriving associations before the reputation had developed, or a real incentive for preserving ethnic community life, the bad name might not have had such a devastating effect. Where a minority group has some initial solidarity, informally imputed collective responsibility may stimulate it further; but where the fundamental disposition of group members is towards personal withdrawal, it seems to boost this tendency and make community controls all the more impracticable.

The vicious circle of reputation and disorganisation

The massive dissociation of Maltese from the ethnic group is part of a vicious circle in which group disorganisation and a bad collective reputation have progressively reinforced each other. As experienced settlers retire to pursue a private salvation from group blame as best they may, the potentiality of the community for exercising internal controls is reduced. This continuing disorganisation confirms the view of those who are able to look after themselves that the group is incapable of imposing a general will on malefactors, and justifies their own reluctance to put themselves at risk by attempting to promote this.

Most of the informants were emphatic that the ethnic community was too incoherent to be able to contemplate corporate action, and it could never hope to offer any inducements which would compete with the attractions of the disorganised life. One ex-convict remarked that:

> Not even Jesus Christ himself can change their minds. These people get into the habit of getting the easy money. You don't have to force the girls to give you the money. Maltese enjoy having a good time and make good companions. So you are not going to change them easily.

The general view was that whether you were law-abiding or not was something that was entirely up to you personally.

> I don't think there are any ways to stop them. They come here because they say the English women are so easy to put on the streets. Friends who are on holiday in Malta tell them how much they can earn but don't warn them about the jail. And there is no community here – not that that can do any good and control them. All that you can do is to work regular yourself and behave yourself in general. No one can help you.

> Not even family ties have any effect.

I don't think anything can stop it. If they're used to that business you can't do anything about it. My brother is like that now. We are different now. I respect him as my brother but I can't live with him any more. When I came here (just after him) he took me to the club in Cross Street. I went there to get help about tax. After a while I stopped going every day. I heard a lot of stories while I was there. I only go there occasionally now – it's not my type of place. When I first heard that a friend of mine was in jail I felt ever so embarrassed. It's not nice what they do. When they come here and find freedom they just go berserk and you can't do anything about it.

These attitudes to criminality among Maltese were generally based on first-hand experience of café society, and personal recollection of how the respondent himself had overcome its charms and settled down to a more orderly life. Most of the non-involved settlers had circulated in club life for a period after arriving in London; and a proportion had acquired criminal convictions at the time. The fact that they had made good by their own efforts only served to convince them that it was up to the individuals themselves to look to their own reform.

The very nature of Maltese criminality was sufficient evidence to most respondents that community controls were out of the question. They appreciated that a fundamental reason for delinquency among Maltese newcomers was that they were young and single and had few permanent or close ties in Britain. In an impersonal and apparently indifferent social environment, they behaved irresponsibly because they felt accountable to no one. Their personal disorganisation reflected the lack of influence that the ethnic group had over them. It was unrealistic to suppose that the community could save them after the event. If it had been possible for the group to restrain the behaviour of young, liberated newcomers, then it *would* have done so already, and the present situation would not have arisen. The occasional attempts to counsel disorganised compatriots usually ended up by confirming this interpretation.

What can you do. I've said to them that they should be ashamed of themselves – but they turned nasty and told me to mind my own business. I don't think you can do anything about it.

I come here because people tell me it is a good country, with easy money and plenty of girl friends. Then when you come you find £11 a week is no good. So you grumble and put girls on the game and pinch the money. Because it is easy money. They are lazy. I had a chance to put a girl on once, but I was scared of jail. I wouldn't do it now (I am married); I wouldn't lower myself. When I talk to them I say they are silly and they say '£11 a week for working all day! You should get some easy money.' When I say they are silly to put girls on, they say 'Bugger off'. They take no notice. I can't do anything. I say good luck to them now. If they get caught they do the jail.

Several established migrants complained that they had gone out of their way to help Maltese in trouble to find steady jobs, but that they soon slipped back to their old ways. The old-timers wielded no real sanctions to back up their advice, and could expect little thanks. Moreover their own experience told them that in practice personal disorganisation was not overcome by being drawn into a Maltese community, but, on the contrary, by forging of relationships outside of it. So any efforts to regulate compatriots tended to be half-hearted.

London Maltese understood only too clearly the importance of marriage in providing restraints for an individual, and several respondents had deliberately used it as a means of escaping from the wild lives they had been leading as bachelors. As most Maltese marriages in Britain are contracted outside of the ethnic group, they take away from the community the very men who could by remaining in it play a central part in working out a collective way of life acceptable to migrants in Britain. But once an individual has set up a satisfactory home life of his own and has become independent of the community, the last thing he will want to do is endanger his family by reviving contacts with criminals. So people's interest in following an orderly life themselves is anti-thetical to participation in a collective response to group blame.

Enhancement of factionalism

The second dimension of fundamental weakness in the Maltese community, of disagreement over the most suitable forms of

G*

association, is also exacerbated. Although the overwhelming response of Maltese is one of individual dissociation, there are some interesting minor variations which coincide closely with the different styles of involvement within the community. Each main sector of the group has slightly different ideas about the nature of the problem, and how it may best be dealt with, and consequently their reactions tend to extend the gulfs between them, instead of providing a possible bridge for concerted action.

One such difference is between members of café society and those settlers who have withdrawn to a position of ethnic non-involvement. These sectors of the community, which together make up the bulk of the settlement, have many similarities, and can be regarded as different stages in what is basically the same process of adjustment. Both are individualistic, anti-authoritarian, and hostile to the Maltese church. Members of café society are wilder, more strident, and inward-looking; but the majority will settle down later to ethnic non-involvement, just as most of the latter have themselves passed through café society.

Reaction to the Maltese reputation maximises the contrast in attitudes of these two sectors. Members of café society were much less willing to admit the existence of a collective problem. They argued that Maltese criminality was a fabrication of the press, or that if there were any actual crime there was no group reputation arising out of it, or that if there was a group reputation then not all Maltese suffered its consequences – only the criminals themselves. Withdrawn settlers on the other hand were ready to concede the existence of a group bad name, and asserted that all Maltese found themselves obliged to share in the inter-group reprisals it invited.

This difference in response may have been related to variations in experience. Café society devotees might perhaps have come into less contact with English people, although they would perhaps be more likely to incur stereotyped treatment when they did so. The primary cause of variation in response is that the means of dissociation available to the two sets of respondents were different. The bad name is based on the exploits of the café society fraternity, and participation in this style of life is probably eased by the supposition or assertion that an individual's behaviour is not the source of problems for others. Denial of the bad name by café associators affirms their atomistic view of society, and at the same time rejects any personal culpability on the grounds that there is nothing to feel responsible *for*. Some compatriots may get themselves into trouble – though this is debatable – and should be prepared to carry the consequences. These respondents avoided any personal implication by asserting that whatever may be going on is none of their business: they blamed Maltese crime firmly on to individual perpetrators, and stated that it was up to individuals, criminal or otherwise, to look after their own interests in whatever way they thought best.[1]

Ethnically non-involved respondents were in a sense already dissociated by the fact of having withdrawn from ethnic participation; and what they felt the need to justify was their *lack* of involvement. More of them accordingly located the blame for Maltese crime within the community itself and considered that no solution from within the group was feasible, so that the most realistic means of tackling the problem would be through British governmental action, in the form of more severe penalties, deportation and so on. Since many of these interviewees regarded any form of Maltese association as dangerous, they were able to present their own withdrawal as being corporately desirable as well as personally expedient; the less association among Maltese, the smaller the volume of disorganisation to earn a bad name.[2] Such men dismissed the concept of internal community controls.

In addition to enhancing the division between established individualists and those in café society, differential reaction to the problems arising out of the collective reputation also helps seal off from the rest of the community those settlers with an interest in recreating a traditional Maltese society in London. Internal community controls administered through priests are a fundamental postulate of traditionalist thinking, so in this group of respondents there was a much greater willingness to entertain notions about corporate solutions to the problem, and a substantial minority of them were prepared to assume some collective responsibility for the situation. Middle-class, nationalist,

[1] Different types of response to the Maltese reputation are analysed in detail in Table D.4 in Appendix D.

[2] Disapproval of association was endorsed by the Malta High Commission in its administration of the work voucher system. Until the present administration took over, every attempt was made to distribute the jobs for which vouchers are granted as widely and thinly over the country as possible, to prevent concentrations building up outside of London, and a spreading of the reputation.

religiously-active respondents involved in formal Maltese associations showed a much stronger disposition to regard Maltese crime as being due to aspects of life within the community, and for declaring that the most appropriate means of dealing with it would be through ethnic group action.

These reformists were however the people with least real commitment to the community in London. They were mainly sojourners, whose reflexes were more indicative of moods and ideas in Malta than of consideration about the local situation. They were a Maltese presence rather than part of the London settlement. The programme of church-based reforms which they put forward for the community was completely contrary to the body of experience, interests and common sense of most ordinary settlers, and served only to maintain the moral and social isolation of this group. By the same token, though, this reformist sector did have the backing of traditional institutions and agencies in Malta, and their ideas accordingly were consistent with the one attempt which has been made to grasp collectively the nettle of group blame – that is the officially sponsored Catholic Mission.

Attempted reform through the Catholic Mission

A sizeable minority of middle-class Maltese associators in the 1967 sample believed that much could be done to improve the tone and prestige of the community through vigorous missionary work to bring back disorganised men into regular communion. Curiously, many of these respondents did not realise that this had been one of the principal objectives of the Malta Catholic Mission at its foundation in London fifteen years earlier, and that by the time of the investigation the task had been abandoned as hopeless. The general history of this mission has already been reviewed in Chapter II but it is worth looking at it in more detail here as it does represent an attempt at internal community reform.

The precipitating event in the setting up of the mission does in fact seem to have been the Messina Brothers affair, which gave official opinion in Malta a sharp jolt, and may have conjured up in Valletta the spectre of migration restrictions even before they were discussed in Britain.[1] A Maltese priest was posted to London

[1] The Maltese archbishop flew to London a few days after the exposure started in the British press. This suggests a very swift reaction by the church – although in reality the visit may have had some other purpose.

in 1951, and in 1953 was made official chaplain to the community, with financial support from the Maltese government. This move towards assumption of group responsibility and the cultivation of a traditional church-centred community in London to retrieve the Maltese good name, was made by Maltese outside of the London settlement. It was from the outset a response to inter-national feeling, not inter-ethnic; and the movement never adapted itself to the thinking of Maltese on the spot.

During the 1950s the chaplaincy grew into a larger mission and then, in 1963, with the assistance of the diocese of Westminster, a fully equipped church and community centre was opened in the East End as a lifeboat for the Maltese caught up in the whirl-pool of café society.

The missionaries worked on the theory that Maltese migrants turned to crime as a result of spiritual and material neglect. By providing accommodation for newcomers, and a variety of social services, the Fathers hoped they could establish themselves locally as patrons, and develop some real influence among settlers.[1] But as already pointed out the venture was not a success. The Fathers failed to find a satisfactory relationship with ordinary migrants, and their spiritual and moral impact was minimal. One priest who had been working in Britain for some years admitted this at the time of the main London enquiry.

It is practically impossible to bring them back when they are so rooted in vice. All we can do is visit them and try to bring them to their senses. But in my experience I didn't serve to get *one* back! I go to see them in prison; one said to me 'I assure you I won't go back to it when I am out', and he's out now and I saw him a week ago in Soho. He said to me 'I needed the money and my girl doesn't want to leave me.' They won't come to the Catholic Centre, and the devout

[1] The Mission was given a warm reception by Lena Jeger in the *Guardian*. 'But why do even a few, usually young men who were well-behaved, God-fearing and priest-respecting at home, get "into trouble" and what can be done to prevent it? Seeking the answers is a Franciscan Friar, Fr. Coppola, who has been living here for ten years, serving his homesick countrymen, visiting them in hospital, baptising their children, talking to the straying, encouraging the others. Now, for the first time, there is to be a sort of Malta parish in London ... this enthusiastic priest, with a few other Franciscan Friars and Sisters, is preparing a church, a community centre, a day nursery, a hostel for twenty-five young men and twenty-five young women.' Lena Jeger, 'London Maltese'.

Maltese don't want to mix with them. When I go to Soho they treat me with the greatest respect, but they try to avoid me as they are ashamed of themselves. I get letters from Malta asking me to search for husbands – and in the cafés they wink at each other not to say a word to me. But we have only a handful in trouble – two or three hundred out of twenty or thirty thousand. It used to be much worse in Cardiff!

By 1968 the mission in the East End had been closed, and the priests had moved back to headquarters in Westminster where they were concentrating on the performance of spiritual functions for middle-class visitors and transients.

This lack of impact cannot be attributed to the personal inadequacies of the Fathers. The reaction of Maltese settlers against the role of the church in Malta, the divergent approach of priests and ordinary settlers to the question of blame for Maltese criminality, the comparatively weak position occupied by priests in this country – all these eroded the stoutest efforts of the missionaries. As material patrons, they could not compete with the bosses of café society. A café or club proprietor could find someone lodging far more cheaply than could the Fathers, and was in a better market position to offer or find employment. Although such a person might not be really trusted by a newcomer, at least he did not embarrass his guests with sermons, which were often enough exactly what they had come to London to get some relief from.

The welfare and social services offered by the priests were met with cynicism by ordinary migrants – especially those most in need – and many respondents voiced criticism of the mission.

The priests won't help you. According to what I hear there is only one who comes round the East End, and all he is after is making money out of the people he houses. If they've got nowhere to sleep he's got a house with six beds in one room and charges them as though they are living in a first class hotel – £5 for a bed. *He's* the biggest Maltese crook in London. My brother was living there. That's what he does. I'm not just saying that because he's a priest; he's never helped no one. He wants people to go to church so he can make a profit out of them.[1]

One day I been so hungry I go and ask the priest for help; but he give me nothing. Not even a cup of tea. I've not met the other priest, but somebody told me he is greedy.

Soon after I came here I was destitute and went to the Fathers to help find a flat. After a while he summoned me again and said he could offer me a couple of rooms in Poplar at the top of a four storey house, for £9 a week plus £160 key money and a donation to the church. Later I saw him in the street on his bicycle and I tried to push him off it.[2]

The criminal Maltese, whom the Friars were the most anxious to confront and influence, were the most antagonistic.[3] Conversely, those Maltese who wanted sermons were not keen to associate with the criminals whom they supposed would be hanging round the Mission, and so avoided it themselves. The two main functions of the centre, of rescuing the wayward and ministering to the faithful, did not dovetail at all neatly. The job of the Fathers was more difficult than in Malta where, although the church could not prevent vice, it was at least in a position to restrict it to a few areas where it could be covered up and denied. In London the priests neither wielded sanctions to control Maltese nor had power to conceal their criminality for the comfort of the faithful. The crime, after all, was what the Mission was supposed to be doing something about.

The Fathers tried to resolve their dilemma by acknowledging the existence of crime and the need for reform but playing it down as far as they could. This is where an inflated estimate of the size of the settlement was convenient. A specific volume of crime looks much better shared among 30,000 Maltese in London than among 3000 or less. But in practice this sort of propaganda defeated its own purpose. The main audience for it were the few faithful who did go to Mission functions, and the over-

[1] Some of these allegations are grounded in reality. The Centre had to borrow quite a lot of money to establish itself, and was obliged to charge quite heavily for some services, in order to discharge its capital debt.

[2] Statement by a family man with Maltese wife and several children, who had subsequently lapsed from religious activity.

[3] Two-thirds of serious offenders interviewed expressed strong sentiments against the Maltese priests in London.

estimate of the settlement made them feel their isolation and the lack of impact of the Fathers all the more acutely.

The Fathers' inability to exercise traditional authority in a secular society was cumulative, failure promoting further failure. Several respondents who had started out with favourable attitudes towards the church had lapsed in London because of disillusion with the performance of the priests. So the attempted missionary function gravely hindered the practice of ordinary religious activities.

But perhaps the major factor preventing the missionaries from having any real success with ordinary settlers was the refusal of the Maltese church as an institution to understand the resentment which many migrants harboured towards it, and the escapist nature of Maltese migration to Britain. A large proportion of Maltese here blame the church for the ills besetting their island. They feel that if only the church had put more resources into capital developments, practical education and so on, and less on magnificent buildings and expensive rituals, then Malta would be a far better place to live in.[1] They condemn hallowed Maltese institutions as being inappropriate in a modern world. And although many respondents attached primary blame for Maltese criminality to the individuals concerned, most of them judged that in the last resort everything was the fault of the church. It was because of the church that the individuals had become what they were.

> I suppose it's all the fault of the church really for bringing them up wrong. They're afraid of change as they don't want to lose their position there. Everyone is Catholic in Malta. You are brought up to believe that you are committing a sin everytime you step out of your home. So over here persons are like birds let out of a cage. Other nationalities don't do this [living on prostitution] on the scale that Maltese people do.

This analysis is of course diametrically opposed to that around which the Catholic Centre was organised. Religiously active Maltese were more prone than others to cite the Maltese community as responsible for the crime in London; but they did

---

[1] An article by John Greally in the *Catholic Herald* on 17 June 1966 quoted a number of Maltese migrant workers who were very critical of the role of the church in Malta, and who blamed their individual and national problems on to it.

not mean by this that Maltese institutions were at fault. In their view the causes of disorganisation were negligent parents who failed to instil values into children, or established settlers who did not bother to look after newcomers, or even officials who had not properly checked the credentials of potential migrants. Everything could be traced back to human error and negligence; and the reforms for which this group was prepared to regard itself as collectively responsible were simple matters of rectifying mistakes and repairing damage brought about by ineffectual implementation of traditional institutions and procedures. The fundamental validity of these institutions was unquestionable.

The remedial programme which these attitudes inform was therefore so straightforward that it amounted to little more than a reiteration of the problem. A senior priest interviewed in 1968 summarised the task ahead in these terms:

> Most of the Maltese who are in trouble here abandon family life on account of the liberty they find themselves in here. A man on his own here feels lonely so he then tries to attach himself on the first occasion that comes along. He is far from home, and can live with a girl easily. What we [the Catholic Centre] must do is give good advice to Maltese here to keep them in the same old traditions that they were brought up in, in Malta.

This was hardly a realistic platform for corporate action, and it is not surprising that settlers with experience of life in London should have been so unenthusiastic. Those aware of the history of the mission considered that this sort of approach had already proved inadequate.

Even some of the reformist respondents may not really have rated very highly the chances of a successful operation. It must be suspected that a major attraction of the religious reform programme for many middle-class Maltese was that – apart from being a purely conventional reflex – it helped absolve them from the need to think about doing something themselves. It was easy to leave the initiative to the priests in this way; whereas middle-class Maltese would be reluctant to become personally involved with lower classes, especially the criminal element, this role would be congenial to the religious. It is gratifying to a devout priest to be called to assume responsibility before God for other people's weaknesses, provided there is no question of also sharing blame. And this was exactly the role available to the missionaries in this programme of action. The faithful Maltese in Malta who knew about and supported them would not have dreamt of holding the church to blame for the disorganisation that had taken place in Britain. So the Fathers could go about their business in London unimpeded by any sense of personal or institutional guilt.[1] Their mission was simply a rescue or salvaging operation, undertaken in charity, and underwritten by a finely-developed awareness of the inevitability of sin. The fact that most Maltese in London did not see things in the same terms maintained the deep gulf between them and the priests.

The approach of the priests may have been inappropriate to the problem, but there was no real alternative basis for internal community controls. One or two reformist respondents appreciated that the priests were in a weak position here, and suggested compromise projects in which the work of the Catholic Centre would be supplemented by secular social workers. But if the inefficiency of religious controls is conceded, the rationale for internal group action is undermined. If the priests had no authority the emphasis had to be shifted to agencies which did have some, such as local authorities and the state. This was the position taken by withdrawn settlers and MLP supporters on the issue, who located *blame* for crime within the Maltese community, but saw the best source of controls in action through local British institutions.[2]

---

[1] There was one priest who did substantially agree with criticisms made by settlers about the church in Malta, and he was the most popular and influential among ordinary settlers. But his views made his position within the Mission ambiguous and insecure. It is very doubtful whether the Maltese church could be flexible enough to allow open discussion of such viewpoints. And anyway it is unlikely that anything which the missionaries did in London as individuals would be sufficient to dissociate them in the minds of migrants from the position and attitudes of the parent national church. The healing of the MLP-church rift may in the long run enhance their standing; and the church is certainly the natural basis for an organised community, and the best vessel for conveying internal group sanctions. But it is improbable that in a largely secular society the Fathers could ever repeat the successes of Maltese priests in Catholic and Muslim countries.

[2] MLP supporters were willing to help compatriots where they could, by serving as court interpretors for newcomers, helping them find jobs and so on. But their general political philosophy, which located responsibilities within the territorial community, was antagonistic to the concept of an inward-looking, separate community; so they were fundamentally opposed to ethnic group controls. This was consistent with, and gave some additional justification to, the individualism of settlers here.

It is conceivable that traditional community controls could develop in the future – though at the moment the priests are not seeking this type of role. As immigration restrictions have become harsher, with more extensive deportation powers, the hand of the missionaries is however being strengthened. For where they can act as mediating patrons and guarantors their power within a community is much greater. Severe migration controls can give migrants more of a stake in their adoptive country, and those who want a secure life are provided with a real incentive to submit to group authority and impose the same on compatriots who may endanger the common interest. As migrants' individual rights are progressively removed, they become more dependent on those which may be available to them as members of a corporation.

All this has happened in the past in other Maltese settlements, and it could happen in Britain too. But for it to do so either a revival of migration would be needed, or a much stronger emphasis on descent in future British citizenship legislation than contained even in the 1971 Immigration Act. Most of the current settlers have no need for the priests' assistance and thus no compelling reason to submit to their authority. There is accordingly little immediate prospect of the missionaries establishing the sort of local influence which they came here intending to create.

VII

IN CONCLUSION:
MINORITIES IN BRITAIN

The preceding chapters illustrate that the actual response of
Maltese in London to the experience of group blame does not
conform at all closely to the general minority reaction postulated
in Chapter V. The immediate effect of shared liability on the
Maltese is an exacerbation of disorder and criminality. Far from
promoting compliance to moral and legal norms, the mechanics
of collective responsibility reinforce those very tendencies,
deriving primarily from the nature of the migratory process,
which lead to community disorganisation.

As already pointed out, it is perhaps misleading to suppose that
group blame does normally result in social control in the narrow
sense. The main influence of collective responsibility is to
reinforce a receiving group's minority status. Whether or not it
is able to regulate its members makes little difference in the last
analysis to the designation of their behaviour as anti-social. A
disorderly minority can be portrayed as a public nuisance; an
orderly one as subversive. Either kind can have something to
answer for to a majority.

What therefore is distinctive in the Maltese case is not so much
the failure of the group to regulate its disorderly component –
which is perhaps in some degree a commonplace – but the extent
to which this has entailed a virtual breakdown in the life of the
rest of the community. The operation of collective responsibility
depends upon a certain level of group solidarity, since any desire
to exercise mutual controls must be grounded in some sense of
mutual dependence. A group with some original cohesion will
probably find its solidarity enhanced by the experience of group
blame; for even if it is unable to bring a troublesome element
under control, the community can cushion the law-abiding

members against harsher points of inter-group conflict, and prevent their further demoralisation.

The London Maltese do not seem to reach this initial threshold of basic solidarity, both because of the individualistic nature of migration to Britain, and because of the comparative ease with which migrants can become independent of compatriots and drift away from the ethnic group. Most Maltese can soon learn to look after themselves economically, sexually and to some extent socially; so ties between them are often purely sentimental. Such bonds are too slender to bear the sort of demands made on them by imputed collective responsibility, and become even more attenuated if they are exploited in this way. No reliable procedures or channels exist within the community for passing on sanctions; and this fact is so obvious to most Maltese that very few of them have ever wasted any energy in this direction. Consequently there is no real incentive to defend ethnic honour, either by mutual vigilance or through an anti-defamation programme; and the main attempt to do so originated outside of the local settlement, at the instigation and expense of public authorities in Malta afraid of losing a valuable migration outlet. Maltese in London have steadfastly denied communal responsibilities and have, instead, endeavoured with even greater determination to improve their positions on a personal basis.

So the experience of shared discrimination has not mobilised and cemented the community; it has confirmed and hastened dissociation from it, especially by those older and more settled migrants with a stake in this country, and who might have formed the backbone of a viable ethnic association. Joint moral accountability has not created common interests which can override individualism and factionalism; both have in fact been sharpened by it.

It is important to keep in mind how far this rapid assimilation is from being a natural and easy process for the individuals passing through it. Quite apart from any ordeals and privations of the disorganised life beforehand, the act of dissociation by which the new identity is sought may itself be extremely disagreeable. The massive renunciation of national origin by Maltese migrants betrays a very low level of morale throughout the community. Ethnic honour is almost non-existent; many Maltese themselves accept as broadly true the stereotype of the vicious ponce, and in the course of the London enquiry several children of respondents remarked, presumably echoing their fathers, that the Maltese are a 'rotten people'. What is worse, this dissociation may not be entirely successful, and many settlers who have taken the decision to abandon their ethnicity find that they are still sometimes treated as Maltese, and are obliged to live out their lives in Britain in an ambiguous status.

This problem applies less to their children, of course, and the signs are that most of the second and third generation will complete the transition and participate fully in the life of local society. Few Maltese in London think of their offspring as anything other than English, and there is little danger of this being disputed by other people; for even where the mother is also Maltese, most children can pass quite readily. The fact remains though that this act of passing, or rather the need to do so, implies that being Maltese still leads to painful experiences that are worth avoiding.

It is therefore altogether too bland to regard the assimilation of Maltese as a spontaneous, even instinctive, process of absorption. The conspiracy of silence which has for so long enveloped the Maltese rests on the assumption that if they are indeed assimilating, then fundamentally there could not be much wrong. This is very wide of the mark. On the evidence of this present study it seems clear that any 'assimilating' tendency the Maltese have is in fact intimately bound up with and dependent on their criminality and reputation. The individualism which prompts early adoption of a new ethnic identity is the same spirit as that which leads to disorganised behaviour. Furthermore, the *strength* of the desire for personal assimilation is a direct consequence and function of the virulent group reputation which the problem of criminality has created. The difficulties experienced by Maltese as a result of their image are not just a marginal factor in Maltese life in Britain; they are severe and central to their situation, and it is largely because of the apparent impossibility of salvaging ethnic honour that Maltese are so eager to abandon ethnic loyalties by seeking incorporation to the majority group. For an individual and his descendants, this appears a quick and conclusive escape route from a highly uncomfortable minority status.

As the process of incorporation is not automatic or natural, it is not necessarily self-sustaining. In this respect it is important to distinguish between the implications of this escapist assimilation for those individuals who actually pursue it, and for the group as a whole, since this course of action is by its nature not equally available to all group members. Thus if the intensity of the urge to assimilate with the majority is contingent on the existence of a vicious collective reputation, some continuing community may be essential to the maintenance of the process. If dissociation is painful and is undertaken more readily when there is something even less tolerable to be avoided, then personal incorporation to the host group would be expected to take place most rapidly at times when visible members of the minority were attracting the most hostile treatment. Also the act of dissociation by those individuals in a position to carry it through is itself likely to make things worse for remaining group members. During the 1950s, it was partly as a result of the massive dissociation and assimilation of mature Maltese, in response to stereotyping and imputed group liability, that Maltese criminality became so blatant. For such moderating influence as the older men did possess, albeit limited, was withheld. And their failure to stand up as visible contradictions of the vicious stereotype allowed public antagonism to fasten all the more tightly on Maltese who were identifiable.

Conversely, as the image improves, the impulse to dissociate may weaken. The personal assimilation of relatively mature Maltese in the 1950s was continuously provoked by the exploits of rebellious Maltese youngsters flocking to Britain to sow their wild oats, who kept ethnic honour sullied. But the migration controls introduced by the Commonwealth Immigrants Acts have hampered the recruitment of adventurous young men to café society, and have started to dismantle the vicious circle of criminality and group disorganisation. By the mid-1960s, this had set in motion an amelioration in the group reputation which might eventually have allowed the emergence of a more respectable and self-confident ethnic community.

For as the group reputation declined in severity, some resurgence of communal pride might begin to take place. With more family migration, and fewer incentives to dissociation, the organisation and solidarity of the community could be expected to revive, further hastening the abatement in disorganised criminality, and eventually permitting a facsimile Maltese culture to take root here. As the difficulties arising out of the group reputation eased, they might even come within the scope of collective action, opening the way for movement towards a more corporate, inward-looking community, as happened in the Mediterranean settlements in similar circumstances.

However in this case the condition of the community is unlikely to completely reverse itself in this way, as in the event the reduction in casual migration has not been accompanied by commensurate growth in regulated movement of responsible migrants. At the end of the 1960s the indications were that Maltese migration to Britain was stopping altogether. Some of the reasons for this, like the overall drop in emigration from Malta, and unemployment in Britain, may be temporary phenomena. But more fundamentally it does now seem as though the sort of Maltese who are able to enter this country under regulated conditions are not the sort who really want to, or indeed have ever wanted to in appreciable numbers. Maltese have mainly come to this country in the search for individual freedom. When this is not necessary, or not possible, few will come at all. Maltese families prefer warmer climates if they have to leave Malta; and only if there is a large frustrated demand in Malta for passages to Australia, as occurred briefly in the early 1960s, will Maltese families seriously contemplate coming north to Britain. And even then this will often be for the traditional reason of using it as a jumping-off point for some other part of the globe. The Maltese bad name in London may have been some deterrent in its own right to respectable settlement here; but it has been a last straw, not a prime consideration, and its removal would not materially affect the desirability of Britain as a site for permanent family life.

Thus over the last few years immigration from Malta has declined to below the level needed to replace losses to the existing community, through death, re-migration and assimilation; and the chances of a more coherent community emerging in the future must be dwindling. By the time that the collective reputation has subsided to a point where it no longer serves as an incentive to dissociation, the majority of existing settlers and their children will have effectively done so already. A small residual colony of middle-class sojourners may be enabled to celebrate Maltese feasts with higher heads than at present, but they will make little impression on public opinion, and even less of a permanent contribution to the population of this country. So in all probability any real ethnic grouping here will soon have ceased to exist, and escapist assimilation will have resulted in the fading away of the whole minority group in a single generation.

The significance of Maltese individualism

The fact that most people in this country of Maltese origin and descent will soon become incorporated to the majority can only at the most superficial level be seen as a vindication of the traditional liberal model of immigrant behaviour. This individualistic solution to the problem of minority status has been possible only because of the coincidence of a peculiar constellation of factors which is not likely to hold for many minorities. The escapist character of Maltese emigration, the comparatively small size of the community and its internal factionalism, the cultural and racial affinity of the migrants with the host population – allowing a high rate of intermarriage and physical absorption – and the rapid emergence of a severely damaging group reputation; each of these influences has made an indispensable contribution to the rate of assimilation, by maximising the incentives and opportunities for Maltese to perceive themselves as independent and isolated actors, in command of their personal destinies, instead of as members of a cohesive and consensual ethnic group.

It is misleading to define the individualism of these migrants as normal, and equally so to regard the process of assimilation which it stimulates as orderly. For it is when the young Maltese are most free, between cutting themselves off from parents and parental surrogates in the ethnic community, and before binding themselves by marriage into British society, that their behaviour is most disorganised and anarchic. Without stable and demanding personal relationships to give boundaries and meaning to their lives, the migrants find themselves in an egoistic condition where objectives become more volatile and personal interests increasingly hard to calculate and assess. Life in a social system occupied by unattached individuals is extremely disorienting for the participants, and it is worth recalling from the discussion in Chapter IV that the crucial step in assimilation for many Maltese, marriage with a local girl, is undertaken as a voluntary curbing of personal freedom, a furnishing of the individualistic vacuum with constraints to render it habitable. Not only is this freedom difficult to bear for long; it is also corrosive of social order, for migrants in their individualistic stage are receptive neither to formalised, public sanctions on their behaviour nor to inter-personal mutual controls.

It is therefore suggestive that it should be just the type of behaviour which results from this anarchic individualism which eventually encounters a *communalistic* reaction, attempting to influence individuals through presumed or imposed group loyalties, on the part of the British majority. For regardless of the self-perception of the migrants, the dominant majority does *not* consider the Maltese to be a mass of independent individuals. This fact, perhaps more than any other finding in the study, has far-reaching implications for the liberal analysis of British society, both in relation to immigrant groups and to social and political relations in general. These implications are obscured in the first instance by the fact that, paradoxically, the highly collectivist attitudes of the British serve in this case to arouse even further the individualism of the Maltese, as it is the majority group's refusal to judge Maltese *as* individuals which ultimately presses them to denial of Maltese identity. Only when the unusual nature of the Maltese response to group blame is appreciated can it be understood that their propensity to assimilation is in the last analysis sustained by forces in the British social system which in the case of most minorities would help to inhibit it.

However, it is at the same time precisely because the Maltese tendency to individualism reverses the normal effect of majority sentiments and behaviour that the Maltese case study is able to provide such valuable evidence of the real nature of British attitudes. The popular concept of the Maltese community as a cohesive group is so far from being an accurate reflection of its real nature that our attention is inevitably drawn to the ideological character of British majority views about minority groups. Where a minority does actually exhibit solidarity and internal organisation then it may be difficult to realise that this cohesion is in the interests of the dominating group, and may indeed often be the outcome of discrimination by the majority. It is popularly assumed that ethnic groups are exclusive because they want to be; and even Freedman, as shown earlier, suggests that British Jews are projecting their own feelings when they suppose that they are judged collectively by the British majority.[1] But on the evidence of the

---

[1] See the passage referred to on p. 167, Chapter V.

1969 study of non-Maltese attitudes, it seems clear that the majority representation is pre-eminent; for where the minority in question is weakly articulated, like the Maltese, the exploitative and exclusive nature of the presumption of solidarity stands out starkly. And, as further indicated by that survey, the conceptual-isation of the Maltese as a cohesive group cannot be dismissed as mere error or pre-judgment arising out of ignorance, as it is adhered to even more tenaciously among people who know Maltese personally and have Maltese friends.[1]

It is important to note that this exclusive attitude towards minority groups on the part of the British is not necessarily racialist in nature. Many respondents in the 1969 enquiry who supported the principle of collective liability did not regard Maltese individuals as distinguishable from the British population. So their belief in the need to take ethnicity into account in the allocation and organisation of social and political rights cannot be regarded as simply deriving from erroneous biological assumptions.

Some theorists, for example John Rex,[2] would argue that this sort of distinction is not worth making, and that any ascription of group status or rights according to involuntary criteria should be condemned as racialist. But this proposal would have the effect of confusing two completely separate issues – the descriptive and scientifically amenable question of the distribution of human characteristics, and the prescriptive issue of which legal principles and conventions are preferable in the ordering of social relations.[3] By lumping the two together in this way, what Rex appears to be doing is setting up a position from which he can hope to discredit as equally odious and irrational any statements which do not conform wholeheartedly to universalistic, individualistic criteria. His real concern is not so much with combating racialism – which he defines so broadly as to render meaningless – as with

---

[1] See Tables 6 (p. 153) and F.5 in Appendix F.

[2] John Rex, *Race, Colonialism and the City*, Appendix to Ch. 17 ('Letter to Professor Michael Banton').

[3] As pointed out by Benn and Peters (*Social Principles and the Democratic State*, p. 116), discrimination based on purely prescriptive criteria is morally irrefutable: 'Impartiality, as a criterion of morality, implies only that all those who are the proper objects of moral consideration be considered equally: but since it is the most general or the ultimate criterion, we cannot go behind it to show who are the proper objects of moral consideration.'

wielding the slur of racialism against anyone bold enough to utter propositions antithetical to dogmatic liberalism.

This is significant, because it is arguable that the real issue underlying the crisis in community relations in Britain is *not* racialism as such, but the more fundamental question of whether liberal individualism still provides a relevant language for social and political relations. As the debates on immigration and race relations have unfolded, it has become increasingly evident that the values of a large proportion of the British public are now basically anti-liberal, and indeed may never have been anything else. When the findings of this present study are set in the general context of class and political relations in Britain, they lend support to the view that ethnic consciousness and particularism have been much more important in our social history than liberal accounts, beguiled by the notion of a homogeneous native population, have generally credited. This conclusion has widespread repercussions for the prospects of inter-group relations in this country, and although this is not the place for a detailed discussion of the problem, it is possible to outline the main issues briefly, in order to show the full implications of the Maltese case.

Liberalism as an élite ideology

Liberalism is the declared value-system of modern western democracy, and its basic premises are ostensibly shared by many modern societies. British people however are disposed to entertain the idea that its principles are especially strongly rooted in our way of life, and that whereas in many countries they are merely pious ideals, in Britain they represent a practical and well-tried system, understood and respected by all the main political formations. Consequently liberal intellectuals have welcomed the immigration of colonial citizens, as an opportunity to demonstrate to the rest of the world the superiority of our own institutions in setting a context for a peaceful multi-racial society.[1]

A society which has provided the model for other societies by evolving democratic forms that respect the individual, and which has known how to combine tolerance with dissent, now has the chance to set a further example by proving that men of many races can live together in justice and harmony.

[1] E. J. B. Rose (ed.), *Colour and Citizenship*, p. 756.

The cornerstone of liberalism is commitment to the concept of the 'open society', in which all men are free to determine for themselves their own destinies, and are at the same time seen as being able to serve the common good most effectively by seeking to express themselves fully as individuals. This happy coincidence of private with public interest hinges on the principle of unrestricted individual competition for important and prestigious social positions. Men who can develop their capacities freely will, it is assumed, feel a stake in the social order; and their legitimate efforts to gain honour in society will ensure that the most capable come to perform the most arduous and exacting roles, thereby maximising efficiency to the benefit of all. In order to bring about this desirable state of affairs, liberal social policies aim at creating conditions of universalism, in which everyone is enabled as far as possible to compete as a free individual, on an equal basis, and to enter voluntarily and rationally into associations and alliances with others sharing similar objectives and interests. Arbitrary and exclusive social divisions, like nationality, are regarded as hindrances to the full implementation of universalism, and are to be tolerated only for so long as unavoidable. The ultimate goal is a society of all humanity, in which each can unimpededly promote the welfare of all.[1]

In spite of its humanitarian claim to impart benefits to everyone, this individualistic philosophy has less to offer some sectors of society than others. At a material level the claim to promote general betterment has some substance, since with economic expansion we can all become richer than our forbears. But it breaks down when it comes to status and prestige, which must always be distributed unequally in a 'zero-sum' manner. Liberalism cannot overcome the logic of this, and if it has any impact on the matter at all it is probably to sharpen inequalities, as the insistence on the need for competition to get the best people recruited to élite positions, implicitly devalues the social contribution of everyone else.

Liberal individualism offers an élite a highly flattering picture

[1] 'The root principle of liberalism is not merely freedom in general, but the specific, personal freedom of the individual, even the self-imposed obligation, to make *no* unconditional commitments to *any* organisation. All loyalties to movements or organisation, parties or states, are, for the liberal, conditional upon his own principles and conscience.' C. W. Mills, *The Marxists,* p. 24.

of itself, as the product of a bracing competitive system in which the fittest and most useful people find themselves at the pinnacle of a prestige hierarchy, performing tasks (as only *they* could) which are advantageous not just to themselves, but to the whole of society or even humanity. Not only are their egos gratified, but an apparently impregnable justification for their privileged position is thrown in too. For if it is submitted that society is open, with equal opportunities for all, then the masses can have only themselves to blame for their inferior status – either for not having tried hard enough, which is avoidable and reprehensible, or for being inherently incapable, which is jolly hard luck.[1]

So by the same token, liberalism is not at all congenial outside of the élite. If the unsuccessful masses endorsed this philosophy, they would be obliged to see themselves as morally and intellectually inferior, and heavily indebted to a talented élite who, on their behalf, exercised the more demanding social activities. There is no joy in this; and in any case it does not correspond to the social reality they experience, in which the existing élite is in practice seen to be careful to preserve for its own members and their offspring a better than equal competitive chance. Even if society were to be made truly 'open', it is doubtful whether the doctrine of individualism would be more attractive to ordinary people, as it is not rational to commit oneself heavily in a highly competitive game, in which there are few winners and many losers, unless the dice are heavily loaded for one. If they favour someone else it is better to withhold one's stake. Competitive individualism is something which only members of a protected élite can indulge in with confidence,[2] and most participants in a social system would be well advised to embrace a different kind of philosophy.

And in practice they do seem to. Even in Britain, where liberal values have enjoyed almost unchallenged formal hegemony in

[1] The legitimacy of liberal ideology is not undermined by the presumed existence of inherent, and therefore involuntary, differences in human talent and behaviour. In an open society, the rewards of membership to *all* are seen as outweighing differentials according to social utility. Social justice can permit some disparities, and (it is asserted) reasonable men could be expected to voluntarily accept membership of such a society even before knowing what talents they might be born with and what social position they could occupy. See W. G. Runciman, *Relative Deprivation and Social Justice,* pp. 263 ff.

[2] Just as in the economic sphere, the liberal proponents of free trade were thickest on the ground and loudest in their declamations when British industry dominated the world.

social and political affairs, and where – if anywhere – they might be expected to be widely diffused among the general population, a large proportion of the citizenry does in fact appear to subscribe to an alternative set of social values, in conflict with individualism at almost every point. As would be expected, the main focus of the contrasting value-system is located in working-class culture, and specifically in its fraternalistic aspects which assert the priority of communal interests over individual fulfilment and self-expression.[1] In this milieu, individual opportunism, the byword of liberalism, is seen as anti-social and dangerous nonsense threatening the fabric of social relations that give life meaning; since while some selfish and ambitious people may be able to better themselves socially, it is appreciated realistically that this can never be true for many in a group, so that success for the few necessarily takes place at the expense of the rest. The moral person therefore is one who seeks his own satisfaction in contributing to the well-being, security and good name of his community, and in sharing the enjoyment of jointly experienced benefits.

There is no reason to suppose that this fraternalistic philosophy is in the last analysis less self-seeking than individualism, or requires a different type of human nature. It is more to the point to see them as expressing opposite strategies, appropriate to different circumstances, for achieving fundamentally similar aims. A powerful, privileged or talented person can get by in most situations on his own resources, and individualism provides a convenient doctrine for laying an exclusive claim to benefits accrued. Less advantaged people stand a greater chance of acquiring valued rights, or even of just hanging on to them, if they act in solidary combination, and press their personal claims through the exercise of group membership. So, although fraternal communities do provide some purely intrinsic satisfactions for members, such as conviviality and the assurance of some mutual personal respect, they are at the same time a means by which their members seek access to scarce resources in the way most appropriate to them. The potential rewards of collective action are smaller than those for freely acting individuals, as the pooling of interests in a corporation entails the division of any spoils. But this is made up for by greater security, as a loyal member can expect

[1] See for example Richard Hoggart, *The Uses of Literacy*, 1958; J. Klein, *Samples from English Culture*, 1965; E. Bott, *Family and Social Network*, 1957.

some automatic entitlement to a share of the resources commanded by the group.

The anti-liberal nature of the communalism of the British masses is usually ignored by the convention of assuming it to be a manifestation of 'class' cohesion, emergent in conflictual opposition to the hierarchical domination of a capitalist élite. And some substance is given to this belief by the fact that its instrumental collectivism is exercised most obviously and frequently in trade union activities. If class is seen as the natural axis of communal sentiments and formations, these can be dressed up in the guise of rational, voluntary associations, and accommodated without undue embarrassment to an individualistic analysis of British society. But this interpretation completely distorts the real character of the alternative philosophy, which is collectivistic, particularistic, and in the last resort deeply ethnocentric.

A communalistic social philosophy moves inexorably away from the principle of universalism. True liberals believe that it is possible for individuals to serve and identify with all of humanity. A communally-oriented person on the other hand has to take a more sectional view of things, since if meaning can only be found through participation in a specific group, the definition of outsider groups is obviously vital. Communal identifications are invariably exclusive, and to some extent competitive, for otherwise no practical expression or measure of group welfare or loyalty would be possible. Consequently communalistic moral evaluations are likewise inherently relativistic.

This relativism holds on two levels. Firstly moral judgments are relative to group membership, and secondly the conceptualisation of group membership itself may be relative to the situation a person finds himself in. In almost all societies group memberships tend to fit together into structures of 'pyramidal-segmentary' loyalties,[1] in which members of any specified community are able to see themselves as in some contexts owing prior loyalty to constituent sub-groups, and in yet others to higher-level more inclusive collectivities. This relativity of identification gives individuals some room to manipulate group allegiances without abandoning the communalistic principle of axiomatic, unquestioning loyalty to group. Thus while people's places may be fixed

[1] For a discussion see Robert A. Levine and Donald T. Campbell, *Ethnocentrism: Theories of Conflict, Ethnic Attitudes and Group Behaviour*, 1972. In particular ch. 4.

involuntarily in the sense that they should not change their position in the general scheme of inter-group relations, it is quite feasible for them to expand or contract the boundaries of the group to which they declare prime allegiance, according to whether they are trying to gain access to a group commanding valuable resources, or to exclude fraternalistic claims to some already under their effective control. The politics of instrumental collectivism are therefore played out around highly particularistic conceptions of social good; and even though the whole world may be populated by brothers, in practice some brothers turn out inescapably to be closer, and share more interests, than others.

The natural axis for communal identifications is ethnic or tribal, as the language of common origin and shared destiny provides at the same time a perfect medium for expressing the enduring and permanent nature that communal relationships ought to have and a conveniently segmentary framework for gradations of group membership and solidarity.[1] This may appear to have very limited relevance for a study of Britain. Political modernisation is conventionally defined in terms of a progressive movement away from ascriptive loyalties towards rational, universalistic association; and this country is widely believed to have travelled the furthest along that road. Apart from the marginal case of the Irish, the British population is celebrated for its ethnic homogeneity, and sectional identifications are presumed to survive only in the vestigial forms of music-hall jokes and occasional rivalry in sports. But as I will try to demonstrate briefly below, this assumed detribalisation of the British people may have been more apparent than real, so that the whole edifice of individualistic theory is founded on an illusion.

Liberalism and imperialism

The ethnic homogeneity of the British population is generally

---

[1] A number of studies have suggested that tribal societies organise inter-group relations around the idea of descent not because groups *are* related in this way, but because the idiom of kinship provides a convenient fiction for organising and understanding political obligations and behaviour. See for example Laura Bohannan, 'A Genealogical Charter', *Africa*, vol. 22. Weber makes the same sort of point in a more general, sweeping manner. 'All history shows how easily political action can give rise to the belief in blood relationship, unless gross differences of anthropological type impede it.' *Economy and Society*, Roth and Wittich edition, 1968, vol. 1, p. 393.

H

held to be due in some way to the development of urban, industrial society, which created new, universalistic sets of interests, such as class in relation to shared position in the productive process, which superimposed and obliterated sectional loyalties.[1] The various accounts which follow this line have in common an individualistic basis, as they posit the gradual rationalisation and internationalisation of individual action. In socialist theory, for instance, the conflict between capital and labour is expected to transcend national boundaries. As capital, which abhors artificial restrictions, becomes ever more international in its ramifications, so too should be the class consciousness and the collectivism of the workers opposed to it.

Actual social and political behaviour in Britain does not begin to measure up to these expectations. There is perhaps an unparalleled adherence to universalistic criteria in political life here, and class is more relevant in national politics than in any other country. But this class solidarity, among the lower class at any rate, does not seem to derive from a rational appreciation of interests, so much as out of an *alliance* between local, particularistic communities, and is therefore essentially a segmentary type of grouping, suggesting a *suspension* rather than an obliteration of sectional loyalties. The working-class communities in Britain which exhibit the strongest class consciousness and greatest commitment to fraternalism are precisely those in which there is the most powerful sense of regional identity mediating, and logically preceding, membership of the national class movement.[2] The wider unity of this group is therefore not axiomatic, but contingent on a convergence of sectional interests; and in order to explain the apparent detribalisation of the British people what we need to do is to specify a long-term community of interest which would have enabled the component segments to come together for a sustained period in recent history.

The experience of empire clearly meets this requirement, as the joint domination of alien groups by a combination of British

[1] Robert R. Alford, *Party and Society*, 1964. See in particular the Preface, chapter 6 and Conclusion.

[2] Alford (op. cit., p. 292) misses the significance of this, and ends up by arguing that strong class loyalties in, say, Wales imply that sectional loyalties are *weak*. However, class voting does not mean that regional and ethnic ties are weak, necessarily. The success of the British Labour movement has been due in large part to its success in *subsuming* regional sentiments to class action.

tribes would obviously have been such a rewarding and prestigious exercise that a sinking of internal rivalries is easily accounted for. This hypothesis also furnishes a more convincing explanation of recent trends in British political life. On the conventional view, continuing industrialisation in Britain should have lead to a steady growth in rational voluntary loyalties and associations, whereas in fact there has been a resurgence of regionalism and Celtic nationalism. If tribal unity is seen as contingent on over-riding common benefits, this is understandable. For with the loss of empire, the main sources of wealth and status left are now *internal* to Britain, so that the dormant issues of how they should be distributed between competing segments of the nation are bound to revive and assume once more a primary significance.[1] When the wealth of Britain was augmented by imperial tribute, and colonial and military service provided wide avenues to power and status for ambitious men from all parts of the country, internal disparities were less obvious and created less sense of discrimination. But over the last decade or so regional groupings which receive less than their due proportion of the national income, or are relatively poorly represented in the national élite, have shown an increasing tendency to define themselves as minorities, even as exploited colonies, inside the nation-state. As the shared glory of empire continues to fade, further demands for some measure of self-determination can be expected, and the particularistic, ethnocentric disposition of working-class solidarities will be exposed more clearly.

The reopening of these ancient fissures in British society, revealing purely domestic minorities, has been rather over-shadowed by the simultaneous arrival of new minorities from former colonies. These immigrants have been given a poor reception on the whole, and this has been generally attributed to 'racialism' on the part of the British population. As I suggested

[1] One of the few authorities on race relations in Britain to begin to take the imperial experience into account in the analysis of domestic social structure is Philip Mason. As he puts it: 'Now the question is how to transform what was once an essentially homogeneous nation-state into a society in which a variety of different groups can live side by side. The old nation had been united by a common culture, a language, a pride in past achievement, a sense of imperial power.... Regional and ethnic differences had been forgotten in the aura of the successful nation-state but today they revive; if the colonies are independent – ask the regions – why are not we?' *Patterns of Dominance,* p. 330.

earlier, though, it is misleading to suppose that British attitudes
to immigrants are intrinsically racialist, in the sense of flowing
from a belief in the inherent individual inferiority of coloured
people; and the revival of exclusive solidarities within the British
nation, which are ethnocentric without being racialist, perhaps
strengthens this contention. The level of discrimination experienced by, say, Celts is admittedly much less than that for colonial
immigrants; but this can be explained readily enough in terms of
segmentary principles of relative closeness of common histories,
and shared interests, without any necessary recourse to notions
of biological inferiority or incompatibility.[1]

Ethnocentrism can certainly take on racialist overtones, but
logically it does not need to do so unless its initial premise of the
prior rights of a group of people with feelings of common origin
and destiny to extend preferential treatment towards each other
is placed in question. This sort of challenge will typically originate
from a doctrine of individualism, and so in practice racialism is
likely to be generated as a response to liberal demands for the
opening-up of society, and to be a dressing-up of the communal
sentiments of an under-class in a guise which meets some of the
conventions of the élite philosophy. Liberalism argues that the
enjoyment of differential rewards should be dependent on the
contribution made by individuals to society, and it assumes that
the capacity to make this contribution varies. Racialism asserts
that a whole *category* of people are inherently incapable of performing certain socially important roles, so that it is justifiable to
withhold from them the opportunities to do so. Thus as an
ideology racialism consists of a translation into collectivist terms
of the Darwinist, élitist conception of human ability which
underlies liberal humanist thought.

This analysis of racialism fits in closely with Blalock's recent
proposal that inter-group discrimination can be understood best
as a deviant response to frustration in the context of formally

[1] The Irish are a slight exception here, as they have never really seen themselves
as British and yet, as a result of the arrival of new and more alien minorities, they
have become incorporated into the category 'British' in English cities in recent
years. It would seem that the entry of relative outsiders has in some contexts
served to hold the British together, and hindered the process of segmentation, by
importing the imperial situation into British cities. This has had the effect of
drawing *into* the British group that Celtic minority which had previously remained
partly outside of it.

individualistic competitions, whereby losers adopt an alternative means for achieving or defining success.

> An individual may succeed 'legitimately' through his own efforts or he may attempt to form a coalition to block his competitors. If he lacks the resources to make use of the first solution, then he may be more motivated to try the second (even though it is not legitimate) . . . (p. 115).

Blalock's argument cannot be fully endorsed in the British case if it is applied to ethnocentrism as well as racialism. The collectivism of the British masses may be labelled by the élite as deviant, but it does not seem likely to have been developed in response to failure in an individualistic competition, because the lower classes have traditionally held back from such an engagement. As Downes has recently contended, in spite of decades of propaganda by the middle classes about equal opportunity, lower-class children in Britain are still remarkably realistic in their occupational and social aspirations, so that their non-acceptance of middle-class values must be interpreted as a refusal to be bullied into accepting an inappropriate ideology, and not as a reaction to the status frustration which adopting this ideology would make them liable to.[1]

If, as argued here, the bulk of the British population has not conformed in either thought or action to the precepts of liberalism, it may seem odd that this value-system should have appeared to hold such undisputed sway for so long. This is itself almost certainly closely connected with imperialism. Conventional wisdom dictates that the breakdown of tribalism in Britain was a consequence of the rise of universalistic individualism. But the opposite formulation may have more truth in it – that the temporary tribal unity achieved through the imperial exploit allowed a flowering of universalistic interests and sentiments. It is perhaps no accident that the emergence of similar philosophies, such as Stoicism, has tended to occur in analogous circumstances. And it is possible that many of the institutions which we lovingly interpret as marks of progress and modernity are the normal currency of old-fashioned empires.

Among the lower orders in the metropolitan society, the

---

[1] David Downes, *The Delinquent Solution,* 1966, pp. 261 and 268.

creation of an empire induces a degree of ideological complicity with their masters, by extending élite status to them in relation to subject peoples. Whatever its avowed ideology, an imperial system is implicitly ethnocentric, so that for example, although the British sometimes declared the intention of exporting democratic institutions to dependencies, in practice all British nationals enjoyed highly preferential status throughout the empire, and occupied a protected position which enabled them to embellish the doctrines of individualism in some security. So long as liberal principles were not in practice implemented outside of the metropolis, the inclusion of the British lower classes in a categorically superior group was assured and they had little incentive to question the validity of the liberal value-system; indeed its declaration served for them almost as a badge of élite membership.

There was of course no great danger of liberalism spreading to the administration of the colonies, because the universalist ideology of the British operated as a neat device for perpetuating their dependence, by putting colonial citizens in a double-bind situation. If they made nationalistic noises, then the British could argue that they had clearly not yet achieved sufficient political maturity to be given their own democratic governments; if they expressed the proper universalist sentiments, then they undermined their own claim to autonomy. So it was very much in the interests of all British nationals, whatever their station in life, to uphold the liberal humbug.

Acceptance of this value-system in Britain was further assisted by the fact that it was much less hypocritical when applied to purely domestic relations, as during the period in which liberal ideas assisted the maintenance of élite status for British nationals in the empire, they also provided a comparatively plausible account of society and politics internal to that élite. The primary conflict of interests in the empire was between Britain and the colonies, who had little say in the disposition of their material surpluses or the staffing of prestigious bureaucracies. Consequently divisions within the mother parliament at Westminster were only really concerned with the secondary task of sharing out tribute and honours between competing factions of the imperial élite, and the idea of a liberal political system, conceived as a maximising game played between rational associations of free individuals, was not too gross a fiction.

In Conclusion: Minorities in Britain

It is unwise to extract a general theoretical model from British society before the 1960s, without trying to take into account the effects of the imperial context. Metropolitan Britain was only part of a much larger social and political unit, and the fact that ethnic loyalties seem relatively unimportant within the nation does not mean that they are not in fact a primary source of political motivation. Similarly, the fact that class was able to acquire an unusually high level of national political significance does not mean that these interests were truly predominant. For in so far as universalist ideas have been generally accepted in Britain, it has been because the ethnocentric dimension of our behaviour has coincided with the boundaries of the nation, where it can easily be overlooked or disguised. When this is no longer the case, the formal consensus of liberal opinion may not be able to survive. Once we appreciate this, we must surely be less confident that our heritage of colonial experience uniquely qualifies us to create a peaceful and democratic multi-racial society within Britain.

The dilemma of universalism

The self-deception and hypocrisy of liberal ideologists, maintained so effortlessly during the imperial era, has faltered badly over the last fifteen or twenty years as we have returned to the condition of an ordinary, if still quite powerful, nation-state. Reassessment of the character of British political principles has advanced furthest at the level of international relations, where a greater honesty about the place of British interests in determining imperial policy has accompanied the transition from empire to common-wealth. With the passing of sovereignty to dependent territories, the British have lost the power to conceal real conflicts of interest – as illustrated by the issue of migration between Britain and the commonwealth. When immigrants started arriving in Britain in substantial numbers and putting their formal legal equality to practical test, the principle of universal British citizen-ship within the commonwealth was rapidly modified. For a few years in the early 1960s, liberals declared themselves outraged at the protectionist response of the British public; but looking back now, what seems genuinely remarkable is that the real nature of the empire should have escaped the notice of British observers, and that so many of them should have expected liberal dogmas to be upheld when they no longer served the national interest.[1]

Britain has now abandoned the pretence of universalism in dealings with commonwealth partners, but internal community relations policies are still informed with liberal ideals, even though the recipient minorities have long since lost faith in their efficacy and no longer seem to share a common language with native reformers.[2] Almost all policy recommendations for the alleviation of communal and racial antagonism issuing from government departments, responsible agencies and universities are couched in terms of augmenting or defending the rights of *individuals,* and in particular the sacred right to equal opportunities. The reaction of liberals to the discovery of ethnocentric or racialist sentiments in the British population has been to broaden their objectives to include the simultaneous eradication of *all* inequality in Britain, in order to prevent any frustrations, whether within minorities or among deprived sections of the general population, from spilling over into inter-group tensions.[3] If British society can be opened up, and a general onslaught made on lack of opportunity, general social justice and multi-racial harmony can be achieved in the same stroke.

This analysis, however well-intentioned, fails to understand the dynamics of the sort of frustrations it is ostensibly trying to reduce, as it is the emphasis on an open society of freely competing individuals which appears to be a major factor provoking a racialist response in the majority. Not everyone can be successful; and disenchantment can easily lead to retreat within a deviant and more rigidly communalistic world-view than would be necessary in a less competitive society. The more truly equal the opportunities of contestants, the longer, harder and nastier the race, and the more crippling its aftermath of disappointments. The attempt to create an open society may in practice end by producing a more competitive but closed one. As Blalock points out (p. 116):

[1] Some commentators have revealed a talent for double-think on this issue. Paul Foot for example roundly condemns liberalism for its hypocrisy, then carries on to make a thoroughly Victorian plea for individualism and universalism. *Immigration and Race in British Politics,* 1965.

[2] See, for example, Dilip Hiro, *Black British, White British,* 1971.

[3] Rose (op. cit.) reaches this general conclusion.

Presumably, whenever certain goals such as the success goal become generally encouraged for all participants, there will be strains within the system that create pressures to change the norms defining the range of behaviours considered to be legitimate. Where large numbers of majority-group individuals are blocked from upward mobility, we would anticipate that norms will be restructured in such a way that minority discrimination becomes defined as being perfectly legitimate.

In a sense, therefore, liberalism both defines and creates the problem of racialism. Defines it by arguing that all individuals must be completely free and serve the community through competing with each other, and by attacking as irrational any non-individualistic conceptions of social order. Creates it by unleashing more personal aspirations than it is able either to adequately fulfil or control, and which can only find release in competitive *group* aspirations. Hence it is mainly in societies with a strong commitment to liberal individualism – and thus particularly in Protestant countries – that racialism erupts most insidiously as a threat to morality and order.[1] This racialism is generally interpreted, as by Myrdal in relation to the American Creed, as a failure to implement perfectly an agreed and viable social philosophy. But the real problem seems much deeper than this, and to point to an irreducible tension in such societies between formally accepted principles and their implications for ordinary members of society.

It is fashionable to argue, in criticism of reformist solutions, that what would do most to combat racialism in Britain is revolution and the inauguration of socialism. But in the forms generally proposed, socialism does not dispense with an élite grouping, so that problems of differential social status and honour are not removed. If the experience of societies in Eastern Europe is anything to go by, disparities of prestige and economic rewards, and competition for social mobility, are as marked as in capitalist societies.[2] This should hardly come as a surprise, for European socialism is the quintessence of the liberal tradition.[3]

Both marxism and liberalism embody the ideals of Greece

---

[1] See Philip Mason, op. cit., p. 326.
[2] Frank Parkin, *Class Inequality and Political Order,* 1971, ch. 6.
[3] C. W. Mills, op. cit., pp. 13–14.

H*

and Rome and Jerusalem, the humanism of the renaissance, the rationalism of the eighteenth century enlightenment . . . Much of the failure to confront marxism in all its variety is in fact a way of *not* taking seriously the ideals of liberalism itself, for despite the distortions and vulgarisations of Marx's ideas, and despite his own errors, ambiguities and inadequacies, Karl Marx remains the thinker who has articulated most clearly – and most perilously – the basic ideals which liberalism shares.

Socialism shares with conventional liberalism the objective of an open, universalistic society, and diverges from it chiefly by asserting the need to adopt even more radical measures to realise it – in particular by dispensing with private property. This political aim, like that of liberal revolutionaries in earlier centuries, arises more out of the aspirations of deprived sectors of an existing élite than from lower-class experience, so that socialism requires the constant intervention and interpretation of bourgeois intellectuals in order to retain its universalistic commitment. As Kautsky has recognised: 'socialist consciousness is something introduced into the proletarian class struggle from without and not something that arose within it spontaneously.'[1]

Thus socialist ideology operates structurally in a similar manner to liberal ideology, even down to the way in which its universalist doctrines can be used to maintain an empire, by discrediting or dissipating the opposition of dominated groups. Russians are as condemnatory of national or ethnic sentiments among their dependent minorities – both within the USSR and in orbital states – as any traditional liberal in the British context.

Some revolutionary programmes in Britain eschew élitism altogether, and put forward properly egalitarian goals in which individuals would share equal rewards and honour irrespective of their contribution to society. Leaving aside the question of the feasibility of such schemes, they would in principle seem consistent with the eradication of racialism, but only because they necessarily abandon altogether the commitment to universalism. Fraternalism is inveterately particularistic in its statement of priorities, and an egalitarian communism would surely be as ethnocentric as any pre-industrial tribalism.

[1] Quoted in Parkin, op. cit., p. 101.

This brief discussion shows the intractable dilemma faced by liberalism now that its limitations are no longer obscured by imperialism. The principle of individualism is not, and on the face of it cannot be, shared by the majority of a population, for whom it provides no assured reward for participation in society. Liberalism cannot now stand still without discrediting itself, as it has created aspirations which if not fulfilled will fester and undermine its legitimacy. But no more can it move forward, for every step that is taken towards the truly open society the stronger the reaction from unsuccessful and disappointed competitors, and the grosser the disparity between promise and performance. The very concept of a peaceful, multi-racial, individualistic society may in fact be a contradiction in terms, as it is the insistence on rational individualism which often triggers off irrational collectivist behaviour in a majority group.[1]

On the other hand, any step backward from individualism is held to lead certainly to a rapid descent into the pit of totalitarianism; once any legitimacy is accorded to communal loyalties, a rationale is forged for the oppressive domination of minorities. As Popper has colourfully expressed it:[2]

> Nationalism appeals to our tribal instincts, to passion and to prejudice, and to our desire to be relieved from the strain of individual responsibility, which it attempts to replace by a collective or group responsibility ... [But] We can never return to the alleged innocence and beauty of the closed society ... Once we begin to rely upon our reason ... once we feel the call of personal responsibilities ... we cannot return to a state of implicit submission to tribal magic. For those who have eaten from the tree of knowledge, paradise is lost. The more we try to return to tribal heroism, the more surely do we arrive at the Inquisition, at the Secret Police, and at romanticized gangsterism. Beginning with the suppression of reason and truth, we must end with the most brutal and violent destruction of all that is human. There is no return to a harmonious state of nature. If we turn back, then we must go the whole way – we must return to the beasts.

[1] It is possible to analyse in this light the emergence of the Ku Klux Klan as a response to Reconstruction, the passing of the Mines and Works Act of 1911 as a reaction to the fanatical *laissez-faire* of liberal mine-owners; and so on.

[2] K. R. Popper, *The Open Society and Its Enemies*, 1945, vol. 2 p. 47 and vol. 1 p. 177.

The universalistic value-systems of liberalism and socialism appear to be unable to deal with the problems of ethnic and race relations, as whichever way their proponents move their aims appear to be fading. Whether we like it or not, we must look elsewhere for principles to order inter-personal and inter-group relations in the future. For as concluded by C. Wright Mills,[1]

> Both marxism and liberalism bear the trademark of a period of human history that is ending; both are marred by inadequate attention to leading facts and problems with which the world scene now presents us. It is the crisis of this humanist tradition itself, I believe, that is at the bottom of our crisis in political orientation.

Ethnocentrism and British democracy

Retreat from extreme individualism need not however be so calamitous as is often supposed. Totalitarian domination of ethnic minorities is not the inevitable outcome of the recognition of community rights, and is a real threat only where a majority group is able, in Hegelian fashion, to take control of a highly centralised, autonomous state, and to use the power and machinery of that state to pursue its collective destiny at the expense of other groups. If political powers are not concentrated at a single level, the risk of severe exploitation of minorities is greatly reduced. The real problem is not ethnocentrism in itself, but forms of political representation and institutions which afford minorities insufficient self-expression and self-determination.

Obsessive fear of totalitarianism ultimately rests on the assumption that the only viable form of political organisation in the modern world is the independent, highly unified state. Once this concept is abandoned, it is possible to devise political

---

[1] C. W. Mills, op. cit., pp. 12 and 140. The flight from liberal ideology in America has a very similar basis to that in Britain. This is not immediately obvious as the States have never been an imperial power like Britain; however, the relation of the dominant WASP group to immigrant minorities has been structurally analogous. Behind a screen of universalistic propaganda about America as a 'melting-pot', the dominant group maintained its position by exercising a *de facto* indirect rule of immigrants via their ethnic communities. Since the First World War this exclusiveness has come under increasing attack, and efforts have been made to create one nation. It is the failure of this individualistic reform programme which has led to loss of faith in liberal ideals and the American way of life.

structures which give reasonable protection and expression to minority interests and sentiments. Significantly, this could only take place in Britain at the expense of the strong principle of universalism contained in our institutions. Our highly centralised political system is built on the proposition that minority groupings do not exist, and is formulated for the participation in the political process of 'rational, independent, individual persons'.[1] The winner-take-all, simple-majority voting system – both in parliament and electorally – effectively excludes minority groups from having a voice, let alone from sharing executive power.[2] The fundamental issue which we in Britain are being obliged to confront, perhaps now for the first time in centuries – and which Ulster has helped to illuminate – is that the pursuit of status, security and material comfort is for many in our population an activity to be undertaken collectively, through membership of cohesive communities, and that the individualistic bias enshrined in our current political institutions favours the majority at the expense of any minorities. It is arguable that exporting these institutions to our ex-colonies has accordingly sharpened competition between their constituent ethnic communities, and that countries like Guyana, Cyprus, Nigeria and so on have experienced greater communal strife since independence, than have former dependencies of less individualistic states.[3]

Alternative forms of democracy are available which could help redress the balance, if we are prepared to relinquish the traditional notion that they are unnecessary, inappropriate or alien in Britain. For instance, proportional representation helps to give a voice to minorities, although it does not give them much real power unless combined with a modification of legislative voting rules

[1] Hanna Pitkin, *The Concept of Representation*, 1967, p. 190. 'In England, Utilitarianism not only favoured the representation of persons, but made interest an increasingly personal concept. The theorists of Liberalism generally thought of representation as being of individuals rather than corporate bodies, "interests" or classes. In harmony with the individualism of their economic outlook, they also thought of representation as based upon rational, independent, individual persons.'

[2] See Benn and Peters, op. cit., p. 347.

[3] For a brief discussion of this point see C. Bagley, *The Dutch Plural Society*, 1973, concluding chapter. Mauritius illustrates the same point in a slightly different way, as it has only managed to contain communal rivalries since independence by keeping up a state of emergency which suspends liberal sections of its constitution. For details of measures adopted see M. M. Minogue and S. K. Joypaul, 'Notes on the Constitution of Mauritius', Occasional Paper No. 3, School of Administration, University of Mauritius.

to the effect that decisions require a substantial majority, or some specifications are also made about group representation at ministerial level, so that any government is necessarily a coalition of ethnic interests. An alternative solution lies in decentralisation and devolution of powers within the state, in order that minorities can have the chance of attaining some measure of self-determination, and no single group can exercise a complete monopoly of power. Minority aspirations are better met by the provision of *more,* not more *equal,* opportunities.

Decentralisation as a means of protecting minorities is sometimes objected to on the grounds that since ethnic identities are relativistic, and capable of seemingly endless sub-division into ever smaller segments, any concession made to minority sentiments will trigger off a fracturing of the nation into a host of tiny components. For instance, it might be envisaged that if Scotland, Wales and other Celtic groupings were to be accorded self-government within Britain, this would reinforce secessional demands from areas inside the new units, such as the North Country, or Wessex or whatever within England, and then inside these from yet smaller territories until the state crumbled away entirely, and a thousand years of political progress had been squandered.

This anxiety pays insufficient attention to the fact that, although communal identities and allegiances may indeed be relative, the tendency of segments to sub-divide around divergent interests is matched and balanced by their capacity to merge in wider combinations, so that there would be strong forces to prevent any absolute splintering. Dread of anarchy, just like the fear of totalitarianism, attaches an undue importance to the integrity of the centralised state. For once you allow some stretching out of sovereignty through a multi-level federal system, it is possible to accommodate a range of minority interests without spawning a multitude of tiny states. Limited decentralisation allows for the relativity of group identifications, at the same time as reducing the danger of group exploitation.

Part of the failure of liberal individualism to comprehend the nature of ethnocentrism in Britain is due to its inability to appreciate the positive contribution to social order made by communal loyalties in our society. If fears about anarchy and oppression can be dispelled, it becomes evident that not only are vertical, segmentary divisions a natural part of our social structure, but they play an indispensable part in maintaining its overall cohesion. Far from being only sources of conflict or disorder, they provide powerful moderating influences against the egoistic and divisive individualism proclaimed, if not actively practised, by the élite.

This is particularly true in relation to the bond between élite and masses. The élite may believe that acceptance of its privileged position by the rest of society hangs solely on the principle of the open society, by which everyone is declared to have had 'a chance'. But this seems very doubtful. As Michael Young has demonstrated in his penetrating satire, if too much importance is attached to individual 'merit' in the allocation of social position and rewards, the whole legitimacy of a political order may fall apart.[1] Unsuccessful members of the subordinate masses cannot identify with an élite that is too obviously superior. So where a political system requires the consensual identification of subjects with the ruling class, as it presumably does in a democracy, then it seems likely to occur most spontaneously along an ethnic dimension. For in this way the members of an ethnic community who do not occupy positions generally regarded as socially important can share fraternalistically in the honour of those who do.

It is very easy for members of the élite to sneer at this vicarious[2] striving for power and status by 'poor whites', but in fairness we should concede that the component of fantasy it involves is no greater than that in the liberal tenet that every tinker's son should think of himself as a potential minister of the realm. Collective definitions of gratification are in the last analysis both more realistic and equitable than the individualistic alternative, and give some dignity to many people who would otherwise have none. Until a social system is devised which dispenses with leaders or élites, and distributes honour and rewards evenly throughout society, this communal sharing of status must be considered a useful procedure. Even for members of ethnic groupings unable to identify with the élite in this way, the fact of belonging to a cohesive community can impart intrinsic satisfactions and compensations which render members better off in many ways than

[1] Michael Young, *The Rise of the Meritocracy,* 1958.
[2] It is, of course, vicarious only in terms of individualistic statements of the nature of society.

unsuccessful individualists, who have little comfort in their predicament.

It is of course *because* group membership makes subordinate status more bearable that dominant groupings are able to monopolise élite activities so readily, and minorities are created which are liable to long-term exploitation. This is politically hazardous and morally objectionable. But it is no remedy to open up society in a competitive free-for-all; because in an open situation of this sort, the aspirations of all members of the incumbent majority will be mobilised, and the group will be likely to use its dominant position to hinder the progress of minorities by 'closing' the competition. Nor is a free-for-all even necessary. What is really needed in order for a minority group to improve its standing in society is for a reasonable proportion of its members to join the wider élite and to be seen to contribute to the common good. In this way, all members of society can to some extent identify, and *be* identified publicly, with prestigious functions. Multi-racial harmony is more likely to be achieved through ensuring appropriate representation of groups at élite level, including the policy and decision-making processes, than by insistence on individualistic participation. What is important is not that all individuals should have equal opportunities, but that the hierarchical relation between élite and masses should cut across, instead of coinciding with, ethnic divisions.

In this respect it is interesting to note that an overtly pluralist society like Holland, which falls short of our own universalistic moral standards, has been much more successful in incorporating new minorities to its social system. As Bagley has pointed out in his recent study, there are essentially two levels of social and political behaviour in Holland, one within communities or 'blocs', and the other between them. Members of different blocs do not attempt to treat each other *as* individuals, but as parts of social units which have their own, separate share in the national stake. Inter-group relations are conducted in a diplomatic manner at an élite level.[1] By analogy with the Dutch case, if we in Britain really want to alleviate inter-ethnic or inter-racial tensions, the best means of doing so would be to ensure the promotion to

[1] C. Bagley, op. cit., p. 231. This analysis derives from Arend Lijphart's model of 'consociational democracy'. For a fuller exposition see his discussion in *World Politics*, January 1969.

honourable élite status of some members of under-represented minority groups, and to qualify the concept of the 'open society' which we are currently pursuing. It probably does not matter very much how individuals are selected for sponsorship, merely that it is done according to considerations which do not simultaneously excite the aspirations of lower-class members of the dominant community.

It is interesting to contrast the traditional position in Britain with that in tribal societies, as in many respects they illustrate the contrasting dangers of opposite extremes. Before the formation of state agencies capable of defining and protecting a wider concept of citizenship and providing legitimate leadership for arbitration of disputes, the formal structure of societies tended to be segmentary, with lineage groupings, recruited on the involuntary principle of descent, and commanding the automatic and permanent allegiance of members, serving as the framework of political life. As Gluckman and others have shown,[1] this sort of system cannot unaided regulate conflicts between tribal groups, as it only recognises particularistic loyalties which by their nature preclude consideration of moral claims outside of a mobilised group. Consequently the peaceful settlement of disputes is dependent on the intervention of unaligned individuals – either complete outsiders or individuals with marriage ties cutting across groups and creating a conflict of loyalties for them – who are by virtue of their anomalous position able to put forward impartial, universalistic criteria by which a settlement can be reached. It is significant that legalistically-minded tribesmen consider any such mediation as most improper, since it violates the formal ideology of absolute submergence of individual interests and sentiments within the tribal segment.

In British society the situation is reversed. The only conduct which is publicly endorsed as legitimate is that which keeps closely to individualistic, rational-bureaucratic norms. Particularistic favouring of kinsmen or fellow-tribesmen is condemned outright as corrupt and immoral, and counted as putting the efficient operation of the system in jeopardy. Such deviant practices are known to occur, but are generally judged to be survivals from

[1] Max Gluckman, *Politics, Law and Ritual in Tribal Society*, 1965, ch. 3.

less civilised days which will vanish with the complete transition to modernism. But by analogy with the opposite condition in tribal society, it is very likely that kinship and ethnic loyalties are more than vestiges of bygone days, and play a valuable part in modern society. Over the last twenty years or so, sociological studies have shown that in modern society kinship does much more than perform the breeding and socialisation functions allowed it by liberal ideology; and the same may be found to be true of communal loyalties. Just as it is important in a formally collectivist society, which recognises only ascribed or involuntary group allegiances, for 'deviant' individuals to proclaim universal morality, so in an officially individualistic society like our own, which strongly emphasises voluntary relationships and achieved status, it may be imperative that some 'deviant' groups hold on to communalistic values. Both types of value and relationship serve useful purposes in society, and to declare only one of them legitimate cannot invalidate the actual contribution of the other.

Ideologically these two sets of principles are of course antithetical, and it would be hard to imagine a society in which both were fully and equally supported. But some coexistence is certainly possible, with adherents of each value-system conceding a marginal validity for the other, but disputing how much and in what contexts. Outside of the Anglo-American democracies, these two basic philosophies do indeed tend to coexist in practice, and the debate between them constitutes a natural major axis of political life. This is potentially true in Britain too. At the moment parties of both Left and Right share a sizeable common fund of liberal premises. But following the retreat from empire, which sustained this consensus, adjustments are taking place in our political vocabulary which could lead to a realignment on this sort of basis.

The most obvious manifestation of this tendency is Powellism. Support for Powell's ethnocentric platform comes from both sides of the present house, although more from Labour than his own party. Powell himself appears to be increasingly sceptical about the utility of the existing axis of political choice, and the formation under him of an anti-liberal, protectionist, nationalist party, with segmentary potentialities, no longer seems as fantastic as it would have done a few years ago.

At the same time as the development of Powellism, there has

been the drift towards a Mogg-Levinist grouping,[1] of liberal, universalist, internationalist persuasion, and broadly distinguishable as the pro-European alliance at the time of Britain's entry to the EEC. A party of this ilk would appeal to the outward-looking élite and those who believe in Britain's capacity to recreate her former greatness on new shores. The creation of two major parties on these lines would presumably leave a third party, or cluster of parties, socialist in character, to cater for the universalist rump of the Labour Party, and which might support either of the main formations on particular issues.

This restructuring of political forces has shown itself most coherently over the issue of Britain's entry to Europe, and whether or not a more permanent reshaping along these lines takes place will probably depend very much on the future political development of Europe itself. For present purposes, the most important aspect of membership of the European community is that Britain has now herself become a minority within a larger totality, and one way or another this is bound to have many repercussions for the strength and form of national cohesion. On one hand, it is conceivable that the new minority experience could pull back together again in a joint endeavour the tribal segments of our society which have shown signs of drifting apart. However, this seems likely to occur only if Britain is successful in gaining acceptance quite quickly for a strong regional development policy to offset the centripetal tendencies in the market. If no such policy is forthcoming, the interests and fortunes of southern England will increasingly diverge from those of the regions, and a growing awareness of sectional differences can be expected. As the dominant partner in British union, the English have in principle the most to lose from decentralisation. But if the other regions become heavy burdens, then separatist feelings could be expected to grow in England too, leading to a majority acceptance of political devolution.

By entry into Europe, Britain has moreover already become

---

[1] So known because advocated relentlessly in *The Times*. It should be noted, in view of its recent successes, that this movement cannot be identified with the current Liberal Party. The revival of the Liberals may help spark off realignment, by unsettling the Tory and Labour parties; but at the time of writing the eclectic nature of their platform, drawing as strongly on communal as on individualistic principles, would appear to rule out their coming into direct opposition with Powellism.

committed to participation in a federal structure. The interests of member countries are at present too different to allow any rapid movement to centralisation at a supranational level, and sovereignty is likely to remain split between EEC and member nations. This creates a framework of political ideas in terms of which decentralisation and reorganisation of sovereignty *inside* Britain will no longer seem such a radical deviation from normal and proper practice; and so the stretching out of powers through several tiers of legislative bodies, giving expression to minority feelings and fostering political élites within minority groups, may not be such an unlikely eventuality as it seems at first glance.[1]

But either way, whether resulting in decentralisation or not, our political debates must in the future surely give increasing recognition to vertical divisions of interest – regional, ethnic, national or whatever – and proportionately less to the traditional area of conflicts between horizontal formations such as class. This should mean that minorities will cease to be regarded as problems in the sense that they now are. By becoming incorporated to a model of normal political behaviour, minorities and minority interests could be transmuted into an integral and accepted facet of political life, instead of a topic for furtive insinuation and secret anxiety. The general solution to the situation of minorities in Britain lies therefore in an honest acceptance that, in all but exceptional circumstances, ethnic groupings are natural political forces which need to be allowed for in political organisation. The Maltese are unlikely to participate in any flowering of minority sentiments in Britain, as on present trends they will soon have faded away as a distinct group. But they may help to bring it about, even if only by being the exception which helped to illuminate a rule.

[1] Since this was written the Kilbrandon Commission have reported in favour of some executive devolution within Britain – although their proposals do not yet seem to have much popular backing among the English.

APPENDIX A
SUPPLEMENTARY TABLES

TABLE A.1 *Frequency of religious observance in Malta (percentages)*

Number of Mass attendances per month	Number of Holy Communion participations per year					
	Wives			Husbands		
	1–12	13–363	364	1–12	13–363	364
Up to 5	8	7		20	11	
6 to 29	7	22	1	12	15	1
30 or more	4	26	25	9	20	12
n (100%)	574			450		

Source: adapted from tables 4 and 5, Floriana Parish Enquiry, 1961. Research Agency Malta.

TABLE A.2 *Family size in Malta, 1948 and 1960 (compared with Great Britain, 1946) (percentages)*

Number of live births	Great Britain 1946	Malta 1948	Malta 1960 by cohorts		
	Women married in 1925	Women married between 1900–9	Women married over 45 years of age	Women married before 1920	Women married 1920–9	Women married 1930–9
None	17·2	10·3	11·3	6·4	7·7	8·5
1–3	63·6	48·2	17·8	15·7	19·2	21·0
4–9	18·6	37·8	45·0	54·9	52·2	52·9
10 and over	0·6	3·7	25·9	23·0	20·9	17·6
Data	R.C. on Population 1949–50, vol. 2	1948 Census	Malta Enquiry into Family Size		

Sources: H. Bowen-Jones, *et al.*, *Malta: Background for Development*, 1961, table 29. Malta Central Office of Statistics, *An Enquiry into Family Size in Malta and Gozo*, 1963, table 5.2.

Appendix A

TABLE A.3 *Relation between Maltese emigration rate and party in office*

Year	Emigrants	Party in office	Party in opposition
1950	8,503	Nationalist	Labour
1951	7,692	,,	,,
1952	5,345	,,	,,
1953	4,532	,,	,,
1954	11,457	,,	,,
1955	9,007	3 months Nationalist, then 9 months Labour	
1956	4,492	Labour	Nationalist
1957	3,285	,,	,,
1958	3,152	3 months Labour, then 9 months colonial rule	,,
1959–61		Colonial rule	
1962	3,641	2 months colonial rule, then 10 months Nationalist	Labour
1963	6,579	Nationalist	,,
1964	8,987	,,	,,

Source: Voice of Malta, February 1968.

TABLE A.4 *British statistics of Maltese immigration*

Period	Maltese passengers admitted			Immigrants admitted*	Net balance of Maltese passengers		
	Men	Women	Children		Men	Women	Children
1962–5†	12,263	8,337	3,250	4,283	1,044	1,345	840
1966–70	25,815	15,760	5,508	4,301	1,619	297	87
1971–2	12,815	8,363	2,565	1,230	−823	−979	−174
1962–72	50,893	32,460	11,323	9,814	1,840	663	753

Source: Control of Commonwealth Immigrants Acts Statistics.
* i.e. Voucher-holders, dependants and 'other settlers' admitted.
† July 1962 onwards.

TABLE A.5 *Maltese success in applications for UK employment vouchers,*
1962–72

Year	Vouchers issued to Maltese applicants	Maltese voucher-holders admitted to UK	Voucher application success-rates		Proportion vouchers going to Maltese %
			Maltese %	Overall %	
1962	359	154	59	50	1
1963	1,212	679	67	14	3
1964	1,406	793	66	21	7
1965	1,071	716	63	46	7
1966	806	651	90	34	13
1967	762	537	93	45	9
1968	746	539	87	60	9
1969	770	468	99	51	11
1970	846	478	96	38	15
1971	634	331	99	39	17
1972	468	294	73	34	20

Source: Control of Commonwealth Immigrants Acts Statistics.

TABLE A.6 *Sex composition of official Maltese migrant flow to the*
United Kingdom, 1923–8, 1950–72

Period	Total migrants	Total males*	Males as % of total	Unmarried % of adult males
1923–8	2,065	1,890†	92+	
1950–5	8,736	6,122	70	
1956–60	4,548	3,098	68	71
1961–5	6,614	4,145	63	72
1966–70	3,909	2,456	63	77
1971–2	1,124	688	61	75

Source: Annual Demographic Review, Malta.
* Assuming that half of children male, where specific figure not given.
† Adult males only, as no figures for children included.

Appendix A

Sex composition of Maltese population in Australia, 1921–61

Census year	Maltese enumerated	Male %
1921	1,330	88
1933	2,782	80
1947	3,238	76
1954	19,988	62
1961	39,108	58

Source: Australian national censuses.

TABLE A.8 *Maltese seamen on British ships, 1901, 1906 and 1911*

Year:	1901	1906	1911
Total number	270	220	344
Ratings			
Mates	7	7	4
Able seamen	42	29	36
Firemen	101	67	143
Donkeymen	19	16	19
Stewards	64	51	67
Ages			
20–9	84	80	137
30–9	87	59	93
40–9	60	43	59
50+	22	33	41

Source: Merchant Shipping Act statistics.

TABLE A.9 *Estimated approximate mid-point populations of men of specified ethnicity, living in Metropolitan police area* (in thousands)*

			Country of origin			
Period	Malta	West Indies	Eire	West Africa	Cyprus	Britain
1951–4	1·5	8	75	2·5	8	2,700
1955–9	2	30	85	5	14	2,600
1960–4	2·5	55	100	10	20	2,400
1965–9	3	75	100	14	24	2,300

Sources: Censuses of England and Wales, and ch. 10 of *Colour and Citizenship*, ed. E. J. B. Rose (1969), adjusted as far as possible to remove UK nationals born in specified countries.
* Excluding minors, i.e. under *16*.

Appendix A

TABLE A.10 *Deportations of Maltese offenders under the Commonwealth Immigrants Acts*

Period	Court recommen-dations	Offence-types (recommendations)				Deportations ordered
		Vice	Violence	Property	Other	
	1	2	3	4	5	6
1962–4	39	17	3	15	4	28
1965–7	29	15	2	7	5	16
1968–70	24	9	4	9	2	16
1962–70	92	41	9	31	11	60

Source: Home Office.

TABLE A.11 *Offences against White Slave ordinances, Malta 1922–60 (years for which figures available*)*

Administrative year	Decade 1910†	1920	1930	1940	1950	1960
0/1			12		4	7
1/2			15		2	
2/3	5	4	5		18	
3/4	0	7	11		6	
4/5	2	7	10		10	
5/6	11	2	7		3	
6/7	7	3	13	1	1	
7/8		7	7	1	0	
8/9		5	1	2		
9/0		5		3		

Source: Annual Reports of Police Department, Malta.
* Blank space indicates no report found for that year.
† Before 1918, the figures given are for instigating or facilitating the seduction or prostitution of minors – as defined in the criminal code before the White Slave ordinances.

APPENDIX B

ESTIMATING THE VOLUME AND DISTRIBUTION OF MALTESE SETTLEMENT IN BRITAIN

British censuses grossly overstate the size of the Maltese community, by compounding Maltese nationals with non-Maltese British born in Malta. This is betrayed by the consistently low proportion of Malta-born *males* recorded, which bears no comparison with the known composition of the migratory flow. Between the wars, when almost all Maltese coming to this country were men, there were never more than 50 per cent of males among the Malta-born population enumerated in England and Wales. And even since the war, after heavier migration, the level has not surpassed 52 per cent.

To help unscramble the census figures and arrive at more realistic population figures for the Maltese community, I made a thorough investigation into the probable size and fertility of the non-Maltese British population of Malta, and its likely impact on British censuses this century. This is not the place for a full exposition of the demographic sources drawn on for this analysis, nor of the procedures adopted and computations made; in fact I hope to publish this material separately at a later date. In the meantime, all that is required for present purposes is a broad statement of the main conclusions. This is given in Table B.1, which indicates the general standing of the various components of the Malta-born population at censuses from 1911 to 1971.

As can be seen from the table, the male proportion arrived at for the category of UK nationals is very similar to that obtaining for the British population as a whole at respective censuses in question. This suggests that the unscrambling process has been reasonably accurate. It should be borne in mind however that many of the pre-war figures are very small, especially for Inner

London, so that the margin of error for many of these estimates is accordingly broad.

TABLE B.1 *Probable breakdown of Malta-born population in Britain, 1911–71*

Census	Malta-born population enumerated	Maltese nationals				UK nationals	
		Probable total	Service brides	Others (migrants)	Male % †	Probable total	Male %
a. England and Wales							
1911	5,703	450	100	350	87	5,253	46
1921	6,736	1,100	150	950	78	5,636	46
1931	8,000	1,250	300	950	93	6,750	46
1951	14,503	6,500	1,400	5,100	70	8,003	47
1961	24,679	12,500	2,000	10,500	65	12,179	48
1966	31,580	15,500	2,200	13,300	66	16,080	48
b. Inner London							
1911	1,011	50	15	35	*	960	47
1921	1,096	100	20	80	*	996	46
1931	1,134	120	30	90	*	1,014	46
1951	2,724	1,600	150	1,450	77	1,124	47
1961	4,362	2,800	200	2,600	72	1,562	48
1966	5,600‡	3,600	220	3,380	69	2,200	48
1971	4,810	2,600	220	2,380	73	2,210	48

* Figures too small for useful estimates.
† i.e. Percentage of Maltese nationals *excluding* service-brides.
‡ Estimate only.

Distribution of Maltese settlement in Britain

Within the framework set by these broader estimates of the settlement of Maltese in Britain, it is possible to identify fairly confidently the main areas of actual Maltese residence, by picking out localities with the high proportions of Malta-born males. Table B.2 shows the main pre-war communities, and their size if it is assumed that 70–75 per cent of their membership at this period would have been male. It can be seen that most of these colonies were tiny, and were almost entirely based in ports. Table B.3 gives the locations and sizes of the chief settlements in London since the war, on a similar assumption that between 65 and 70 per cent of Maltese nationals would have been males.

TABLE B.2 *Estimates of main pre-war Maltese settlements in England and Wales*

Location		Probable size of Maltese settlement		
	At census:	1911	1921	1931
Plymouth/Devonport		20	150	50
South Shields		10	50	50
Bristol		20	20	20
Gillingham		100	80	40
Liverpool		20	50	50
Portsmouth/Southampton		50	100	130
Cardiff		50	300	200
Swansea/Newport		10	30	100
Manchester/Salford			30	50
London		35	80	90
Minor settlements		35	100	190
Service-brides		100	150	300
Total		450	1,100	1,250

TABLE B.3 *Main areas of Maltese settlement in Inner London, 1951–71*

Location		Probable size of Maltese settlement		
	At census:	1951	1961	1971
Tower Hamlets		600	900	750
Lambeth		125	300	550
Islington		125	350	300
Hackney		25	150	200
Camden		200	100	100
Other areas		375	800	480
Service-brides		150	200	220
Total		1,600	2,800	2,600

APPENDIX C

ADJUSTING 1961 CENSUS MATERIALS RELATING TO MALTESE IN LONDON

Using procedures similar to those adopted for tracing the distribution of Maltese settlements, it was possible to adjust census materials for the Greater London area to remove UK nationals born in Malta, thereby showing more clearly the characteristics of the immigrant community.

A prior problem which had to be disposed of first however lay in the fact that people born in Malta are for most purposes in census tabulations grouped together with those born in Cyprus. Fortunately the Institute of Race Relations had commissioned some special tabulations from the 1961 census which separated these two birthplace categories, and these were made available as the basis for this analysis.

The adjustment which was then made to the 'Malta-born' category to remove non-Maltese people born in Malta was based on the assessment that 55 per cent of the total Malta-born population of Greater London, and likewise 61 per cent of Malta-born *males,* were Maltese nationals. Adjustment was carried out simply by subtracting from the total Malta-born figures the balance – i.e. 45 per cent for both-sex statistics, and 39 per cent for male statistics – distributed in accordance with the characteristics of the overall population of Greater London. (In the absence of contrary information, it was necessary to suppose that UK nationals born in Malta and resident in London were generally similar to the rest of the London population. If they do differ, these adjustments are biased accordingly.)

The estimated break-down of the Malta-born population of Greater London which this process of adjustment assumes is as shown in Table C.1.

Appendix C

TABLE C.I *Estimated composition of the Malta-born population of Greater London in 1961*

	Total Malta-born population	Maltese nationals		UK nationals	
		n	% of total	n	% of total
Male	3,889	2,380	61	1,514	39
Female	3,065	1,420	46	1,640	54
Total	6,954	3,800	55	3,154	45
Male % of total	56	63*		48	
Service-brides		400			
Total migrants		3,400			
Male % of migrants		70*			

* Male proportions lower than for Inner London area, where young, single males are concentrated.

Tabulations of adjusted data

The series of tabulations reproduced below contains a broad outline of information about the Maltese. In order to show the effect of the adjustments made, a number of different categories of subjects are juxtaposed. These categories are as follows:

i People born in 'Malta and Cyprus'. These are the figures given in published census tables on Commonwealth immigrants in the conurbations.

ii 'Malta-born' and 'Cyprus-born' people are also shown separately, following the special tabulations provided by the Institute of Race Relations, which break down the published census figures.

iii A 'Maltese' category, representing the adjusted 'Malta-born' group. (In certain tables there is an additional column for Inner London Maltese; these figures are from the 1967 enquiry reported in Appendix D, and included here for comparative purposes.)

Appendix C

In addition to figures relating to Maltese, statistics for other categories of people are included in some tables – e.g. 'Jamaica-born' persons as an example of a contrasting immigrant group, and also the general population of Greater London. Such figures are extracted direct from published census data.

Finally it should be noted that these tables are taken from the 10 per cent sample section of the 1961 census, so that population totals are smaller than might be expected.

TABLE C.2 *Job status of Maltese men in London (percentages)*

Job status	Greater London total	Born in Malta & Cyprus	Born Cyprus	Born Malta	Maltese	Inner London Maltese	Reg.-General S.E.G. Categories
Managerial	12	12	13	7	4		1. 2. 13.
Professional	5	2	1	5	5		3. 4.
Other non-manual	23	9	6	19	16		5. 6.
Total non-manual	40	23	20	31	25	25	
Skilled manual	35	36	37	34	33	36	8. 9. 12. 14.
Other manual	25	42	43	36	42	39	7. 10. 11. 15. 16. 17.
n (100%)	269,640	1,373	1,097	276	168	139	

Sources: i Commonwealth immigrants in the conurbations. Table A.5 (Males in employment).

   ii Greater London total from occupation volume, table 28 (N.B. economically active males).

   iii Inner London Maltese figures – from 1967 enquiry (see Appendix D) (economically active males).

Appendix C

TABLE C.3 *Occupation type of Maltese men in London (economically active males) (percentages)*

Occupation type	Greater London total	Born in Malta & Cyprus	Born Cyprus	Maltese	Inner London Maltese	Born Jamaica	Reg.-General occupation categories
Manufacturing engineering & gen. production	23	13	11	16	19	29	1. 2. 3. 4. 5. 6. 7. 10. 13. 14. 17.
Wood, leather and clothing	4	17	20	5	6	11	8. 9. 11.
Food, drink, catering and personal services	9	36	41	24	24	8	12. 23.
Transport and communications	10	4	3	11	14	11	19.
Building, decorating and gen. labouring	12	10	8	19	13	27	15. 16. 18.
Sales, packing, storekeeping	13	7	7	7	6	5	20. 22.
Clerical, technical, professional	26	9	6	14	14	4	21. 24. 25.
Other and no information	3	4	4	4	3	5	26. 27.
n (100%)	269,640	1,453	1,161	178	139	2,023	

Sources: i Commonwealth immigrants volume, table A.4.
      ii Greater London total from occupation volume, table A.

TABLE C.4 *Housing tenure and relative overcrowding of households with Maltese head or spouse (percentages)*

Nature of tenure	Greater London total	Born Malta & Cyprus	Born Cyprus	Maltese	Born Jamaica
Owner-occupied	37	38	38	28	31
Held by employment or rented with business	3	3	4	3	1
Rented from local authority	18	7	5	9	1
Rented privately: unfurnished	33	30	28	33	13
Rented privately: furnished	9	23	25	27	54
n (Households)		1,291	944	191	1,603
Overcrowding (% households with more than 1½ persons per room)	4	22	27	16	41

Sources: i Commonwealth immigrants volume, table B.3.
ii Greater London total – Housing volume, tables 13 and 22.

TABLE C.5 *Household type of London households with Maltese head or spouse (percentages)*

Household type	GLC total	Born Malta & Cyprus	Born Cyprus	Maltese	Born Jamaica
Non-family households	18	14	12	20	31
Married couple only	22	13	11	20	15
Married couple and children	44	45	44	50	29
Other one-family households	10	21	26	8	18
Two or more family households	6	7	8	2	7
n (100%)		1,291	944	191	1,603

Sources: i Commonwealth immigrants volume, table B.2.
ii Greater London total – from household composition tables, in housing volume.

TABLE C.6 *Intermarriage by Maltese in London (percentages) (households with children where head or spouse immigrant)*

| Marriage type | | Birthplace of immigrant | | | Maltese | | | Inner London Maltese* Households | |
Husband	Wife	Jamaica	Cyprus	Malta & Cyprus	Total; incl. service-brides	Total excl. service-brides	Maltese head only	with children	All† households
Immigrant	Immigrant	84	75	63	24	26	29	37	35
Immigrant	British	10	14	20	47	53	59	52	54
Immigrant	Other	4	8	8	9	10	11	11	11
British	Immigrant	2	2	8	18	8	—	—	—
Other	Immigrant		1	1	2	2	—	—	—
Total intermarriage with British (rows 2 + 4)		12	16	28	65	61	59	52	54
n (100%)		576	602	755	84	76	68	79	103

Source: Commonwealth immigrants volume, table B.5. (N.B. adjustment taken further by making separate allowances for *all* Maltese women, on one hand, and Maltese service-brides only, on the other.)

* *All* households with Maltese head – by nature of sample.

† Includes all households with married couples and Maltese head, even if no children.

Appendix C

TABLE C.7 *Numbers of children in households with Maltese head or spouse (percentages)*

Children in household	Greater London total	Born in Malta & Cyprus	Born Cyprus	Maltese	Inner* London Maltese	Born Jamaica
None	61	37	31	43	40	56
1	19	23	24	21	19	20
2	14	22	24	19	21	13
3	4	12	13	13	10	6
4	1	5	6	3	5	3
5 or more	1	2	2	1	5	1
Children per 100 households:						
a All households	69	134	147	122	136	86
b Households with children	177	212	214	214	226	195
n (100%) households	270,556	1,291	944	191	131	1,603

Sources: i Commonwealth immigrants volume, table B.4.

ii Greater London total – housing volume, household composition, table 37.

* Maltese *head* of household only.

APPENDIX D
REPORT ON THE ENQUIRY AMONG MALTESE MEN IN LONDON

Introduction

This enquiry was the main empirical investigation undertaken. Its objective was to provide measures of the overall state of community articulation and participation among Maltese settlers living in Inner London, and general indications of the character of the settlement. Some interviews had been carried out with leaders of Maltese associations before this enquiry was planned, and a few arbitrary contacts established with ordinary settlers; this more systematic investigation attempted to test the validity of these tentative findings. Originally two phases of investigation were planned. Firstly a large sample of Maltese men would be interviewed, to map out the main pattern of participation in affairs of the ethnic community. At a later stage a sub-sample would be re-interviewed in greater depth to provide more detailed case material. However, as the first phase took longer than intended this second level was never reached.

Interviewing was started in the summer of 1966 and was not finally completed until nearly Easter 1968. For convenience the enquiry is referred to here (and sometimes in the text) as the '1967' investigation, as this was when the bulk of the work was done, and its respondents as the '1967' sample.

The problem of sample design

The very first contacts with Maltese in London indicated that a primary focus of attention must be the low level of involvement of settlers in community activities. Given this definition of the area of study, it was clearly essential that some attempt be made to take a properly representative sample of all Maltese living in London, and not to fall back on the easy expedient of examining only those areas where Maltese activity was concentrated. But the difficulties of designing a suitable sample were considerable.

In the first place, no Maltese agencies possessed anything approaching a register of Maltese people in London, and the task of creating one to order would quite obviously be out of the question. The only possible way of proceeding seemed to be to select a number of areas which could be supposed to contain a reasonable cross-section of Maltese migrants, and then locate them individually by making local registers from voting lists, by sifting out persons with identifiably Maltese names, and supplementing this with local enquiries among those Maltese initially located in this way.

But it was also clear from the outset that the UK census provided a far from perfect sampling frame for selecting these areas. A proportion of people enumerated as Malta-born was known to be UK nationals, but it would have been extremely hazardous to attempt to adjust the population figures for areas small enough to be convenient sampling units, as the numbers of Maltese were in most cases tiny, and the relative proportions would have been liable to very substantial chance variation.

The sample design eventually adopted was therefore very much a compromise. Its main features were a minimisation of the physical labour of interviewing, through the use of area sampling, and a rather elaborate weighting procedure intended to make the sample as representative as possible in the circumstances. The resulting sample is probably as precise as could be expected; unfortunately however, owing to the smallness of numbers and the complexity of the sampling procedure, it is nigh impossible to calculate any confidence levels for the findings. Given the objectives of the investigation, however, it seemed better to try to take a representative sample, even though no formal statistical significance could be attached to its results, than not to attempt a representative sample at all. Formal confidence levels may be absent, but subjectively the conclusions are far more satisfactory.

Sampling procedure and design

The enquiry concentrated on adult Maltese males (aged sixteen or more) who had arrived in Britain after the age of fifteen, having spent their childhood (or most of it) in Malta. Inclusion of other categories of men would have introduced many additional variables, for little gain – as before the investigation was carried out it was assumed that such people would constitute the backbone of any community life. Women were not included because of the smallness of their numbers and relative unimportance in communal activities, and practical difficulties of making contact and establishing the right sort of rapport.

The aim of the area sampling procedure was to select a package of areas which could be expected to contain about two hundred such men resident within them, and who would be generally representative of the settlement. Inside the areas selected a 100 per cent sample of eligible individuals would be taken – that is, all Maltese would be sought out by all means available. The area sampling was restricted to the Inner London region, because detailed information on a ward basis was available on the distribution at the 1961 census. From the overall figures, two hundred adult males seemed likely to be about 10 per cent of the total eligible in the area, so a sample of wards was drawn which seemed likely to contain a representative 10 per cent of the Maltese.

Since the main emphasis of the enquiry was on the extent of contact with other Maltese, and involvement in community activities, the factor which it seemed most important to control in order to get a representative (for this purpose) sample was the *density* of Maltese settlement within the ward. In the 356 wards in the area, this density ranged from 4·2 per cent of the overall population ('Tower Hamlets' ward in Stepney Borough) to nil (in 23 wards).[1] Wards were listed in order of this density, so that a fixed interval sample would in terms of this factor contain a fair cross-section of Maltese.

There were two complicating issues. First the wards varied greatly in their size of general population, from a few hundred persons to over thirty-five thousand. Because of this variation, simple sampling could not be relied on to yield a precise sample. This problem was dealt with by stratifying wards by size, and weighting large wards against selection. Thus two stages of sampling were involved. In the first stage wards were selected from the ordered list, on a fixed sampling interval. This interval was not measured in terms of the ward number in the list (e.g.

[1] Maltese of course here means Malta-born, as this was the basis of census categorisations.

every tenth ward), but in terms of cumulative population. That is, those wards containing every 30,000th person were picked out, then placed in strata according to the size of their population. Twelve strata were used, around mid-points that were multiples of 3,000. The first stratum (notional mid-point 3,000) received wards sized up to 4,499, the second (mid-point 6,000) wards between 4,500 and 7,499 and so on. The second stage sampling fraction assigned to each stratum was simply the reciprocal of the number of population units by which admission to the stratum was defined. Thus the chance of selection at this stage for wards in the first stratum was 100 per cent, that for wards in the second stratum 50 per cent, in the third stratum 33 per cent and so on. Selection within each stratum was on a fixed-interval basis with a random starting point between 1 and n. The overall chance of selection for wards of all sizes was thereby kept at 10 per cent, and a reasonable distribution along the spectrum of Maltese densities maintained at the same time.

The second complicating issue was that one fifth of all Malta-born persons enumerated in London County in the 1961 census were concentrated in twelve wards, each with at least 0·5 per cent Maltese density, and grouped together at the head of the ordered density list. The sampling procedure adopted for the rest of the wards would not be suitable here, because chance inclusion or exclusion of one or two of them would greatly affect the size and representativeness of the sample as a whole. However, since these wards were also clustered geographically, there were fewer potential difficulties involved in compiling complete registers of Maltese individuals in them and adding a further stage of sampling. So a different sampling fraction was used for these twelve wards, which was corrected by a suitable sampling fraction of eligible individuals within the wards picked. In brief, four of the twelve wards were selected, and an internal, individual sampling fraction of 28 per cent used to adjust this component of the general sample to the proportion of Malta-born persons contained in these twelve wards in the 1961 census. Altogether therefore 39 wards were picked.

Conduct of the 1967 enquiry

Pilot interviewing was carried out in spring 1966, in wards not selected for the main sample. By the summer a final questionnaire had evolved and the main interviewing began. Groups of neighbouring wards were dealt with together, but interviewing within a ward was carried out in as short a span of time as possible, to avoid ambiguities created by changes of residence. The general rule adopted was that Maltese resident in a ward when interviewing was started there were eligible. Those moving into a ward during interviewing were not included, but those moving out after the starting-date were traced to new addresses when this was feasible.

Because of the part-time nature of the research, and the distances involved even within the London area, this programme was not considered adequately tackled until Easter 1968, at which time those remaining sample-members who had not been contacted and interviewed were finally abandoned. In the course of this rather drawn-out process, 139 eligible Maltese men were interviewed (of which 130 were seen personally, and nine seen only by Ed. Zammit, a Maltese researcher who was interested in an overlapping field). This figure was short of the intended 200 – but the returns for extra effort were diminishing fast and time was needed to pursue other enquiries.

The contact and response figures for the enquiry were as follows:

GROSS SAMPLE	(i.e. total known or believed to be eligible)	166
NET SAMPLE	(eligible men interviewed)	139
REFUSALS	(eligible men contacted but not interviewed – for whatever reason)	21
NON-CONTACTS	(Men probably eligible but not properly contacted and checked)	6

It is likely that in addition to these there were also a number of eligible men with whom no contact was made at all. This would include a number of young, highly mobile newcomers, not living with established settlers and not yet on the voting lists in their own right. Because of the weakness of the Maltese community, very few contacts were in fact made through personal information, and almost all respondents were located via the voting lists. By the same token, any Maltese in the areas who were passing as English, and using non-Maltese surnames, would also have been missed and this is likely to have been the main group missed by

the sampling method. The main bias in the enquiry is thus
inevitably towards those Maltese involved in the ethnic community.

Estimating the size and composition of the London settlement

Although it is not possible to attach confidence levels to estimates
derived from the 1967 enquiry, the data it provides on Maltese
households and people is definitely useful as a guide to the
probable constitution, and even volume, of Maltese settlement
in London. The total numbers of Maltese persons contained in
the households of the 1967 net sample members was as follows:

TOTAL MALTESE IN NET SAMPLE HOUSEHOLDS		371
a. *Total Malta-born Maltese*		207
i.e. Eligible men interviewed	139	
Ineligible men (e.g. grew up in U.K.)	6	
Malta-born Maltese women	38	
Malta-born Maltese children	24	
b. *Total UK-born Maltese*		164
Full descent	55	
Maltese father only	109	

It is not possible to give household composition for Maltese
men *not* interviewed; but the following figures of adult men of
Maltese descent or part-descent who were contacted in the course
of the enquiry (i.e. in the sampled wards) gives a rough indication
of the number of households which may be involved:

ADULT MALES OF MALTESE BIRTH OR DESCENT		228
a. *Malta-born men*		176
Gross sample	166	
Ineligible men (who grew up outside of Malta)	10	
(i.e. within net sample households	6)	
outside net sample households	4)	
b. *Adult men of Maltese descent only*		52
Born Egypt, Tunisia, France etc.	44	
Born UK (in net sample households)	5	
Born UK (not in sample households)	3	

As argued above, there is some understatement of young, mobile
bachelors by the 1967 sample, and of established 'passers'. But

even when some allowance is made for failure to locate such people, the maximum total of adult males in these wards born in Malta is unlikely to have been much higher than 200 to 250; and the total Malta-born Maltese would be somewhere between 275 and 350. This is broadly in line with the overall estimates given in Table B.1 in Appendix B.

The findings of the 1967 enquiry also generally support the estimates put forward in Appendix B of the sexual composition of the settlement. The male proportion of Malta-born persons in the net sample households was 76 per cent. After allowance has been made for service-brides, some of whom were contacted in sample areas as originators of migration chains, the true proportion is still not very likely to move below 70 per cent. If young newcomers, mainly bachelors, are indeed under-represented in this sample then the real figure may even be higher than this. In so far as this is an accurate sample, it might suggest that estimates given of the size of the settlement in Table B.1, especially from the 1966 sample census, are if anything on the large side.

Questionnaire used in the 1967 enquiry

(N.B. When the schedules were printed some element of pre-coding was included in the hope that responses would fall within set patterns. No prompting was used, and in fact for most questions the anticipated response categories were not very useful. The pre-codes were not used in the final analysis, and are not reproduced here. Most of the personal information about respondents was amassed through the construction of detailed kinship charts before the formal questions were put. In addition to recording a great deal of data, these charts served to establish rapport before systematic interviewing took place. The questions reproduced below constituted the formal part of the interview.)

1 How old were you when you left school? (What further training have you had since?)
2 What was your first job after leaving school?
3 What was your last job in Malta?
4 What was your first job in Britain?
5 What is your present job?

6 How long have you had it?

7 Are you satisfied with your present job? (i.e. for the next few years at least)

8 How old were you when you first left Malta to live abroad?

9 How old were you when you first came to live in Britain? (Where did you live between Malta and Britain?)

10 Have you been back to Malta since you came to Britain? IF YES How long have you spent there altogether since you first came to Britain?

11 Why did you leave Malta?

12 Why did you come to *Britain*?

13 When you were first coming to Britain, how long did you expect to stay for?

14 How long do you now expect to stay for?

15 How long have you been living at this address?

16 What other parts of London, or other towns, have you lived in? (List in order.)

17 What part of London, or England, would you most like to live in? Why?

18 Do you think of yourself now as Maltese or English?

19 Where do your nearest Maltese neighbours live? (i.e. outside same address)

20 How much do you see of other Maltese people in London?

21 Where do you meet them?

22 Would you like to be able to meet *more* Maltese people?

23 Do you think the Maltese in London should get together more to preserve Maltese culture and way of life?

24 Have you ever belonged to any Maltese societies in London? (If NO Why not?; If YES What and how found out about?)

25 Do you think that the Maltese in London are a very united group? (What factions, section etc.?)

26 Who would you say are the leaders of the Maltese community?

27 Do you think that Maltese from Tunisia/Egypt etc. form separate groups from the Maltese from Malta?

28 Do you ever go to the Malta Catholic Centre? (Or even know of it?)

29 Do you consider yourself a good Catholic?

30 When did you last attend Mass?

31 When did you last make a confession?

32 Do you or will you send your children to a Catholic school and church?

33 Why is it that some Maltese stop being good Catholics when they come to Britain?

34 Have you ever had any difficulties in Britain just because you were Maltese?

35 Have you ever had any trouble finding work in Britain? (i.e. ever out of work for more than three months?)

36 Have you ever had any trouble with the police in Britain? (What happened about it?)

37 Why do you think it is that some Maltese *do* get into trouble with the police in Britain? (Which Maltese are they?)

38 Who is to blame?

39 What can be done to prevent or stop it?

40 Do you think that these Maltese (who get into trouble) have given the rest a bad name?

41 How did you first find out about this?

42 Have you personally suffered any insults or other trouble because of this bad name? (If YES How do you feel when this happens?)

43 Is there anything that ordinary Maltese can do to save their good name?

44 Do you think that the community of good Maltese should do anything to control the bad ones? (Any attempts known of?)

45 Do you think that the Maltese Priests have had success in this yet?

46 Have you ever thought of changing your name so that people would not know that you come from Malta?

47 Do you know (of) anyone who *has* done this?

48 Do you think Maltese people need to change much, to be happy in Britain? How? Are you happy?

49 If you won the football pools or the lottery, would you go back to Malta then?

50 What are the main differences between life in Britain and life in Malta?

51 What do you miss most, away from Malta?

Tabulations of results of the enquiry

A series of tables is presented below to show the findings of the investigation which have a close bearing on the argument in the main text. In these tabulations the relationships between sets of variables are expressed through 'indicators of association'. This index is a simple device which describes more clearly than percentaging the two-way association of variables in a matrix where cell sizes differ considerably. Essentially each index value represents the cases actually found in a cell as a factor of the cases which would be expected in that cell if there were no association between the variables – and is computed therefore in a very similar way to a chi-square test. *Index values above unity indicate a positive association between variables, values below unity* (including nought) *a negative association, and values close to unity itself no particular association either way.* The index does not itself measure the significance of relations, and so a 'p' value is also given, from the standard chi-square test, to show the probability of observed deviations from unity in the matrix as a whole being due to chance.

Appendix D

TABLE D.1 *Summary of factors associated with types of involvement in the ethnic community (indicators of association)* *

	Café society	Formal associations	Non-involvement	Private socialising	n	p
			Types of involvement			

a. Nature of migration

	Café society	Formal associations	Non-involvement	Private socialising	n	p
Reason for leaving Malta						
Escape and adventure	1·5	0·0	1·1	0·5	33	
Economic	1·0	0·9	0·9	1·2	68	0·015
Other reasons	0·4	2·3	1·0	1·1	28	
Age at arrival in Britain						
15–25	1·1	0·4	1·0	1·2	86	0·05
26 and over	0·8	2·0	1·0	0·5	46	
Period of arrival in Britain						
Before 1951	0·9	0·2	1·4	0·5	47	
1951–60	0·9	0·9	1·0	1·2	50	<0·001
Since 1960	1·2	2·1	0·5	1·4	36	

b. Economic status

	Café society	Formal associations	Non-involvement	Private socialising	n	p
Job status						
Non-manual	0·4	2·7	1·2	0·5	32	
Skilled manual	0·9	0·6	1·2	1·0	48	<0·001
Unskilled manual	1·5	0·3	0·7	1·4	53	
Tenure of current job						
Less than 2 years, & OOW	1·5	1·1	0·8	0·5	50	
2 years but less than 10	0·6	1·0	1·1	1·6	52	0·02
10 years or longer	0·8	0·7	1·3	0·6	25	

c. Family life

	Café society	Formal associations	Non-involvement	Private socialising	n	p
Period as bachelor in Britain						
None	0·7	2·0	1·0	0·6	27	
Less than 5 years	1·1	0·9	0·9	1·3	62	0·3
5 years or more	1·0	0·5	1·2	0·8	41	
Marriage type						
Not married	1·7	1·4	0·4	1·0	33	
Wife Maltese	0·5	1·8	0·9	1·8	37	<0·001
Wife not Maltese	0·9	0·3	1·4	0·5	63	

Table D.1—*continued*

Children per household						
No children	1·4	0·6	0·7	0·8	48	
1 or 2	0·7	1·0	1·1	1·4	53	0·05
3 or more	0·8	1·7	1·3	0·4	24	

d. Attitudes to Maltese institutions

Last Mass attendance						
Within one year	0·3	2·7	1·0	1·2	48	
Between 1 and 5 years ago	1·9	0·0	0·7	0·8	31	<0·001
5 or more years ago	1·2	0·0	1·2	0·9	53	
Attitudes towards Maltese Priests in London						
Hostile	1·7	0·0	0·9	0·7	35	
Tolerant or neutral	0·7	1·7	1·0	0·9	73	0·003
Don't know of them	0·7	0·0	1·2	1·9	16	
Maltese political party supported						
Not interested/None	0·9	0·9	1·2	0·9	58	
Malta Labour Party	1·2	0·9	0·8	1·0	46	0·65
Nationalists/Constitutional Party	0·7	1·7	1·0	1·3	18	

e. Conception of the community

View on unity of London Maltese						
NO we are not united	1·4	0·9	0·9	0·7	53	
YES we are united	1·2	1·9	0·4	1·7	24	0·004
Yes THEY are united	0·3	0·0	1·6	1·2	20	
Don't know	0·6	1·2	1·3	0·8	31	
View on desirability of greater degeee of association with other Maltese in London						
No objection/would welcome it	1·8	1·5	0·4	1·0	44	
Association bad or dangerous	0·7	0·7	1·3	1·0	68	<0·001
No time personally	0·0	0·8	1·7	0·7	12	
n	42	14	61	16	133	

Source: Questions 20 and 21, against various others.
* See note preceding table for explanation.

TABLE D.2 *Summary of characteristics of criminal offenders* in London Maltese sample (indicators of association)†*

	None known	Minor offences	Serious offences	n	p
		Criminal record			

a. Position in the ethnic community

	None known	Minor offences	Serious offences	n	p
Type of involvement in community					
Café society	0·7	1·2	2·5	42	
Formal associators	1·4	0·0	0·0	14	0·0001
Informal – withdrawn	1·1	1·1	0·4	77	
Period of arrival in Britain					
Before 1951	0·8	1·2	1·7	52	
1951–60	1·0	1·2	0·7	51	0·035
Since 1960	1·2	0·6	0·4	36	

b. Occupation type

	None known	Minor offences	Serious offences	n	p
Job status					
Non-manual	1·1	0·4	1·0	35	
Skilled manual	1·0	1·1	0·9	50	0·3
Unskilled manual	0·9	1·3	1·2	54	
Tenure of current job					
Out of work	0·8	0·5	2·2	13	
Less than 2 years	1·0	1·3	0·8	37	0·1
2 years but less than 10	1·1	1·1	0·4	53	
10 years or longer	1·0	0·6	2·0	27	
Ever had catering job in Britain					
Yes	0·7	1·7	1·6	59	
No	1·2	0·4	0·5	73	0·001

c. Family life

	None known	Minor offences	Serious offences	n	p
Marriage type					
Not married	1·1	0·6	1·1	36	
Wife Maltese	1·2	0·7	0·3	38	0·1
Wife not Maltese	0·9	1·5	1·2	65	
Period as bachelor in Britain					
None	1·2	0·4	0·6	27	
Less than 5 years	1·0	1·1	0·6	62	0·08
5 years or more	0·8	1·1	1·8	44	
Served in Merchant Navy since came to Britain					
Yes	0·7	1·8	2·0	32	
No	1·1	0·8	0·7	99	0·04
n	98	21	20	139	

References to table on facing page

TABLE D.3 *Relation between ideas about group unity and frequency of ethnic contacts (indicators of association)*

Contacts with Maltese	Yes THEY are united	Don't know	Ideas about group unity		n
			NOT United	Yes WE are united	
Weekly or more often	0·1	0·7	1·1	2·0	43
Less often than weekly	1·5	1·2	0·9	0·5	82
n	20	31	50	24	125
p	< 0·001				

Source: Questions 20 × 25.

* Classification of offenders in the sample is based on findings of the 1968 court record analysis (see Appendix E) *plus* information given in interviews. So the group includes men convicted at courts other than those used in the 1968 analysis, and is slightly broader than the 'net criminal sub-sample' discussed in Appendix E.
† For explanation see note preceding Table D.1.

TABLE D.4 *Summary of factors associated with types of response to the Maltese bad name (indicators of association)*

	Attribution of blame for Maltese crime in London			Action proposed to prevent Maltese crime in London			
	Maltese community	Individual perpetrators	English community	Maltese community reforms	None: up to individuals	Action by English agencies	n
a. Class							
Non-manual	2·3	0·6	1·1	2·1	0·7	1·5	28
Skilled manual	0·7	1·1	1·1	0·8	1·0	1·1	45
Unskilled manual	0·5	1·2	0·9	0·5	1·2	0·6	45
n	21	82	18	14	83	24	121
P	0·015			0·015			
b. Type of involvement in the ethnic group							
Café society	0·4	1·2	0·9	0·4	1·3	0·3	39
Formal associations	1·1	1·0	0·9	3·2	0·8	0·4	13
Private socialising	0·7	1·1	0·9	1·6	0·7	1·6	16
Non-involvement	1·4	0·9	1·1	0·7	0·9	1·5	57
n	22	82	18	15	86	24	125
P	0·5			$< 0·0001$			

c. Last Mass attendance

Within one year	1·3	1·0	0·7	2·2	0·9	0·7	46
Between 1 and 5 years ago	0·8	1·0	1·4	0·3	1·1	1·1	30
5 or more years ago	0·9	1·0	1·0	0·4	1·0	1·2	46
n	22	82	18	14	84	24	122
P		0·6			0·02		

d. Political support in Malta

Nationalists/Constitutional Party	1·7	0·8	0·8	3·4	0·6	0·9	17
Malta Labour Party	1·3	1·0	0·6	0·8	0·9	1·4	42
Not interested/None	0·6	1·0	1·4	0·3	1·2	0·7	53
n	20	77	17	13	78	21	112
P		0·15			<0·001		

Source: Questions 38/39 × 5, 20/21, 30 and 24.

APPENDIX E
THE COURT RECORD ANALYSIS

Introduction

The purpose of this analysis was to provide some fairly hard evidence about the overall pattern and trend in Maltese criminality in London, against which arguments about the origin and consequences of the Maltese reputation could be assessed more realistically. The Metropolitan Police had prepared annual tabulations since 1951 showing the countries of origin of men convicted of living on immoral earnings; but for earlier periods, and other types of offence, there were no separate statistics available. Following the Commonwealth Immigrants Act the Home Office has kept figures, by country of origin, of individuals recommended for deportation. But this was too limited, and too late in period, to meet the points at issue. The critical questions of when the Maltese had started to be associated with vice offences in London, and what share of their total criminality this accounted for, could not be tackled on the officially prepared data.

Materials analysed

The most important single consideration governing the choice of source materials was the need to keep the task to a minimum. In principle the most detailed and reliable figures could have been obtained from central police records, but this would have entailed an enormous amount of work, for information not of central importance in the study considered as a whole.

In view of the small size of the Maltese community in London, the best course to take seemed to be to select one or two areas where Maltese crime was known to occur relatively frequently, and to use the accessible and comprehensive source of local magistrates' court records. The courts were chosen which seemed likely to have handled a large part of Maltese criminal activity in London, throughout the main period of settlement. These were Thames Court in Stepney, covering a major section of the principal Maltese settlement in London, and Marlborough Street Court, dealing with an important part of Soho in which Maltese clubs and cafés have traditionally operated.

During late spring and summer 1968 the registers of these courts were examined in the following manner. Starting with the most recent issues made available to me (1966 at Thames and 1964 at Marlborough Street) and working backwards, I scanned through the main court registers and listed the details of all court appearances of people with Maltese surnames. Secondary court registers, dealing almost solely with very trivial offences, and matrimonial court registers, were not examined. Next, wherever possible, the ethnicity of supposed Maltese offenders was verified by reference to the evidence notebooks in which details of the hearing and of the defendant's background and previous convictions were set out. It was extremely rare for offenders selected in this way to turn out not to be Maltese (there were one or two Italians); so the method seems to have been quite reliable in that direction. On the other hand, of course, Maltese with non-Maltese names would have been missed altogether. The Messina Brothers, some of whom appeared at Marlborough Street Court, were not counted as Maltese.

Classification of offences used in tabulations of findings

Vice Living on immoral earnings. Keeping, managing or allowing a brothel. Controlling or aiding prostitutes or procuring to become a prostitute.

Sex Indecent assaults and unlawful intercourse. Soliciting (either for homosexual act, or on behalf of prostitute). Allowing prostitutes to assemble (in club etc.).

Violence Murder, attempted murder and all grades of physical assault and bodily harm. Possession of offensive weapons and assaults on police.

Property All forms of larceny. Breaking and entering. Robbery, with and without violence. Receiving and being in possession of stolen property. Fraud. Forgery.

Gaming Keeping or being found in illegal gaming house; allowing illegal gaming. Street betting.

Nuisance Drunk. Possessing drugs. Loitering and wandering. Obstructing footway or police. Insulting and threatening behaviour. Resisting arrest.

Other (Most common offences) Illegal trading and obstructing street. Driving while drunk, disqualified, uninsured, unlicensed, without care etc. Taking and driving vehicle. Perjury. Allowing children to reside in a brothel.

Findings of the analysis

In both courts, appearances of Maltese began in the early war years and built up steadily through the 1940s. A small sample of registers was examined to well back before the First World War, but appearances by Maltese seemed to be pretty well non-existent before 1941, and no systematic analysis was made for earlier than 1935.

Tabulations have been made, starting with the year 1941, for male Maltese convicted in these courts or sent to a higher court. In the period covered, 2,680 convictions involving Maltese were found in the registers. The tabulations count each identifiable individual once per calendar year in which convicted, per court. Consequently the totals of annual offences given in these tabulations are greater than the annual *offender* totals. Similarly, where five-year periods are used, the totals would overstate even more the number of different individual offenders, since each person would be counted for each year in which he was convicted. For example, in Table E.2, column 8 shows the total of offenders in the years making up each period, column 9 the number of types of offences of which they were convicted (counting each type of offence as in columns 1–7, once per person per year) and column 10 gives the gross total of counts on which the offenders were convicted. Columns 1–7 show the numbers of men convicted of an offence of that type; thus the total for columns 1–7 is provided by column 9.

The main findings of the analysis are summarised in the following tabulations.

Appendix E

TABLE E.1 *Annual numbers of convictions* of Maltese men, by court, 1941–66*

	Marlborough Street Court			Thames Court		
	Decade					
Year	1940	1950	1960	1940	1950	1960
0		35	35		70	95
1	5	54	29	5	105	58
2	17	97	27	19	64	69
3	24	63	33	29	64	78
4	17	50	47	29	60	64
5	39	22		32	181	95
6	33	11		27	155	131
7	24	13		24	117	
8	18	15		27	145	
9	60	25		22	114	

* Figures given are totals of *offences* for which Maltese men convicted in year in question, not totals of offenders.

TABLE E.2 *Types of offences of Maltese men convicted in two London courts, 1941–66*

Period	Types of offence							Men convicted	Totals* Offences by types	Convictions
	Vice	Sex	Violence	Property	Gaming	Nuisance	Other			
	1	2	3	4	5	6	7	8	9	10
1941–5	20	1	13	45	46	32	19	154	176	215
1946–50	31	1	28	52	83	61	23	239	279	339
1951–5	62	12	38	82	276	96	28	542	594	757
1956–60	103	12	93	89	97	149	53	529	596	735
1961–5†	41	9	46	118	11	102	59	345	386	513
1966†	4	3	10	22	9	9	13	57	70	121
Totals	261	38	228	408	522	449	195	1,866	2,101	2,680

* For column 8, each person counted once per calendar year in which convicted; for column 9, each person counted once per calendar year, per offence category (as in columns 1–7) for which convicted.
† Figures for 1965 and 1966 for Thames Court only.

TABLE E.3 *Types of offences* for which Maltese men convicted in London, 1941–66 (two London courts) (percentages†)*

Period	Vice	Violence	Property	Gaming	Sex & nuisance	Other	n (100%) Men‡
			a. All offenders				
1941–50	13	10	25	33	24	11	393
1951–5	11	7	15	51	20	5	542
1956–60	19	18	17	18	31	10	529
1961–6	11	14	35	5	31	18	402
1941–66	14	12	22	28	26	10	1,866

		b. Serious offenders§			
Period	Vice	Violence	Property	Other	n (100%) Men
1941–50	35	22	40	29	111
1951–5	38	20	33	32	133
1956–60	48	26	21	22	188
1961–6	27	20	48	31	143
1941–66	38	22	34	28	575

* Each offender counted *once* per calendar year convicted, per offence category in which convicted, regardless of the number of their sentences.

† Percentages given are of total people convicted, not of total offences. Since some offenders were convicted in the same year for offences of different types, the summation of category proportions leads to a total in excess of 100 per cent.

‡ Again, total column refers to number of men, counting each individual once only per calendar year in which convicted.

§ Offenders imprisoned or sent for trial in calendar year. N.B. Figures indicate per cent of serious offenders convicted (or sent for trial) in respect of that type of offence – but not all *offences* counted are *serious*.

TABLE E.4 *Locations of Maltese convictions for living on immoral earnings in London, 1941–64*

		Convictions found in court registers			
Period	Total*	Thames Court	Marlborough Street Court	2 courts as % of total	Balance (other courts)
1941–5	—	3	8	—	—
1946–50	—	12	11	—	—
1951–4	60	26	6	53	28
1955–9	171	88	3	53	80
1960–4	113	30	5	31	78
1941–64	344	159	33		186

* Figures from Metropolitan Police.

TABLE E.5 *Location of Maltese vice convictions in London, 1941–66 (two London courts)*

| Period | Number of offenders | | Vice offenders as % of total offenders | |
	Marlborough Street Court	Thames Court	Marlborough* Street Court	Thames Court
1941–5	13	7	17	9
1946–50	18	13	15	11
1951–5	11	51	5	15
1956–60	3	100	4	22
1961–6	10	35	10	12
1941–66	55	206	10	16

* To 1964 only.

TABLE E.6 *Ages of Maltese men convicted in London, 1941–66 (two London courts) (percentages)*

| Period | All offenders | | | | Serious offenders | | | |
	15–25	26–35	36+	n (100%)	15–25	26–35	36+	n (100%)
1941–50	19	37	44	393	21	35	44	111
1951–5	32	37	31	539	35	41	24	133
1956–60	38	35	27	525	43	35	22	187
1961–66	42	28	30	395	49	31	20	141
1941–66	33	35	32	1,852	38	35	27	572

TABLE E.7 *Occupations of Maltese men convicted in London, 1941–66*
(two London courts) (percentages*)

	Type of work			Class of occupation				
Period	Seaman	Café/ club	Other	Unemployed/ No job stated	Unskilled manual	Skilled manual and small bus.	Non-manual	n (100%)†
	1	2	3	4	5	6	7	8

a. All offenders

Period	Seaman	Café/club	Other	Unempl.	Unskilled	Skilled	Non-manual	n
1941–50	32	29	32	7	67	25	1	393
1951–5	16	27	42	14	67	18	1	542
1956–60	14	24	36	25	54	20	2	529
1961–6	8	18	47	27	50	21	2	402
1941–66	17	25	39	19	60	20	2	1,866

b. Serious offenders

Period	Seaman	Café/club	Other	Unempl.	Unskilled	Skilled	Non-manual	n
1941–50	32	21	33	14	58	28		111
1951–5	14	23	35	28	56	16		133
1956–60	10	24	26	40	43	16	1	188
1961–6	6	16	36	42	41	16	1	143
1941–66	14	21	32	33	49	18	1	575

* Counting each person once per calendar year in which convicted.
† Columns 1–4 inclusive = 100%, and columns 4–7 inclusive = 100%.

The 1967 'criminal sub-sample'

Some of the offenders detected in the 1968 court record analysis were members of the 1967 general sample, and can usefully be regarded as constituting a criminal sub-sample. Thirty-four of the net (interviewed) 1967 sample were discovered in the 1968 analysis, and 45 members of the gross sample. Their share of the convictions analysed is shown in Table E.8.

The 1967 sub-sample of offenders have an average of about four convictions per person, over the period covered. If this is assumed to be representative of all offenders (and no analysis was made of non-members of the 1967 sample) then about 650 different individuals would be needed to account for the total offences found in these courts.

TABLE E.8 *Share of offences in two London courts attributable to 1967 sub-sample*

Sample	Net individuals*	Gross individuals†	Gross convictions‡
1967 net sample	34	104	154
1967 gross sample	45	127	185
1968 analysis total	650§	1,866	2,680

* Each person counted once only.
† Each person counted once for each year in which convicted.
‡ Total counts on which individuals convicted.
§ Estimated.

The 1967 offender sub-sample appears to be reasonably representative of all the men listed in the 1968 analysis (which itself is of course only a 'sample' of Maltese offenders in London), as it is close to the average in its overall distribution of characteristics. Most of the items on which the sub-sample do differ seem to be reducible to the period in which the offence was committed. Not surprisingly, there are fewer early offenders in the 1967 sub-sample. This can easily be accounted for by deaths of older offenders. The other differences, such as more serious offenders and more unskilled workers, can be related to the relative recency of offences.

TABLE E.9 *Characteristics of 1967 sub-sample (percentages)*

Item	1967 sample		1968 analysis
	Gross	Net	Total
a. Period of conviction			
1941–50	14	15	21
1951–5	27	29	29
1956–60	30	27	28
1961–6	29	29	22
b. Job status of offender			
Unskilled manual	64	68	60
Skilled manual and small business	36	31	38
Non-manual			2
c. Type of work of offender			
Seaman	14	15	17
Café/club	30	26	25
Other	38	39	39
Unemployed/none given	18	19	19
d. Age of offender			
15–25	29	32	33
26–35	34	31	35
36+	37	37	32
e. Type of offence*			
Vice/sex	18	14	16
Violence	13	11	12
Property	18	17	22
Other	67	74	62
f. Sentence received			
Discharge/probation	26	29	23
Fine	40	38	46
Prison/trial	34	33	31

* As percentage of *offenders*, not of offences. Since offenders often convicted of more than one type of offence, total adds up to more than 100 per cent.

APPENDIX F
POSTAL SURVEY ON ATTITUDES TO MALTESE IN LONDON

A postal investigation was carried out around Easter 1969 among non-Maltese people in two parts of London, concerning their contacts with and knowledge about Maltese living here. The expenses of this enquiry were covered by a grant from the University of London Central Research Fund.

The purpose of the survey was to provide some estimates of the general distribution of the attitudes towards Maltese and the Maltese community which had emerged in the course of a couple of dozen pilot interviews with non-Maltese individuals at the time of the main 1967 study. Only a postal enquiry could have possibly yielded sufficient material in the time available. In spite of the undoubted drawbacks of self-completion questionnaires, no alternative seemed feasible.

The main items on which information was sought were the extent of respondents' contact with Maltese people, their knowledge and acceptance of the Maltese 'bad name', their assessment of the degree of solidarity of the community and their judgment on whether or not it should be regarded as a collectively responsible group.

Problems of the postal investigation

Any discussion of the Maltese bad name necessarily involves some degree of further publication and promulgation of the reputation, but this creates more of a moral dilemma in a postal survey than in one conducted verbally. In a face-to-face situation one may be able to raise offensive issues obliquely, and avoid provoking antagonism towards third parties by adjusting the terms of a conversation to the sentiments of other participants. This is not feasible in a printed questionnaire, where if the topic

276

of Maltese criminality was going to be dealt with at all, it needed to be stated reasonably explicitly – and equally so for everyone.

Fortunately this moral issue coincided to some extent with practical considerations about the best form to be taken by the questions. One of the major difficulties in a self-completion questionnaire is that since many people will read the whole thing through before beginning to answer it, issues cannot be raised gradually as later questions may contaminate responses to the earlier ones. Also the more specific a question, the more it may suggest or lead responses by providing ideas or information on matters which the respondent *may* not have considered before. A major aim of this investigation was to establish how far non-Maltese people were in fact aware of the Maltese reputation. It would not have been possible to proceed without mentioning at all on the schedule the existence, or alleged existence, of a reputation. But equally it was essential that no reference should be made to the *content* of the bad name; so the practical need to remain vague coincided nicely with the ethical requirement of not fomenting anti-Maltese sentiments too blatantly. The questions referring to the reputation (9 and 10) were therefore left deliberately vague, so that respondents who did *not* know what the reputation was all about would not be prompted into airing (or developing) artificial views on it. This strategem seems to have been quite effective. Those respondents who claimed knowledge of the reputation tended to show in their answers to the open-ended questions 12–14 that they *did* know about the bad name as understood and experienced by Maltese. In some cases the receipt of the questionnaire may have prompted people to ask friends about it before filling it in; but the incentive to do this cannot have been very great, as questionnaires were anonymous and there was no reason to deny ignorance.

The price of this looseness in the formulation of questions is however a certain ambiguity in some of the responses. This can be illustrated by reference to a different question – the very important and central one on collective responsibility (Question 15). Respondents were asked 'Do you feel that the Maltese community in London has any responsibility to try to control Maltese individuals who are leading a bad life here?' The intention of this question was to establish whether the respondent considered that the group should be regarded as accountable to the rest of society for any anti-social behaviour of members. The wording seemed the best of several alternative forms tried out in pilot interviews; but it was nevertheless ambiguous. For example, it makes no precise distinction between moral and legal responsibility. Thus two respondents replied that the Maltese did not have any collective responsibility for members – but that they *should* have. That is, legally they don't have but morally they *do*. Other respondents who interpreted the question in the same legalistic way may simply have replied 'No', although a yes response would have been more appropriate for my purpose. In the piloting of this particular question the formulation 'should have any responsibility' was in fact tried out as an alternative, but was found to be less generally useful than the wording adopted in the postal investigation. The reasons for this were as follows:

i. For most people the concept of 'responsibility' already connotes a prescriptive evaluation, so that 'should' is in fact *implied*; if it is *stated* in addition, the meaning shifts towards formalising the responsibility in some legal accountability, i.e. 'should be *made* to have'.

ii. The question 'should Maltese have any responsibility' somehow also manages to give the impression that they are currently refusing to accept any, and that action may be needed to prompt them, again perhaps by *formalising* the situation. This seemed to be a much more leading question than the one eventually used. Certainly during verbal piloting it often appeared to elicit an automatic response of 'Yes', whereas the wording adopted for the postal questionnaire takes a much more matter-of-fact line and seemed to get closer to respondents' spontaneous feelings about group blame.

iii. Finally, the more conditional question, of whether the Maltese ought or should take some responsibility for controlling compatriots in London can easily, in view of the content of questions 7 and 8, be taken as about whether it is *in their interests* to do so. The form actually used minimises this interpretation.

Similar difficulties arise in relation to the analysis of responses to several of the other questions, and the detailed interpretation of replies is unfortunately very dependent on the insights provided by the depth interviews (relatively speaking) of the verbally-conducted pilot. The postal investigation would be much more difficult to deal with in isolation, and can serve really only to generalise to some extent the findings of the pilot.

The conduct of the enquiry

The sample of non-Maltese respondents was originally intended to provide comparisons between three sectors of the population thought likely to have different ideas about the Maltese:

a)   Male electors in Tower Hamlets, the area containing the largest and longest established Maltese settlement in London;
b)   Male electors in an area where Maltese were only just beginning to settle;
c)   Policemen in Central and East London.

After some deliberation, the police authorities refused to distribute questionnaires to members of the force, so only sectors 'a' and 'b' were completed. The area chosen for 'b' was the industrial part of Lower Edmonton, where some Maltese have been settling in recent years, where the class composition seemed not too dissimilar to that of East London, and which was reasonably near to Tower Hamlets so that in the event of a disastrously low postal response rate, a rescue operation to collect questionnaires by hand could be mounted without too much difficulty.

Three hundred male electors were selected systematically in each area, on a fixed interval procedure. Each sample member was in the first instance sent a questionnaire and covering letter, with an addressed envelope for returning the completed schedule. A large number returned the questionnaires blank, stating that they had no contact with Maltese and no knowledge of them. Two weeks later, all sample members who had not identified themselves as having returned the questionnaire were sent a reminder letter (phrased in a way to allow for those sample members who had chosen to return the schedule anonymously); and two weeks after that a final letter with fresh questionnaire and addressed envelope. Altogether 228 completed questionnaires were received, out of the possible total of 600. Details of the response are as follows:

	Completed questionnaire received after			Totals		Complete response rate
	First letter	*Reminder*	*Last letter*	*Received*	*Possible*	
Edmonton	74	30	15	119	300	40%
Tower Hamlets	54	44	11	109	300	36%
Total	128	74	26	228	600	38%

The questionnaire and main findings

The questionnaire used in the postal enquiry is reproduced here with the responses to pre-coded, closed questions filled in, as percentages of the completed total.

LONDON MALTESE STUDY: NON-MALTESE QUESTIONNAIRE

Note. Please answer questions by putting a tick in the box next to the printed answer which represents your own reply. If none of the printed answers corresponds to your own, *write* your answer in your own words in the space below the question.

1   Have you ever been to Malta?

Never	89
Yes, on holiday	1
Yes, lived there or visited often	
Yes, visited when in Services	7
Yes, stationed there in Services	2

2 Do you know any Maltese people in London?

None to your knowledge	70
You have a few Maltese friends or acquaintances	7
You have close Maltese friends or relatives	2
You meet some Maltese in your work	18
You have Maltese neighbours	4

3 How many Maltese people do you think there are in Greater London?

Less than 500	
Between 500 and 1,000	6
Between 1,000 and 5,000	25
Between 5,000 and 10,000	23
Between 10,000 and 50,000	12
More than 50,000	1
You have no idea	32

4 Do you think that the Maltese in London are a very united (close-knit) community? (Tick ONE answer only)

Yes they are or probably are	43
Some are but not others	23
No they are not	5
You have no idea	28

Do you think that it is easy to *recognise* a person as being Maltese?

Yes easy,	13
Possible but not easy	45
Not easy	28
You have no idea	14

6 Would you classify the Maltese as white, coloured or somewhere in-between?

White	21
Coloured	4
In-between	49
Individuals vary	19
You have no idea	5

Please read carefully before answering question 7

Many Maltese people in London have told me that quite a lot of Maltese immigrants here have got themselves into trouble with the police, and that as a result the whole Maltese community has received a bad name. This bad reputation can make things difficult for law-abiding Maltese people here, because the police are liable to suspect *them* of being criminals just because they are Maltese. When this happens to them they feel that they are being made to suffer, unjustly, for the actions of the other, criminal Maltese.

In order to answer the next two questions, I would like you to try to imagine the likely reactions of Maltese people when this sort of thing happens. (Even if you do not know any Maltese people very well, I would like you to try to imagine what their reactions might be; but if you really have no idea please just answer 'Don't know'.)

7   What do you imagine would be the likely reaction of a law-abiding Maltese person who is suspected of an offence by the police, just because he is Maltese?

Would he a) try to *dissociate himself* from other Maltese, to help himself avoid police suspicion in the future;

or would he b) *join with other* law-abiding members of the Maltese community in efforts to control the criminal Maltese individuals, to prevent them causing further trouble for the innocent ones?

(Tick one answer only)

a. Probably dissociate himself	22
b. Probably join with other Maltese	44
You don't know	32

8   Secondly, what do you imagine would be the likely reaction of a law-abiding Maltese person who is not in any trouble himself, but who hears that a friend is under suspicion by the police just because he is Maltese?

Would he a) try to *dissociate himself* somehow from other Maltese, to avoid possible police suspicion of himself in the future;

or would he b) *join with other* law-abiding Maltese in efforts to control the criminal Maltese, to prevent them causing trouble in the future for innocent persons like himself?

(Tick one answer only)

a. Probably dissociate himself	19
b. Probably join with other Maltese	46
You don't know	33

9 Do you consider that the Maltese in London *do* have a bad reputation among other persons?

Yes	16
Yes, some do	26
No or not really	33
You don't know	23

(*If answer* No *or* Don't know *go on to question 15*)

10 Do you think that the reputation is at all true?

Yes, true	8
Yes, true in part or of some	29
No, false	1
You don't know	4

(*If answer* No *go on to question 15*)

11 Can you distinguish those Maltese who are like this, from those who are not, when you first meet them?

Yes	5
No	23
You don't meet any	9

(*If Yes, How do you distinguish them?*)

12 Why do you think it is that some Maltese in London do behave in this way? (*Write in your answer in your own words*)

13 Whose fault is it that this happens? (*Write in your answer*)

14 What could be done to prevent it happening?
(*Write in your answer*)

15 Do you feel that the Maltese community in London has any responsibility to try to control Maltese individuals who are leading a bad life here? (Tick one answer)

Yes, definitely	24
Yes: has some responsibility	29
No	25
You are not sure	18

16 In what ways do you think the Maltese community can try to control them?

Personal influence	27
Punishment of some kind	7
By cutting them off	4
By good example	36
Some other way	3
You have no idea	21

17 Do you think that people in this country have treated Maltese immigrants fairly?

Yes	55
No	4
You don't know	36

18 Do you think that this country is doing enough to help Malta at present?

Yes, doing enough	37
Could do more	14
Should do more	11
You don't know	33

19 Should more Maltese be encouraged to emigrate to this country, or should those already here be helped to go back?

Some more should be encouraged to come	3
No more should be encouraged to come	40
Some should be helped to return	29
You don't know	22

20 Do you think that the majority of Maltese people already in this country are being assimilated easily into our society?

Yes, most of them	24
Yes, some of them	29
Not really	14
You don't know	29

Finally may I ask one or two things about yourself
a. How old are you?
b. Where were you born?
c. How long have you lived in London?
d. Are you married?
e. Do you have any children (and how many)?

f. What is your job at present (or your last job if you are not working)?
g. How long have you had this job (or did you have it)?
h. What was your previous job (if any)?
i. How old were you when you finished your full-time education?
j. Have you done any military service (if so which Service, and as Regular or National Serviceman)?
k. What is your religion?
l. Which political party do you normally support?

Thank you.

Main findings

The most important results of the investigation are outlined in the following tabulations. Relationships between variables are expressed again through 'indicators of association'. For an explanation of this index, see the note preceding Table D.1 in Appendix D.

TABLE F.I *Relation between views on group blame and ideas about Maltese group unity (indicators of association)*

| Ideas about unity | Group blame views | | | | |
	Definite collective responsibility	Some collective responsibility	No collective responsibility or not sure	n	p
Supposed unity of London Maltese:					
Maltese united group	1·3	1·0	0·8	148	
Maltese not united and don't know	0·5	1·0	1·3	71	0·001
n	54	67	98	219	
Supposed means of group internal controls:					
Punishment by group	2·0	0·8	0·6	33	
Group influence and good example	1·1	1·4	0·7	142	< 0·001
No means of control (and don't know)	0·2	0·1	2·1	49	
n	56	71	97	224	
Supposed interest of members in group control:					
Interest in control	1·4	1·3	0·6	100	
Interest in dissociation	0·9	0·8	1·1	48	< 0·001
Not sure	0·3	0·8	1·5	68	
n	53	65	98	216	

Source: Questions 15 × 4, 16 and 7.

TABLE F.2 *Effect of personal contacts with Maltese in London on knowledge and acceptance of Maltese reputation*
(indicators of association)

Personal contacts with Maltese	Knowledge of reputation			Acceptance of reputation*		
	Reputation known	Reputation not known	n	Reputation accepted	Reputation not accepted	n
	1	2		3	4	
Maltese neighbours and personal friends	1·6	0·6	28	1·1		18
Some Maltese met through work	1·4	0·7	39	1·0	1·3	23
No personal contacts	0·8	1·1	158	1·0	1·3	54
n	97	128	225	85	10	95
p		0·001		0·15		

Source: Questions 2 × 9 and 10.
* i.e. where known.

TABLE F.3 *Summary of characteristics of group blamers*
(indicators of association)

	Definite collective responsibility	Some collective responsibility	No collective responsibility or not sure	n	p
a. Age					
i. No contact with Maltese					
21–35	0·6	1·6	0·8	38	
36–50	0·7	0·8	1·3	48	
51 or more	1·1	0·8	1·1	52	0·002
ii. Contact with Maltese					
21–35	0·4	1·0	1·4	19	
36–50	2·0	1·1	0·3	21	
51 or more	1·6	0·9	0·7	23	
n	54	63	84	201	

b. Class

i. No contact with Maltese					
Non-manual	1·0	1·4	0·8	38	
Skilled manual	0·9	0·9	1·2	68	
Unskilled manual	0·4	1·1	1·3	25	0·25
ii. Contact with Maltese					
Non-manual	1·0	1·0	1·0	14	
Skilled manual	1·7	0·8	0·7	33	
Unskilled manual	1·2	1·2	0·6	12	
n	53	59	78	190	

c. Political support

i. No contact with Maltese					
Conservative	1·1	1·2	0·8	30	
Labour	0·9	1·0	1·1	65	
Other	0·7	0·9	1·2	31	0·7
ii. Contact with Maltese					
Conservative	1·7	0·8	0·7	13	
Labour	1·4	0·9	0·8	30	
Other	0·7	1·1	1·2	20	
n	51	60	78	189	

d. Military experience

i. No contact with Maltese					
Regular servicemen	1·1	0·9	1·0	14	
Conscripts	0·9	0·8	1·2	71	
No experience	0·6	1·3	1·0	52	0·3
ii. Contact with Maltese					
Regular servicemen	2·3	0·8	0·3	8	
Conscripts	1·2	1·1	0·7	29	
No experience	1·1	0·9	1·0	26	
n	54	63	83	200	

e. Area of residence

i. No contact with Maltese					
Edmonton	1·0	1·0	1·0	93	
Stepney	0·5	1·1	1·2	61	0·04
ii. Contact with Maltese					
Edmonton	1·9	1·0	0·5	22	
Stepney	1·2	1·0	0·9	44	
n	54	67	99	220	

Source: Questions 15 × 2 × personal characteristics of respondents.

TABLE F.4 *Relation of personal contacts with Maltese in London to views on Maltese immigration (indicators of association)*

Opinion on further Maltese immigration to Britain	Personal contact	No personal contact	n
Some more should be encouraged to come	2·3	0·3	6
No more should be encouraged to come	1·0	1·0	92
Maltese already here should be helped to return	1·4	0·8	65
Don't know	0·4	1·2	50
n	60	153	213
p		0·001	

Source: Questions 2 × 19.

TABLE F.5 *Effect of personal contacts with Maltese in London on ideas about unity of Maltese (indicators of association)*

Ideas on unity	No personal contact	Some contact through work	Maltese friends or neighbours	n
Maltese united group	0·8	1·4	1·5	150
Maltese not united (and don't know)	1·3	0·3	0·0	75
n	159	39	27	225
p		< 0·001		

Source: Questions 4 and 2.

REFERENCES

ALFORD, ROBERT R., *Party and Society,* London: John Murray, 1964.

BAGLEY, CHRISTOPHER, *The Dutch Plural Society,* London: Oxford University Press, 1973.

BANTON, MICHAEL, *The Coloured Quarter,* London: Cape, 1955.

BANTON, MICHAEL, *Race Relations,* London: Tavistock, 1967.

BASTIDE, ROGER, 'Dusky Venus, Black Apollo', *Race,* vol. 3, no. 1, November 1961.

BENN, STANLEY I. and PETERS, RICHARD S., *Social Principles and the Democratic State,* London: Allen & Unwin, 1959.

BERTHOFF, ROWLAND TAPPAN, *British Immigrants in Industrial America,* Cambridge, Mass.: Harvard University Press, 1953.

BLALOCK, HUBERT M., JR, *Towards a Theory of Minority-group Relations,* New York: John Wiley, 1967.

BOHANNAN, LAURA, 'A Genealogical Charter', *Africa,* vol. 22, no. 4, 1952.

BOISSEVAIN, JEREMY, 'Malta; Church and State', *New Society,* no. 75, 27 February 1964.

BOISSEVAIN, JEREMY, *Saints and Fireworks: Religion and Politics in Rural Malta,* London: Athlone Press, 1965.

BOTT, ELIZABETH, *Family and Social Network,* London: Tavistock, 1957.

BOTTOMS, A. E., 'Delinquency among Immigrants', *Race,* vol. 8, no. 4, April 1967.

BOWEN-JONES, HOWARD, DEWDNEY, J. C. and FISHER W. B., *Malta: Background for Development,* Newcastle: King's College, 1961.

CASOLANI, HENRY, *Awake Malta, or the Hard Lesson of Emigration,* Malta: Government Printing Office, 1930.

CENTRE DE RECHERCHES SOCIO-RELIGIEUSES, *The Socio-Religious Study of Malta and Gozo,* Brussels: CRS-R Report 64, 1960.

DAVIS, ALLISON W., GARDNER, B. B. and M. R., *Deep South,* University of Chicago Press, 1941.

DOWNES, DAVID M., *The Delinquent Solution,* London: Routledge & Kegan Paul, 1966.

ECONOMIST INTELLIGENCE UNIT, *Studies on Immigration from the Commonwealth,* London: EIU, 1961-3.

FOOT, PAUL, *Immigration and Race in British Politics*, Harmondsworth: Penguin, 1965.

FORMA, H. B., 'Immorality – A conscientious appreciation of the past and present attitude of the Church of Malta', *Voice of Malta*, September 1967.

FREEDMAN, MAURICE (ed.), *A Minority in Britain*, London: Vallentine, Mitchell, 1955.

GENERAL REGISTER OFFICE, *Censuses of England and Wales, 1841–1931, 1951, Sample Census 1966, 1971*, London: HMSO.

GIBBENS, TREVOR CHARLES NOEL and AHRENFELDT, ROBERT HENRY (eds), *Cultural Factors in Delinquency*, London: Tavistock, 1966.

GLASS, RUTH, *Newcomers: the West Indians in London*, London: Allen & Unwin for Centre for Urban Studies, 1960.

GLUCKMAN, MAX, *Politics, Law and Ritual in Tribal Society*, Oxford: Blackwell, 1965.

GLUCKMAN, MAX (ed.), *The Allocation of Responsibility*, Manchester University Press, 1972.

GREALLY, JOHN, 'Maltese workers in Britain', *Catholic Herald*, 17 June 1966.

GREENWALD, HAROLD, *The Call Girl*, London: Elek Books, 1958.

HANDLIN, OSCAR, *Immigration as a Factor in American History*, Englewood Cliffs: Prentice-Hall, 1959.

HILL, ROBERT, 'Passport to Vice', *People*, 8 February 1959.

HIRO, DILIP, *Black British, White British*, London: Eyre & Spottiswoode, 1971.

HOGGART, RICHARD, *The Uses of Literacy*, Harmondsworth: Penguin, 1958.

HOME OFFICE, *Commonwealth Immigrants Act, 1962: Control of Immigration Statistics, 1962–1972* (Cmnd 2151, 2379, 2658, 2979, 3258, 3594, 4029, 4327, 4620, 4951, 5285), London: HMSO, 1963–73.

ISAAC, JULIUS, *Economics of Migration*, London: Kegan Paul, 1947.

JACKSON, JOHN A., *The Irish in Britain*, London: Routledge & Kegan Paul, 1963.

JEGER, LENA, 'London Maltese', *Guardian*, 14 February 1963.

KLEIN, JOSEPHINE, *Samples from English Culture*, London, 1965.

KRAUSZ, ERNEST, *Ethnic Minorities in Britain*, London: MacGibbon & Kee, 1971.

LAFERLA, A. V., *British Malta*, Malta: Aquilina, 2 vols, 1938, 1947.

LAMBERT, JOHN R., *Crime, Police and Race Relations: a study in Birmingham*, London: Oxford University Press for Institute of Race Relations, 1970.

LEVINE, ROBERT A. and CAMPBELL, DONALD T., *Ethnocentrism: Theories of Conflict, Ethnic Attitudes and Group Behaviour*, New York: Wiley, 1972.

LIJPHART, AREND, 'Consociational democracy', *World Politics,* vol. XXI, January 1969.

LITTLE, KENNETH, *Negroes in Britain,* London: Kegan Paul, 1947.

MACARTNEY, CARLILE AYLMER, *National States and National Minorities,* London: Royal Institute of International Affairs, 1934.

MALTA: CENSUS OFFICE, *Census of the Islands of Malta, Gozo and Comino, 1967,* Valletta: GPO, 1968.

MALTA: CENTRAL OFFICE OF STATISTICS, *An Enquiry into Family Size in Malta and Gozo,* Valletta: GPO, 1963.

MALTA: CENTRAL OFFICE OF STATISTICS, *Annual Abstract of Statistics,* Valletta: GPO, from 1946.

MALTA: CENTRAL OFFICE OF STATISTICS, *Censuses of the Islands of Malta, Gozo & Comino, 1843, 1851–1931, 1948 & 1957,* Valletta: Government Press & GPO.

MALTA: CENTRAL OFFICE OF STATISTICS, *Demographic Review of the Maltese Islands,* Valletta: GPO, annually from 1957.

MALTA: DEPARTMENT OF EMIGRATION, *Annual Reports* (supplements to Malta Government Gazette), Valletta: GPO, 1922/3–1929/30, 1950–5.

MALTA: DEPARTMENT OF EMIGRATION, LABOUR AND SOCIAL WELFARE, *Annual Reports,* Valletta: Dept Information, 1956–64.

MALTA: DEPARTMENT OF LABOUR AND EMIGRATION, *Annual Reports* (supplements to Malta Government Gazette), Valletta: GPO, 1930/1–1949.

MALTA: POLICE DEPARTMENT, *Annual Reports* (supplements to Malta Government Gazette), Valletta: GPO, from 1913–14.

MANNHEIM, HERMANN, *Social Aspects of Crime in England Between the Wars,* London: Allen & Unwin, 1940.

MASON, PHILIP, *Patterns of Dominance,* London: Oxford University Press, 1971.

MILLS, C. WRIGHT, *The Marxists,* New York: Dell, 1962.

MURTAGH, JOHN MARTIN and HARRIS, SARA, *Cast the First Stone,* London: W. H. Allen, 1958.

PARK, ROBERT EZRA and MILLER, HERBERT ADOLPHUS, *Old World Traits Transplanted,* New York: Harper & Bros, 1921.

PARKIN, FRANK, *Class Inequality and Political Order,* London: MacGibbon & Kee, 1971.

PARLIAMENTARY DEBATES, *House of Commons Official Reports* (Debate on the Street Offences Bill: 2nd Reading: vol. 598, 29 January 1959; 3rd Reading: vol. 604, 22 April 1959; Committee Stage: Standing Committee F. Report, 1958–9, vol. IV, 18 February to 8 April 1959).

PHILPOTT, STUART B., 'Remittance obligations, social networks and choice among Montserratian migrants in Britain', *Man,* new series, vol. 3, no. 3, September 1968.

PITKIN, HANNA, *The Concept of Representation*, Berkeley: University of California Press, 1967.

POPPER, KARL R., *The Open Society and Its Enemies*, London: George Routledge & Sons, 1945.

POWELL, ENOCH, Speech to Rotary Club of London at Eastbourne, on 16 November 1968. Text in *Sunday Times*, 17 November 1968.

PRICE, CHARLES A., *Malta and the Maltese: A Study in Nineteenth Century Migration*, Melbourne: Georgian House, 1954.

REICH, WILHELM, *The Mass Psychology of Fascism*, London: Souvenir Press, 1972.

Report of the Committee on Distressed Colonial and Indian Subjects, Cmnd 5133, London: HMSO, April 1910.

Report of the Committee on Homosexual Offences and Prostitution (Wolfenden Report), Cmnd 247, London: HMSO, September 1957.

RESEARCH AGENCY MALTA, *The Parish of Floriana: Report on a Mail Questionnaire*, mimeographed, Valletta: Research Agency Malta, 1961.

REX, JOHN, *Race, Colonialism and the City*, London: Routledge & Kegan Paul, 1973.

ROLPH, C. H. (ed.), *Women of the Streets*, London: Secker & Warburg for British Social Biology Council, 1955.

ROSE, E. J. B. (ed.), *Colour and Citizenship: a Report on British Race Relations*, London: Oxford University Press for Institute of Race Relations, 1969.

RUNCIMAN, W. G., *Relative Deprivation and Social Justice*, London: Routledge & Kegan Paul, 1966.

SAXON, ERIC, 'The Street that shames Hero Island', *Titbits*, February 1965.

SELLIN, THORSTEN, *Culture Conflict and Crime*, New York: Social Science Research Council, 1938.

SIMMONS, WILLIAM, 'How we rescued women who were lured on to vice ships', *People*, 10 December 1950.

SINGTON, DERRICK, 'Immigration and Crime', *New Society*, no. 57, 31 October 1963.

SWINGLER, NICHOLAS, 'The Streetwalker Returns', *New Society*, no. 338, 16 January 1969.

WEBB, DUNCAN, 'The Messina Gang' and 'Messina Gang Exposure', *People*, 3 September to 22 October 1950, and 15 July to 2 September 1951.

WEBER, MAX, *Economy and Society*, eds Guenther Roth and Claus Wittich, New York: Bedminster Press, 1968.

WILLIAMS, ROBIN M., JR, *The Reduction of Intergroup Tensions*, New York: Social Science Research Council, 1948.

WILLIAMSON, JOSEPH, *Father Joe,* London: Hodder & Stoughton, 1963.

WIRTH, LOUIS, 'The Problem of Minority Groups', in Ralph Linton (ed.), *The Science of Man in the World Crisis,* New York: Columbia University Press, 1945.

YOUNG, EDWYN, RAMSEY, EDITH, PATERSON, M. C., and WILLIAMSON, JOSEPH, *Vice Increase in Stepney,* mimeographed, June 1957.

YOUNG, MICHAEL, *The Rise of the Meritocracy,* Harmondsworth: Penguin, 1958.

YOUNG, PHYLLIS, *Report on an Investigation into Conditions of the Coloured Population in Stepney,* mimeographed, April 1944.

INDEX

Alford, Robert R., 216n
Anglo-Egyptian Aid Society, 62
anti-defamation strategies, 169–71
anti-semitism, 174
assimilation, liberal ideology of,
    3–4, 207–8
assimilation of Maltese
  economic adaptation, 39–40
  ethnic group morale and, 34–6,
    191–4, 202–4
  factors promoting, 207
  intermarriage, 41–5, 54, 60,
    148–51, 191, 207
  manifestations of, 34–45
  'passing', 183–5, 203
  political absorption, 53
  strategy of escape, 151, 188–9,
    203–7
Association of Maltese Communities
    of Egypt, 62
attitudes to Maltese, survey of,
    276–91
Australia, Maltese in, 18, 30, 38,
    53, 62, 131, 135, 148n, 206, 238

Bagley, Christopher, 227n, 230
Banton, Michael, 72, 162
Blalock, Hubert M., 218–19, 222–3
Board of Deputies of British Jews,
    Trades Advisory Council, 166–9
Boissevain, Jeremy, 11, 21n
British in Malta
  attitude to church, 11–14
  domination of economy, 10–11,
    16–17, 19
  fertility, 28–9, 240–1

fortress government, 12–13
paternalism, 9, 13
sexual exploitation, 119–23
since independence, 19–20, 118,
    125

Cable Street, 71–2, 88
Callaghan, James, 72–3
Cana movement, 15
Cardiff, Maltese in, 31, 71–3, 85,
    94, 137, 196
Casolani, Henry, 18n, 52n, 133–5
Catholic Centre, see Malta Catholic
    Centre
Catholic Emigrants Commission,
    50, 54, 148n
class
  of Maltese migrants, 39–40, 245
  political axis in Britain, 214–16,
    221, 231–2
clip joints, 101–2, 106
collective responsibility
  British imputation to Maltese,
    152–3, 156–7, 288–90
  effect on community structure,
    183–94
  loss of individual rights, 158–60,
    201
  Maltese responses, 180–94, 202–3
  means of group suppression,
    158–63
  strategy of group control, 154–8
  'typical minority response to',
    165–8
colonial situation
  double-bind, 220

297

Routledge Social Science Series

Routledge & Kegan Paul   London and Boston

68–74 Carter Lane   London EC4V 5EL
9 Park Street   Boston   Mass 02108

Contents

*Authors wishing to submit manuscripts for any series in
this catalogue should send them to the Social Science Editor,
Routledge & Kegan Paul Ltd, 68–74 Carter Lane,
London EC4V 5EL*

●*Books so marked are available in paperback
All books are in Metric Demy 8vo format (216 × 138mm approx.)*

International Library of Sociology

General Editor John Rex

GENERAL SOCIOLOGY

Barnsley, J. H. The Social Reality of Ethics. *464 pp.*
Belshaw, Cyril. The Conditions of Social Performance. *An Exploratory Theory. 144 pp.*
Brown, Robert. Explanation in Social Science. *208 pp.*
● Rules and Laws in Sociology. *192 pp.*
Bruford, W. H. Chekhov and His Russia. *A Sociological Study. 244 pp.*
Cain, Maureen E. Society and the Policeman's Role. *326 pp.*
Gibson, Quentin. The Logic of Social Enquiry. *240 pp.*
Glucksmann, M. Structuralist Analysis in Contemporary Social Thought. *212 pp.*
Gurvitch, Georges. Sociology of Law. *Preface by Roscoe Pound. 264 pp.*
Hodge, H. A. Wilhelm Dilthey. *An Introduction. 184 pp.*
Homans, George C. Sentiments and Activities. *336 pp.*
Johnson, Harry M. Sociology: *a Systematic Introduction. Foreword by Robert K. Merton. 710 pp.*
Mannheim, Karl. Essays on Sociology and Social Psychology. *Edited by Paul Keckskemeti. With Editorial Note by Adolph Lowe. 344 pp.*
Systematic Sociology: *An Introduction to the Study of Society. Edited by J. S. Erös and Professor W. A. C. Stewart. 220 pp.*
Martindale, Don. The Nature and Types of Sociological Theory. *292 pp.*
●**Maus, Heinz.** A Short History of Sociology. *234 pp.*
Mey, Harald. Field-Theory. *A Study of its Application in the Social Sciences. 352 pp.*
Myrdal, Gunnar. Value in Social Theory: *A Collection of Essays on Methodology. Edited by Paul Streeten. 332 pp.*
Ogburn, William F., and **Nimkoff, Meyer F.** A Handbook of Sociology. *Preface by Karl Mannheim. 656 pp. 46 figures. 35 tables.*
Parsons, Talcott, and **Smelser, Neil J.** Economy and Society: *A Study in the Integration of Economic and Social Theory. 362 pp.*
●**Rex, John.** Key Problems of Sociological Theory. *220 pp.*
Discovering Sociology. *278 pp.*
Sociology and the Demystification of the Modern World. *282 pp.*
●**Rex, John** (Ed.) Approaches to Sociology. *Contributions by Peter Abell, Frank Bechhofer, Basil Bernstein, Ronald Fletcher, David Frisby, Miriam Glucksmann, Peter Lassman, Herminio Martins, John Rex, Roland Robertson, John Westergaard and Jock Young. 302 pp.*
Rigby, A. Alternative Realities. *352 pp.*
Roche, M. Phenomenology, Language and the Social Sciences. *374 pp.*
Sahay, A. Sociological Analysis. *220 pp.*
Urry, John. Reference Groups and the Theory of Revolution. *244 pp.*
Weinberg, E. Development of Sociology in the Soviet Union. *173 pp.*

FOREIGN CLASSICS OF SOCIOLOGY

●**Durkheim, Emile.** Suicide. *A Study in Sociology. Edited and with an Introduction by George Simpson. 404 pp.*
  Professional Ethics and Civic Morals. *Translated by Cornelia Brookfield. 288 pp.*
●**Gerth, H. H.,** and **Mills, C. Wright.** From Max Weber: *Essays in Sociology. 502 pp.*
●**Tönnies, Ferdinand.** Community and Association. (*Gemeinschaft und Gesellschaft.*) *Translated and Supplemented by Charles P. Loomis. Foreword by Pitirim A. Sorokin. 334 pp.*

SOCIAL STRUCTURE

Andreski, Stanislav. Military Organization and Society. *Foreword by Professor A. R. Radcliffe-Brown. 226 pp. 1 folder.*
Coontz, Sydney H. Population Theories and the Economic Interpretation. *202 pp.*
Coser, Lewis. The Functions of Social Conflict. *204 pp.*
Dickie-Clark, H. F. Marginal Situation: *A Sociological Study of a Coloured Group. 240 pp. 11 tables.*
Glaser, Barney, and **Strauss, Anselm L.** Status Passage. *A Formal Theory. 208 pp.*
Glass, D. V. (Ed.) Social Mobility in Britain. *Contributions by J. Berent, T. Bottomore, R. C. Chambers, J. Floud, D. V. Glass, J. R. Hall, H. T. Himmelweit, R. K. Kelsall, F. M. Martin, C. A. Moser, R. Mukherjee, and W. Ziegel. 420 pp.*
Jones, Garth N. Planned Organizational Change: *An Exploratory Study Using an Empirical Approach. 268 pp.*
Kelsall, R. K. Higher Civil Servants in Britain: *From 1870 to the Present Day. 268 pp. 31 tables.*
König, René. The Community. *232 pp. Illustrated.*
●**Lawton, Denis.** Social Class, Language and Education. *192 pp.*
McLeish, John. The Theory of Social Change: *Four Views Considered. 128 pp.*
Marsh, David C. The Changing Social Structure of England and Wales, 1871-1961. *288 pp.*
Mouzelis, Nicos. Organization and Bureaucracy. *An Analysis of Modern Theories. 240 pp.*
Mulkay, M. J. Functionalism, Exchange and Theoretical Strategy. *272 pp.*
Ossowski, Stanislaw. Class Structure in the Social Consciousness. *210 pp.*
Podgórecki, Adam. Law and Society. *About 300 pp.*

SOCIOLOGY AND POLITICS

Acton, T. A. Gypsy Politics and Social Change. *316 pp.*
Hechter, Michael. Internal Colonialism. *The Celtic Fringe in British National Development, 1536–1966. About 350 pp.*
Hertz, Frederick. Nationality in History and Politics: *A Psychology and Sociology of National Sentiment and Nationalism. 432 pp.*

Kornhauser, William. The Politics of Mass Society. *272 pp. 20 tables.*

Laidler, Harry W. History of Socialism. *Social-Economic Movements: An Historical and Comparative Survey of Socialism, Communism, Co-operation, Utopianism; and other Systems of Reform and Reconstruction. 992 pp.*

Lasswell, H. D. Analysis of Political Behaviour. *324 pp.*

Mannheim, Karl. Freedom, Power and Democratic Planning. *Edited by Hans Gerth and Ernest K. Bramstedt. 424 pp.*

Mansur, Fatma. Process of Independence. *Foreword by A. H. Hanson. 208 pp.*

Martin, David A. Pacifism: *an Historical and Sociological Study. 262 pp.*

Myrdal, Gunnar. The Political Element in the Development of Economic Theory. *Translated from the German by Paul Streeten. 282 pp.*

Wootton, Graham. Workers, Unions and the State. *188 pp.*

FOREIGN AFFAIRS: THEIR SOCIAL, POLITICAL AND ECONOMIC FOUNDATIONS

Mayer, J. P. Political Thought in France from the Revolution to the Fifth Republic. *164 pp.*

CRIMINOLOGY

Ancel, Marc. Social Defence: *A Modern Approach to Criminal Problems. Foreword by Leon Radzinowicz. 240 pp.*

Cain, Maureen E. Society and the Policeman's Role. *326 pp.*

Cloward, Richard A., and **Ohlin, Lloyd E.** Delinquency and Opportunity: *A Theory of Delinquent Gangs. 248 pp.*

Downes, David M. The Delinquent Solution. *A Study in Subcultural Theory. 296 pp.*

Dunlop, A. B., and **McCabe, S.** Young Men in Detention Centres. *192 pp.*

Friedlander, Kate. The Psycho-Analytical Approach to Juvenile Delinquency: *Theory, Case Studies, Treatment. 320 pp.*

Glueck, Sheldon, and **Eleanor.** Family Environment and Delinquency. *With the statistical assistance of Rose W. Kneznek. 340 pp.*

Lopez-Rey, Manuel. Crime. *An Analytical Appraisal. 288 pp.*

Mannheim, Hermann. Comparative Criminology: *a Text Book. Two volumes. 442 pp. and 380 pp.*

Morris, Terence. The Criminal Area: *A Study in Social Ecology. Foreword by Hermann Mannheim. 232 pp. 25 tables. 4 maps.*

Rock, Paul. Making People Pay. *338 pp.*

●**Taylor, Ian, Walton, Paul,** and **Young, Jock.** The New Criminology. *For a Social Theory of Deviance. 325 pp.*

SOCIAL PSYCHOLOGY

Bagley, Christopher. The Social Psychology of the Epileptic Child. *320 pp.*

Barbu, Zevedei. Problems of Historical Psychology. *248 pp.*

Blackburn, Julian. Psychology and the Social Pattern. *184 pp.*

●**Brittan, Arthur.** Meanings and Situations. *224 pp.*

Carroll, J. Break-Out from the Crystal Palace. *200 pp.*

●**Fleming, C. M.** Adolescence: Its Social Psychology. *With an Introduction to recent findings from the fields of Anthropology, Physiology, Medicine, Psychometrics and Sociometry. 288 pp.*

● The Social Psychology of Education: *An Introduction and Guide to Its Study. 136 pp.*

Homans, George C. The Human Group. *Foreword by Bernard DeVoto. Introduction by Robert K. Merton. 526 pp.*

● Social Behaviour: *its Elementary Forms. 416 pp.*

●**Klein, Josephine.** The Study of Groups. *226 pp. 31 figures. 5 tables.*

Linton, Ralph. The Cultural Background of Personality. *132 pp.*

●**Mayo, Elton.** The Social Problems of an Industrial Civilization. *With an appendix on the Political Problem. 180 pp.*

Ottaway, A. K. C. Learning Through Group Experience. *176 pp.*

Ridder, J. C. de. The Personality of the Urban African in South Africa. *A Thematic Apperception Test Study. 196 pp. 12 plates.*

●**Rose, Arnold M.** (Ed.) Human Behaviour and Social Processes: *an Interactionist Approach. Contributions by Arnold M. Rose, Ralph H. Turner, Anselm Strauss, Everett C. Hughes, E. Franklin Frazier, Howard S. Becker, et al. 696 pp.*

Smelser, Neil J. Theory of Collective Behaviour. *448 pp.*

Stephenson, Geoffrey M. The Development of Conscience. *128 pp.*

Young, Kimball. Handbook of Social Psychology. *658 pp. 16 figures. 10 tables.*

SOCIOLOGY OF THE FAMILY

Banks, J. A. Prosperity and Parenthood: *A Study of Family Planning among The Victorian Middle Classes. 262 pp.*

Bell, Colin R. Middle Class Families: *Social and Geographical Mobility. 224 pp.*

Burton, Lindy. Vulnerable Children. *272 pp.*

Gavron, Hannah. The Captive Wife: *Conflicts of Household Mothers. 190 pp.*

George, Victor, and **Wilding, Paul.** Motherless Families. *220 pp.*

Klein, Josephine. Samples from English Cultures.

  1. Three Preliminary Studies and Aspects of Adult Life in England. *447 pp.*

  2. Child-Rearing Practices and Index. *247 pp.*

Klein, Viola. Britain's Married Women Workers. *180 pp.*

The Feminine Character. *History of an Ideology. 244 pp.*

McWhinnie, Alexina M. Adopted Children. *How They Grow Up. 304 pp.*

● **Myrdal, Alva,** and **Klein, Viola.** Women's Two Roles: *Home and Work. 238 pp. 27 tables.*

Parsons, Talcott, and **Bales, Robert F.** Family: Socialization and Inter-action Process. *In collaboration with James Olds, Morris Zelditch and Philip E. Slater. 456 pp. 50 figures and tables.*

SOCIAL SERVICES

Bastide, Roger. The Sociology of Mental Disorder. *Translated from the French by Jean McNeil. 260 pp.*

Carlebach, Julius. Caring For Children in Trouble. *266 pp.*

Forder, R. A. (Ed.) Penelope Hall's Social Services of England and Wales. *352 pp.*

George, Victor. Foster Care. *Theory and Practice. 234 pp.*
Social Security: *Beveridge and After. 258 pp.*

George, V., and **Wilding, P.** Motherless Families. *248 pp.*

●**Goetschius, George W.** Working with Community Groups. *256 pp.*

Goetschius, George W., and **Tash, Joan.** Working with Unattached Youth. *416 pp.*

Hall, M. P., and **Howes, I. V.** The Church in Social Work. *A Study of Moral Welfare Work undertaken by the Church of England. 320 pp.*

Heywood, Jean S. Children in Care: *the Development of the Service for the Deprived Child. 264 pp.*

Hoenig, J., and **Hamilton, Marian W.** The De-Segregation of the Mentally Ill. *284 pp.*

Jones, Kathleen. Mental Health and Social Policy, 1845-1959. *264 pp.*

King, Roy D., Raynes, Norma V., and **Tizard, Jack.** Patterns of Residential Care. *356 pp.*

Leigh, John. Young People and Leisure. *256 pp.*

Morris, Mary. Voluntary Work and the Welfare State. *300 pp.*

Morris, Pauline. Put Away: *A Sociological Study of Institutions for the Mentally Retarded. 364 pp.*

Nokes, P. L. The Professional Task in Welfare Practice. *152 pp.*

Timms, Noel. Psychiatric Social Work in Great Britain (1939-1962). *280 pp.*

● Social Casework: *Principles and Practice. 256 pp.*

Young, A. F. Social Services in British Industry. *272 pp.*

Young, A. F., and **Ashton, E. T.** British Social Work in the Nineteenth Century. *288 pp.*

SOCIOLOGY OF EDUCATION

Banks, Olive. Parity and Prestige in English Secondary Education: a Study in Educational Sociology. *272 pp.*

Bentwich, Joseph. Education in Israel. *224 pp. 8 pp. plates.*

●**Blyth, W. A. L.** English Primary Education. *A Sociological Description.*
1. Schools. *232 pp.*
2. Background. *168 pp.*

Collier, K. G. The Social Purposes of Education: *Personal and Social Values in Education. 268 pp.*

Dale, R. R., and **Griffith, S.** Down Stream: *Failure in the Grammar School. 108 pp.*

Dore, R. P. Education in Tokugawa Japan. *356 pp. 9 pp. plates.*

Evans, K. M. Sociometry and Education. *158 pp.*

●**Ford, Julienne.** Social Class and the Comprehensive School. *192 pp.*

Foster, P. J. Education and Social Change in Ghana. *336 pp. 3 maps.*

Fraser, W. R. Education and Society in Modern France. *150 pp.*

Grace, Gerald R. Role Conflict and the Teacher. *About 200 pp.*

Hans, Nicholas. New Trends in Education in the Eighteenth Century. *278 pp. 19 tables.*

● Comparative Education: *A Study of Educational Factors and Traditions. 360 pp.*

Hargreaves, David. Interpersonal Relations and Education. *432 pp.*

● Social Relations in a Secondary School. *240 pp.*

Holmes, Brian. Problems in Education. *A Comparative Approach. 336 pp.*

King, Ronald. Values and Involvement in a Grammar School. *164 pp.*

School Organization and Pupil Involvement. *A Study of Secondary Schools.*

●**Mannheim, Karl,** and **Stewart, W. A. C.** An Introduction to the Sociology of Education. *206 pp.*

Morris, Raymond N. The Sixth Form and College Entrance. *231 pp.*

●**Musgrove, F.** Youth and the Social Order. *176 pp.*

●**Ottaway, A. K. C.** Education and Society: An Introduction to the Sociology of Education. *With an Introduction by W. O. Lester Smith. 212 pp.*

Peers, Robert. Adult Education: *A Comparative Study. 398 pp.*

Pritchard, D. G. Education and the Handicapped: *1760 to 1960. 258 pp.*

Richardson, Helen. Adolescent Girls in Approved Schools. *308 pp.*

Stratta, Erica. The Education of Borstal Boys. *A Study of their Educational Experiences prior to, and during, Borstal Training. 256 pp.*

Taylor, P. H., Reid, W. A., and **Holley, B. J.** The English Sixth Form. *A Case Study in Curriculum Research. 200 pp.*

SOCIOLOGY OF CULTURE

Eppel, E. M., and **M.** Adolescents and Morality: *A Study of some Moral Values and Dilemmas of Working Adolescents in the Context of a changing Climate of Opinion. Foreword by W. J. H. Sprott. 268 pp. 39 tables.*

●**Fromm, Erich.** The Fear of Freedom. *286 pp.*

● The Sane Society. *400 pp.*

Mannheim, Karl. Essays on the Sociology of Culture. *Edited by Ernst Mannheim in co-operation with Paul Kecskemeti. Editorial Note by Adolph Lowe. 280 pp.*

Weber, Alfred. Farewell to European History: *or The Conquest of Nihilism. Translated from the German by R. F. C. Hull. 224 pp.*

SOCIOLOGY OF RELIGION

Argyle, Michael and **Beit-Hallahmi, Benjamin.** The Social Psychology of Religion. *About 256 pp.*

Nelson, G. K. Spiritualism and Society. *313 pp.*

Stark, Werner. The Sociology of Religion. *A Study of Christendom.*
Volume I. *Established Religion. 248 pp.*
Volume II. *Sectarian Religion. 368 pp.*
Volume III. *The Universal Church. 464 pp.*
Volume IV. *Types of Religious Man. 352 pp.*
Volume V. *Types of Religious Culture. 464 pp.*

Turner, B. S. Weber and Islam. *216 pp.*

Watt, W. Montgomery. Islam and the Integration of Society. *320 pp.*

SOCIOLOGY OF ART AND LITERATURE

Jarvie, Ian C. Towards a Sociology of the Cinema. *A Comparative Essay on the Structure and Functioning of a Major Entertainment Industry. 405 pp.*

Rust, Frances S. Dance in Society. *An Analysis of the Relationships between the Social Dance and Society in England from the Middle Ages to the Present Day. 256 pp. 8 pp. of plates.*

Schücking, L. L. The Sociology of Literary Taste. *112 pp.*

Wolff, Janet. Hermeneutic Philosophy and the Sociology of Art. *About 200 pp.*

SOCIOLOGY OF KNOWLEDGE

Diesing, P. Patterns of Discovery in the Social Sciences. *262 pp.*

●**Douglas, J. D.** (Ed.) Understanding Everyday Life. *370 pp.*

●**Hamilton, P.** Knowledge and Social Structure. *174 pp.*

Jarvie, I. C. Concepts and Society. *232 pp.*

Mannheim, Karl. Essays on the Sociology of Knowledge. *Edited by Paul Kecskemeti. Editorial Note by Adolph Lowe. 353 pp.*

Remmling, Gunter W. (Ed.) Towards the Sociology of Knowledge. *Origin and Development of a Sociological Thought Style. 463 pp.*

Stark, Werner. The Sociology of Knowledge: *An Essay in Aid of a Deeper Understanding of the History of Ideas. 384 pp.*

URBAN SOCIOLOGY

Ashworth, William. The Genesis of Modern British Town Planning: *A Study in Economic and Social History of the Nineteenth and Twentieth Centuries. 288 pp.*

Cullingworth, J. B. Housing Needs and Planning Policy: *A Restatement of the Problems of Housing Need and 'Overspill' in England and Wales. 232 pp. 44 tables. 8 maps.*

9

Dickinson, Robert E. City and Region: *A Geographical Interpretation* *608 pp. 125 figures.*

The West European City: *A Geographical Interpretation. 600 pp. 129 maps. 29 plates.*

● The City Region in Western Europe. *320 pp. Maps.*

Humphreys, Alexander J. New Dubliners: *Urbanization and the Irish Family. Foreword by George C. Homans. 304 pp.*

Jackson, Brian. Working Class Community: *Some General Notions raised by a Series of Studies in Northern England. 192 pp.*

Jennings, Hilda. Societies in the Making: *a Study of Development and Redevelopment within a County Borough. Foreword by D. A. Clark. 286 pp.*

●**Mann, P. H.** An Approach to Urban Sociology. *240 pp.*

Morris, R. N., and **Mogey, J.** The Sociology of Housing. *Studies at Berinsfield. 232 pp. 4 pp. plates.*

Rosser, C., and **Harris, C.** The Family and Social Change. *A Study of Family and Kinship in a South Wales Town. 352 pp. 8 maps.*

RURAL SOCIOLOGY

Chambers, R. J. H. Settlement Schemes in Tropical Africa: *A Selective Study. 268 pp.*

Haswell, M. R. The Economics of Development in Village India. *120 pp.*

Littlejohn, James. Westrigg: *the Sociology of a Cheviot Parish. 172 pp. 5 figures.*

Mayer, Adrian C. Peasants in the Pacific. *A Study of Fiji Indian Rural Society. 248 pp. 20 plates.*

Williams, W. M. The Sociology of an English Village: *Gosforth. 272 pp. 12 figures. 13 tables.*

SOCIOLOGY OF INDUSTRY AND DISTRIBUTION

Anderson, Nels. Work and Leisure. *280 pp.*

●**Blau, Peter M.,** and **Scott, W. Richard.** Formal Organizations: *a Comparative approach. Introduction and Additional Bibliography by J. H. Smith. 326 pp.*

Eldridge, J. E. T. Industrial Disputes. *Essays in the Sociology of Industrial Relations. 288 pp.*

Hetzler, Stanley. Applied Measures for Promoting Technological Growth. *352 pp.*

Technological Growth and Social Change. *Achieving Modernization. 269 pp.*

Hollowell, Peter G. The Lorry Driver. *272 pp.*

Jefferys, Margot, *with the assistance of Winifred Moss.* Mobility in the Labour Market: *Employment Changes in Battersea and Dagenham. Preface by Barbara Wootton. 186 pp. 51 tables.*

Millerson, Geoffrey. The Qualifying Associations: *a Study in Professionalization. 320 pp.*

Smelser, Neil J. Social Change in the Industrial Revolution: *An Application of Theory to the Lancashire Cotton Industry, 1770-1840. 468 pp. 12 figures. 14 tables.*

Williams, Gertrude. Recruitment to Skilled Trades. *240 pp.*

Young, A. F. Industrial Injuries Insurance: *an Examination of British Policy. 192 pp.*

DOCUMENTARY

Schlesinger, Rudolf (Ed.) Changing Attitudes in Soviet Russia.
2. The Nationalities Problem and Soviet Administration. *Selected Readings on the Development of Soviet Nationalities Policies. Introduced by the editor. Translated by W. W. Gottlieb. 324 pp.*

ANTHROPOLOGY

Ammar, Hamed. Growing up in an Egyptian Village: *Silwa, Province of Aswan. 336 pp.*

Brandel-Syrier, Mia. Reeftown Elite. *A Study of Social Mobility in a Modern African Community on the Reef. 376 pp.*

Crook, David, and **Isabel.** Revolution in a Chinese Village: *Ten Mile Inn. 230 pp. 8 plates. 1 map.*

Dickie-Clark, H. F. The Marginal Situation. *A Sociological Study of a Coloured Group. 236 pp.*

Dube, S. C. Indian Village. *Foreword by Morris Edward Opler. 276 pp. 4 plates.*

India's Changing Villages: *Human Factors in Community Development. 260 pp. 8 plates. 1 map.*

Firth, Raymond. Malay Fishermen. *Their Peasant Economy. 420 pp. 17 pp. plates.*

Firth, R., Hubert, J., and **Forge, A.** Families and their Relatives. *Kinship in a Middle-Class Sector of London: An Anthropological Study. 456 pp.*

Gulliver, P. H. Social Control in an African Society: a Study of the Arusha, Agricultural Masai of Northern Tanganyika. *320 pp. 8 plates. 10 figures.*

Family Herds. *288 pp.*

Ishwaran, K. Shivapur. *A South Indian Village. 216 pp.*

Tradition and Economy in Village India: *An Interactionist Approach. Foreword by Conrad Arensburg. 176 pp.*

Jarvie, Ian C. The Revolution in Anthropology. *268 pp.*

Jarvie, Ian C., and **Agassi, Joseph.** Hong Kong. *A Society in Transition. 396 pp. Illustrated with plates and maps.*

Little, Kenneth L. Mende of Sierra Leone. *308 pp. and folder.*

Negroes in Britain. *With a New Introduction and Contemporary Study by Leonard Bloom. 320 pp.*

Lowie, Robert H. Social Organization. *494 pp.*

Mayer, Adrian, C. Caste and Kinship in Central India: *A Village and its Region. 328 pp. 16 plates. 15 figures. 16 tables.*

Peasants in the Pacific. *A Study of Fiji Indian Rural Society. 248 pp.*

Smith, Raymond T. The Negro Family in British Guiana: *Family Structure and Social Status in the Villages. With a Foreword by Meyer Fortes. 314 pp. 8 plates. 1 figure. 4 maps.*

SOCIOLOGY AND PHILOSOPHY

Barnsley, John H. The Social Reality of Ethics. *A Comparative Analysis of Moral Codes. 448 pp.*

Diesing, Paul. Patterns of Discovery in the Social Sciences. *362 pp.*

● **Douglas, Jack D.** (Ed.) Understanding Everyday Life. *Toward the Reconstruction of Sociological Knowledge. Contributions by Alan F. Blum. Aaron W. Cicourel, Norman K. Denzin, Jack D. Douglas, John Heeren, Peter McHugh, Peter K. Manning, Melvin Power, Matthew Speier, Roy Turner, D. Lawrence Wieder, Thomas P. Wilson and Don H. Zimmerman. 370 pp.*

Jarvie, Ian C. Concepts and Society. *216 pp.*

Pelz, Werner. The Scope of Understanding in Sociology. *Towards a more radical reorientation in the social humanistic sciences. 283 pp.*

Roche, Maurice. Phenomenology, Language and the Social Sciences. *371 pp.*

Sahay, Arun. Sociological Analysis. *212 pp.*

Sklair, Leslie. The Sociology of Progress. *320 pp.*

International Library of Anthropology

General Editor Adam Kuper

Brown, Paula. The Chimbu. *A Study of Change in the New Guinea Highlands. 151 pp.*

Lloyd, P. C. Power and Independence. *Urban Africans' Perception of Social Inequality. 264 pp.*

Pettigrew, Joyce. Robber Noblemen. *A Study of the Political System of the Sikh Jats. 284 pp.*

Van Den Berghe, Pierre L. Power and Privilege at an African University. *278 pp.*

International Library of Social Policy

General Editor Kathleen Jones

Bayley, M. Mental Handicap and Community Care. *426 pp.*

Butler, J. R. Family Doctors and Public Policy. *208 pp.*

Holman, Robert. Trading in Children. *A Study of Private Fostering. 355 pp.*

Jones, Kathleen. History of the Mental Health Service. *428 pp.*

Thomas, J. E. The English Prison Officer since 1850: *A Study in Conflict. 258 pp.*

Woodward, J. To Do the Sick No Harm. *A Study of the British Voluntary Hospital System to 1875. About 220 pp.*

International Library of Welfare and Philosophy

General Editors Noel Timms and David Watson

● **Plant, Raymond.** Community and Ideology. *104 pp.*

Primary Socialization, Language and Education

General Editor Basil Bernstein

Bernstein, Basil. Class, Codes and Control. *2 volumes.*
1. *Theoretical Studies Towards a Sociology of Language. 254 pp.*
2. *Applied Studies Towards a Sociology of Language. About 400 pp.*

Brandis, W., and **Bernstein, B.** Selection and Control. *176 pp.*

Brandis, Walter, and **Henderson, Dorothy.** Social Class, Language and Communication. *288 pp.*

Cook-Gumperz, Jenny. Social Control and Socialization. *A Study of Class Differences in the Language of Maternal Control. 290 pp.*

● **Gahagan, D. M.,** and **G. A.** Talk Reform. *Exploration in Language for Infant School Children. 160 pp.*

Robinson, W. P., and **Rackstraw, Susan D. A.** A Question of Answers. *2 volumes. 192 pp. and 180 pp.*

Turner, Geoffrey J., and **Mohan, Bernard A.** A Linguistic Description and Computer Programme for Children's Speech. *208 pp.*

Reports of the Institute of Community Studies

Cartwright, Ann. Human Relations and Hospital Care. *272 pp.*

● Parents and Family Planning Services. *306 pp.*

Patients and their Doctors. *A Study of General Practice. 304 pp.*

● **Jackson, Brian.** Streaming: *an Education System in Miniature. 168 pp.*

Jackson, Brian, and **Marsden, Dennis.** Education and the Working Class: *Some General Themes raised by a Study of 88 Working-class Children in a Northern Industrial City. 268 pp. 2 folders.*

Marris, Peter. The Experience of Higher Education. *232 pp. 27 tables.*

Loss and Change. *192 pp.*

Marris, Peter, and **Rein, Martin.** Dilemmas of Social Reform. *Poverty and Community Action in the United States. 256 pp.*

Marris, Peter, and **Somerset, Anthony.** African Businessmen. *A Study of Entrepreneurship and Development in Kenya. 256 pp.*

Mills, Richard. Young Outsiders: *a Study in Alternative Communities. 216 pp.*

Runciman, W. G. Relative Deprivation and Social Justice. *A Study of Attitudes to Social Inequality in Twentieth-Century England. 352 pp.*

Willmott, Peter. Adolescent Boys in East London. *230 pp.*

Willmott, Peter, and **Young, Michael.** Family and Class in a London Suburb. *202 pp. 47 tables.*

Young, Michael. Innovation and Research in Education. *192 pp.*

●**Young, Michael,** and **McGeeney, Patrick.** Learning Begins at Home. *A Study of a Junior School and its Parents. 128 pp.*

Young, Michael, and **Willmott, Peter.** Family and Kinship in East London. *Foreword by Richard M. Titmuss. 252 pp. 39 tables.*
The Symmetrical Family. *410 pp.*

Reports of the Institute for Social Studies in Medical Care

Cartwright, Ann, Hockey, Lisbeth, and **Anderson, John L.** Life Before Death. *310 pp.*

Dunnell, Karen, and **Cartwright, Ann.** Medicine Takers, Prescribers and Hoarders. *190 pp.*

Medicine, Illness and Society

General Editor   W. M. Williams

Robinson, David. The Process of Becoming Ill. *142 pp.*

Stacey, Margaret, *et al.* Hospitals, Children and Their Families. *The Report of a Pilot Study. 202 pp.*

Monographs in Social Theory

General Editor   Arthur Brittan

●**Barnes, B.** Scientific Knowledge and Sociological Theory. *About 200 pp.*

Bauman, Zygmunt. Culture as Praxis. *204 pp.*

● **Dixon, Keith.** Sociological Theory. *Pretence and Possibility. 142 pp.*

●**Smith, Anthony D.** The Concept of Social Change. *A Critique of the Functionalist Theory of Social Change. 208 pp.*

Routledge Social Science Journals

The British Journal of Sociology. *Edited by Terence P. Morris. Vol. 1, No. 1, March 1950 and Quarterly. Roy. 8vo. Back numbers available. An international journal with articles on all aspects of sociology.*

Economy and Society. *Vol. 1, No. 1. February 1972 and Quarterly. Metric Roy. 8vo. A journal for all social scientists covering sociology, philosophy, anthropology, economics and history. Back numbers available.*

Year Book of Social Policy in Britain, The. *Edited by Kathleen Jones. 1971. Published annually.*

Printed in Great Britain by Unwin Brothers Limited
The Gresham Press Old Woking Surrey
A member of the Staples Printing Group